D0209495

BETWEEN BITES

Memoirs of a Hungry Hedonist

BITES

OTHER BOOKS BY JAMES VILLAS

American Taste, 1982

The Town & Country Cookbook, 1985

James Villas' Country Cooking, 1988

Villas at Table, 1988

The French Country Kitchen, 1992

My Mother's Southern Kitchen, 1994

Stews, Bogs, and Burgoos, 1997

My Mother's Southern Desserts, 1998

My Mother's Southern Entertaining, 2000

BETWEEN BITES

MEMOIRS OF A HUNGRY HEDONIST

JAMES VILLAS

JOHN WILEY & SONS, INC.

This book is printed on acid-free paper. ♾

Copyright © 2002 by James Villas. All rights reserved.

Published by John Wiley & Sons, Inc., New York

Published simultaneously in Canada.

This publication is designed to provide accurate and authoritative information in regard to the subject matter covered. It is sold with the understanding that the publisher is not engaged in rendering professional services. If professional advice or other expert assistance is required, the services of a competent professional person should be sought.

Library of Congress Cataloging-in-Publication Data:

Villas, James.

Between bites : memoirs of a hungry hedonist / by James Villas.

p.   cm.

Includes bibliographical references and index.

ISBN 0-471-21420-5 (cloth : alk. paper)

1. Food writers — United States — Biography. 2. Cooks — United States — Biography. 3. Villas, James. I. Title.

TX649.V55 2001

641'.092 — dc21

[B]   2001046815

Printed in the United States of America.

10 9 8 7 6 5 4 3 2 1

DEDICATION

A la très-belle, a la très-bonne, a la bien-aimée

ALEXANDRA MAYES BIRNBAUM

CONTENTS

Mid-Atlantic aboard the S.S. France with Mr. Beauregard Beagle, 1974.

...our votre Toutou . . . . Madame
...our votre fidèle
Compagnon . . . Monsieur

MENU

Le Plat de Tayaut
(Consommé de Bœuf - Toasts - Légumes)

Le Régal de Sweekey
(Carottes - Viande Hachée - Epinards - Toasts)

La Gâterie "FRANCE"
(Haricots Verts - Poulet Haché - Riz Nature
arrosé de Jus de Viande et de Biscottes en Poudre)

La Préférence du Danois
(Os de Côte de Bœuf, de Jambon et de Veau)

Le Régime Végétarien des Dogs
(Tous les Légumes Frais et Toutes les Pâtes Alimentaires)

Biscuit - Ken'l

COMPAGNIE GÉNÉRALE TRANSATLANTIQUE
French Line
PAQUEBOT "FRANCE"

Gourmet canine menu for kennel guests aboard the S.S. France.

"FRANCE"

The Captain
and
The Chief Purser
request the honour of your company for
cocktails on Monday, August 19th at 8.00 PM
in the Monaco Lounge - Veranda Deck -

Invitation to cocktails and dinner at the captain's table.

"FRANCE"

DINER
offert par
le Commandant Igor DOUPLITZKY
à
Madame Denise MULLINS
Madame Roy TITUS
Madame Hans Maria WYMAN
Monsieur et Madame Pierre BEAUQUIER
Monsieur et Madame Sanford GRANOVITZ
Monsieur et Madame Bart JONES II
Monsieur et Madame Gordon SELIG
Sir Joseph LATHAM
Monsieur James VILLAS

A bord, le 15 Septembre 1973

MENU

Le Caviar de la Volga Givré sur Socle

Le Turbot de Gravelines Soufflé au Champagne

Le Cœur de Charolais en Feuilleté Wellington

La Salade Mercédès

La Surprise Glacée des Sous-Bois

Les Mignardises "France"

Les Fruits de l'Eté

————

Vodka Stolitchnaya
Chablis Cruse 1970
Château Pontet-Canet 1967
Mumm Cordon Rouge Brut

I'VE SEEN THE ELEPHANT

WHEN I WAS A YOUNG BOY growing up in North Carolina, my wise father had an expression that he'd use anytime he thought he was being hoodwinked. Daddy was a tolerant, indulgent, fun-loving man fully capable of suffering fools gladly, but stretch his patience to the absolute limit, or try to challenge him about something he deemed important, and he'd stare at you with his piercing, dark, Greek eyes, raise an eyebrow, and say, "Listen, I've been to the circus and seen the elephant"—meaning he'd moved around, covered the territory, taken in the big show, and absorbed a bit of wisdom.

Although the testy expression no doubt has its ambiguities, I know of none other that sums up better the flush, uproarious, refractory, often combative life I've led over the past forty-odd years as a frustrated teacher and scholar, a feisty food journalist and iconoclastic writer, a soi-disant gay blade, and an overall fop perched under the Big Top. I'm fully aware of my reputation as a furtive, antisocial, and sometimes "difficult" individual, and after twenty-seven years as the food and wine editor of *Town & Country* and contributor to other upscale magazines like *Esquire* and *Gourmet*, I've certainly become accustomed to being perceived as a snob, arrogant dilettante, and cad. The fact that such tags are basically so much hogwash only serves to confirm the need for aloofness. Of course some labels I gladly take on. Elitist, proudly. Hedonist, assuredly. Both describe not only my wanton, unbridled approach to gastronomy in general but the way I've cultivated lasting relationships only with those whom I consider to be extraordinary people. As a paid pundit on food, drink, travel, and the good life, I've wandered the globe, ventured into realms that have produced outlandish stories, and encountered unforgettable characters whose encouragement and influence have been profound. I've taken queasy risks, probably made more enemies than friends, reaped the gains and shouldered the losses, and, to paraphrase Mama Cass, made my own kind of music.

I'm not and never have been a conventional food writer, not in my personal conduct, not in my social connections, and certainly not in the books and articles I write. Much to the nervous horror of my peers, I refuse to drink wine at cocktail parties, I smoke, I spurn salsas, sushi, and the food processor, and at table I much prefer the company of an expert pig breeder or hungry whiskey distiller to that of a fatuous foodie waxing ecstatically about Peruvian peppers or some young hotshot chef's latest fusion concoctions. I do not show up at ceremonial dinners to claim my occasional awards and schmooze; I consider it unfair and immoral to review a restaurant that's been in business less than three months. On principle I will not eat any form of raw fresh tuna, blue potatoes, apricot mustard, or Parmesan ice cream. And the recipes that flood my books and articles fairly explode with butter, eggs, rich cheeses, and all the other sinful but glorious ingredients that the Good Lord intended us to eat. None of this is affected to make me appear superior, antagonistic, or wicked. It's just my natural makeup—

the way I work, function socially, eat, and survive, and the pulse that throbs throughout these memoirs.

I've never believed that food writing is any more of an art than eating and cooking, and that to try to elevate the craft to the exalted level of serious literature, music, and painting is a naive attempt by dreamers to transform a quite ordinary discipline into a complex process by which true masterpieces are produced. Just as popular music, however charming, is risibly not as profound and important as the immortal notes penned by Beethoven, so even the best, most trenchant essays and books of authors like M.F.K. Fisher, Waverley Root, and Elizabeth David can hardly be equated with the impact of writings by Montaigne, Nietzsche, or Proust. Much too much careless nonsense is made these days about the so-called art of eating, the art of cooking, and the art of writing about food and restaurants. In fact, the only thing more boring for me than writing (and reading or talking) about food out of the context of human experience is writing abstractly about wine. Yes, since we must eat to survive, it's preferable to approach the act intelligently; since food must be prepared in one way or another, it's good to have practitioners with the necessary skills and insights; and since millions find it useful and interesting to be instructed about food and its relation to the senses, it's helpful to be exposed to dedicated experts willing and ready to dispense all the facts, anecdotes, and romance about food and dining. But to credit such mundane facets of life with the same transcendental creativity implicit in the fine arts is both vain and obtuse.

After some forty years participating in the world's riotous food and beverage scene and associating with dynamic individuals like those portrayed in these memoirs, I have indeed gone to the circus and seen the elephant, and, my, what a spectacle to behold. Connected with prestigious magazines, I've been lucky enough to know many of the era's most respected chefs, restaurateurs, food authors, and exorbitant gourmands. I've hobnobbed on the royal banquettes with dukes and duchesses, the king of Spain, Leslie Caron, Ned Rorem, Truman Capote, Pauline Trigère, and a contingent of other gold-plated swells, while, at the same time, slumming in various low-life dens with delightful creatures who didn't know the difference between a truffle and a dessiccated turnip. Aboard the S.S. *France*, I've shared a lavish pot-au-feu with Salvador Dalí and his pet ocelot and, outrageously, danced with Sir Stephen Spender after dining on coulibiac of salmon washed down with Niagaras of vintage Krug. Once, on a Concorde flight to Paris, I had a memorable discussion with Rudolf Nureyev about the different grades of caviar, surpassed only by a jolly argument with Tennessee Williams at Antoine's in New Orleans about the correct preparation of shrimp remoulade.

I suppose I was on speaking terms with the maitre d' of every restaurant of consequence from Lyon to Venice to San Francisco, but some of my most meaningful relationships have been with Greek fishermen, French geese breeders, Spanish sausage makers, and Midwestern farmers eager to teach me about prime beef, persimmons, and pygmy rabbits. I've lived high on the hog in the plushest hotels and sat in the back of the spiffiest limos, squatted in bug-infested Moroccan huts, zipped around Jamaica in a ridiculous rattle-trap, and bicycled to a remote Norwegian fjord just for the excitement of wading up to my belly in a giant pen with thousands of thrashing farmed salmon.

At possibly no point in history has gastronomy evolved more vibrantly and radically than during the second half of the twentieth century, a phenomenon that we can already look back upon with a certain jaundiced nostalgia and one that should provide the inspiration needed to move ahead to more impressive developments. A lot of gin has flowed over the gold crowns since I first became involved in all the action, strong bonds have been formed with extraordinary people who have contributed so much to my joy and vitality, and if I've learned nothing else, I've learned that to draw a bead on work, human relations, and indeed life, an author must at once be in the center ring and stand on the sidelines—an essential but irrelevant observer. Believing firmly in the hedonistic philosophy of living half as long and seeing twice as much, I certainly don't expect to remain forever under the Big Top, but oh yes, I've seen the elephant, marveled at his fabulous performance, and appreciated the way he's accepted the peanuts of my gratitude so graciously.

With fellow Fulbright scholars (I'm in the center) aboard the Queen Elizabeth en route to France, 1961.

Chef Alexandre Dumaine in the garden of Hôtel de la Côte d'Or in Saulieu. France, 1962.

Pam, my favorite dining companion during my year in Grenoble, before lunch in the Alps.

CHAPTER ONE

FROM GRITS TO GAUL

"IT IS A PLEASURE TO INFORM YOU . . ." began the official letter dated April 10, 1961, from the Department of State in Washington.

Without even taking time to finish reading the sentence, I whooped right there in the middle of the Chapel Hill post office, waving the sheet of paper excitedly in the air like a twenty-two-year-old lunatic as a dignified man checking his postal box close by turned and glared at me.

"I have a Fulbright!" I shrieked uncontrollably. "I've got a Fulbright grant! I'm going to France!"

Finally smiling, the much older stranger quickly began tucking his mail into the sort of shabby leather briefcase that so many professors at the university carried. "Congratulations," he then muttered before heading for the door and leaving me to wonder whether he was truly impressed by my glorious news or simply eager to distance himself from still another crazy student.

I'd waited months and months for this moment, never daring to believe that I'd actually be awarded the grant while hoping against tough odds that somehow it would come through. Having already

7

earned at Carolina two degrees in comparative literature despite a rather reckless social life that kept me on the edge of academic and emotional disaster, I dreamed of nothing more than going to France for an entire year. There I'd expose myself to a culture I'd only read about, perfect a language that infatuated me, and continue my studies in Romanticism before eventually pursuing a doctorate, teaching at some leading American college or university, and becoming . . . a distinguished scholar. That I was involved in the most recent intense and everlasting youthful love affair should have discouraged me from wanting to leave North Carolina, but even this was of secondary importance to the vision of living in France. Nor did it much matter that my grant was worth exactly 578,200 old francs, the equivalent of about $1,100 for the year or all of $93 a month to live on.

Naturally, like most American students of any generation I longed to go to Paris. Advised by a wise professor, however, that my chances of getting a Fulbright would probably double if I requested instead to be sent to the provinces, I applied for the University of Grenoble with the intent of studying under the country's most eminent authority on Gérard de Nerval, the nineteenth-century author on whom I'd written my master's thesis. I'll never know whether or not it was actually this tactic that did the trick, but I was given jealous pause when another candidate who was also my best friend requested Paris and got it.

In any case, on September 21, 1961, Jimmy and I together sailed from New York at midnight on the majestic *Queen Elizabeth* with a rousing send-off from our families and friends, two hotshot Southerners ready to take on new worlds and indulge fully in all the glamour and sophistication and excitement to which we as Fulbrights were entitled. Our first taste of putative glamour was in the form of a tourist-class cabin in the bowels of D Deck no larger than a bear's cave and equipped with sagging upper and lower berths, no porthole, no bath or toilet, and maybe enough luggage space beneath the bottom bunk to accommodate two shaving kits. Most of the fellow Fulbrights we met on board dressed and behaved like refugees on a banana boat. The grub proffered at communal tables in the dreary dining saloon would have been eschewed by swine in any Virginia pigsty. And since the ship had no stabilizers, much of the voyage was spent either heaving up the swill in our bellies or tossing back enough gin at the bars to numb every nerve cell in the disoriented brain. A few years later, when I began to develop a veritable passion for crossing the Atlantic by luxury liner in the comfort of cabin or first class, a few contumelious passengers would often ask if I'd ever traveled "down below." Needless to say, I had a few arresting tales to tell.

Paris in the early sixties was still a Hemingway fantasy, a vibrant, highly cultural, and romantically bohemian city where, under de Gaulle's Fifth Republic, modest postwar prosperity was starting to blend propitiously with a traditional, unique way of life that eventually would be radically or partly shattered by discoteques, *nouvelle cuisine*, high-speed underpasses, McDonald's, and computer technology. Of course, there were no laundromats, toilet paper resembled waxed sandpaper, and deodorant simply didn't exist even in the most well-stocked pharmacies and Prix Unics. Incredible as it sounds today, however, a Left Bank hotel room with shower and *petit déjeuner* could be had for the equivalent of three dollars per night (or eighteen dollars a week); dinner in favorite Latin Quarter bistros like Prolognan, Procope, and Aux Assassins ran about four dollars a head; and even in the finest temples of haute cuisine, we heard that it was hard to spend more than fifteen dollars for a sumptuous meal—wine included.

Piaf was singing her same sad love ballads in louche music halls, Cocteau or Sartre or Giacometti could often be spotted in places like the Odéon, Café de Flore, and Grand Palais. And for the price of a cloudy Pernod or *café filtre*, one could nest for hours on the terrace of Brasserie Lipp while, perched inside on overstuffed banquettes under soaring antique mirrors, powerful cultural and political figures like André Malraux and François Mitterand discussed the future of France over steaming platters of *pot-au-feu*. The gory Grand Guignol was still terrifying audiences up in Montmartre, the Follies Bergères exuded a racy decadence reminiscent of the *belle epoque*, and, though certain streets and avenues could be filled with irate French students demonstrating for or against Algerian independence, in restaurants like Au Pied de Cochon in the ancient food market of Les Halles, it was almost a ritual to meet friends in the wee hours of the morning for bowls of cheese-crusted onion soup, carafes of red wine, and lots of bonhomie.

Paris was all and more than I expected, and the fact that, thanks to my parents, I was one of the few students lucky enough to own a car (a blue Volkswagen Beetle) only enhanced the way I and my cohorts quickly got around a city that I knew instinctively would continue to captivate me for the rest of my life. Although it had come as a shock that the French spoken by Parisians bore little resemblance to the lingo I so confidently and arrogantly thought I'd mastered in college, in just a matter of two weeks I was beginning to communicate halfway intelligently with the personnel at the Cité Universitaire where Fulbrights were housed, with the orientation teachers at the Alliance Française, and even with waiters in cafés and restaurants and the gruff old lady behind the counter of my favorite *tabac*. As for academic pursuits, well, those could wait till all the cultural and social edification was over.

On a rainy, chilly October morning, Jimmy and another Fulbright helped me load a gigantic steamer trunk, suitcase, and portable Royal typewriter (all my worldly goods for a whole year) into the VW in preparation for the 350-mile drive down to Grenoble. Leaving Paris and my friends was traumatic enough, but lighting out on my own into *la France profonde* with little idea of what awaited me was nothing less than frightening. Before I left the U.S., my worldly father, who had already exposed me somewhat to fine dining in New York, Chicago, San Francisco, and even London, said he'd read in *Holiday* magazine about a good restaurant he thought was called La Côte d'Or in Saulieu, a small town almost equidistant between Paris and Grenoble and on my direct route. Maybe, he suggested, I could stop there for lunch.

Not, mind you, that I'd ever heard of or cared about Michelin except as a company that produced good tires and road maps, meaning that I certainly had no copy of the legendary red restaurant guide that would have verified the name and location of the restaurant (and that would one day become my bible in France). Nor, as I made my way guardedly down Route Nationale 6 in the pouring rain with visions of the Alps and French classrooms and lofty scholarly endeavors running through my brain, was I in the least bit aware that at Sens and Auxerre and Avallon and elsewhere in this part of Burgundy existed some of the finest food and wines in the entire country. My most immediate and anxious concerns were getting to Grenoble, finding a place to live, getting officially enrolled at the Faculté des Lettres at the university, and meeting the distinguished professor Léon Cellier.

SAULIEU the sign read through the flapping windshield wipers. It occurred to me that I was peckish, so slowing down, I looked from side to side through the fogged windows, hoping to catch sight of the restaurant Daddy had mentioned. I saw nothing in the village that looked like a restaurant, but across the busy highway from a gas station I did notice the name Hôtel de la Côte d'Or in gold letters framed in a blue band on a nondescript, yellowish, two-story building. Not really caring where I ate, and thinking that in this hotel I could probably get a good omelette with *pommes frites* or a *croque-monsieur* like those I'd had in Paris, I slammed on the brakes and turned into the small parking lot. I did find it strange that next to me was a majestic silver Bentley, but after throwing on a corduroy sports jacket over my crewneck sweater, I made sure the doors to the car were securely locked and raced through the drenching downpour for the hotel entrance carrying only my new and very French satchel containing my important papers and documents.

The lobby couldn't have been less ostentatious or more welcoming: a plain tile floor, wood-paneled walls covered with what looked like lots of family pictures and menus and certificates, simple chairs, a tiny bar, and a desk behind which was a rack of mailboxes and room keys tended by a middle-aged, slim, neatly dressed lady.

After we'd exchanged the appropriate *bonjours*, I huffed, "*Quel temps!*" casually whisking the sleeves of my wet jacket with my hands.

"Oui, c'est affreux," she agreed, rolling her gutteral "r" and pronouncing the difficult "eu" in ways I could only envy.

"I was hoping to have a little lunch," I informed in my most careful French. "Maybe an omelette or sandwich."

Madame appeared somewhat taken back. "Does Monsieur have a reservation?"

Now it was I who was a bit surprised as I uttered, "No."

"I'm sorry, Monsieur," she continued politely, "but we serve no sandwiches in the restaurant." She hesitated a moment, glancing again at me suspiciously before looking down at a thick notebook. "But due to the weather, we have had quite a few cancellations today, so if Monsieur would care to be seated in our dining room and see the menu . . ."

"Ça va," I confirmed offhandedly, now aware of the intoxicating aromas of food wafting in the air and even more hungry.

Coming from behind the desk, she then ushered me into the restful, almost homey, half-empty restaurant and seated me at a small table next to a window outside of which I could hear cars and trucks speeding by on their way to Paris or Lyon. Across the room was a large display table with baskets of fresh fruit, an assortment of cheeses with a little tag stuck in each, and a huge, rosy ham positioned on a silver stand. The impeccable white tablecloth was heavy starched linen, the small vase of flowers unassuming, the silver brightly polished, and the glassware thin and elegant; and just before a plainly dressed, dark-haired lady arrived to ask if I'd like an apéritif and hand me a menu, it suddenly dawned on me that every man in the place except me was wearing a necktie.

This slight shock was nothing compared with the jolt in the pit of my growling stomach when I started to study the menu and saw the strange dishes and hefty prices. *Timbale de Morilles Chatelaine, Quenelles de Brochet Mousseline, Gratin de Queues d'Ecrevisses, La Potée Morvanaise—* I'd just as soon have been trying to decipher Sanskrit. In Paris, I'd had complete meals in bistros for no more than seven new francs; here that was the price of a single appetizer. Remembering that my solvency was all of ninety-three dollars a month, my first urge was to escape with some outlandish excuse to Madame and continue driving till I found a humble café. Then I recognized *Le Coq au Vin à l'Ancienne* priced at eight francs, and detected a half-bottle of some beaujolais for two francs, and was delirious over the fragrances emanating from the next table, and—damnit, I was starving to death.

I tore off a piece of bread from a rugged loaf nestled in cloth in a wire basket and spread butter on one end. The bread was tangy and chewy, the butter sweet, with a slight hazelnut flavor like none I'd ever tasted, not even in Paris. I was beginning to relax.

Pad in hand, the lady returned to the table while I was sipping Pernod and eating bread and listened as I indicated that I'd have just the *coq au vin*.

> NEW YORK, SEPTEMBER 1961—
> *Dinner with Lucius Beebe (clear turtle soup, smoked eel, pheasant with truffle sauce, pear brandy soufflé, and Krug champagne) before sailing to France aboard Queen Elizabeth. "My dear young man," he said at one point, "you'll learn more in five days aboard that liner than you'll learn in a year at any university."*

"*Et pour commencer, Monsieur?*" she inquired, a sudden expression of extreme disappointment or pity on her smooth face when I shook my head. She then smiled, placed a carbon copy of the order on the table, and left.

In a few minutes, a tuxedoed waiter brought the bottle of wine, uncorked it, and very ceremoniously poured a little into the wide-lipped glass for me to taste. It was fine, I nodded with confidence, feeling rather proud of myself and actually quite taken with the wine's fresh and intensely fruity flavor. My eyes followed another waiter carrying a large silver tray to a table of four smartly dressed diners across the room, and as I watched him and a helper begin to carve and serve what looked like two chickens or ducks, I couldn't help but also catch sight of a short, stout, mustached man in a white chef's uniform peeking through what must have been the kitchen door. At first I assumed he was observing all the action with the fowl, but soon it became perfectly clear that the object of his attention was . . . me.

"The chef would like for you to taste his *terrine de gibier*," whispered the waiter, placing a small, meaty rectangle in front of me and a china pot of mustard and ceramic jug of what looked like miniature pickles on the table. Baffled by both the gesture and the word *gibier* (and innocently wondering if I'd be charged for the starter), I nonetheless thanked him and cut into the pâté. Slightly gamy, coarsely textured, and so subtly seasoned that no particular agent could be identified, it was remarkable, and when I added a touch of hot mustard and bit into one of the salty pickles and took a sip of the wine, the sensation was startling.

After a great flurry of scraping bread crumbs off the tablecloth, changing the silver, and replacing my napkin, the waiter then rolled over a handsome wooden cart on top of which rested a large, shiny copper pot, two covered copper containers, and a plate of what appeared to be heart-shaped pieces of bread. By now I should have suspected that I was in no ordinary hotel dining room. I didn't, nor was I fully prepared when the waiter formally announced "*Le Coq au Vin à l'Ancienne pour Monsieur*" as if I'd ordered foie gras studded with diamonds, served a first portion topped with the beautiful fried croutons rubbed with garlic, and spooned a few buttered green peas and parsleyed boiled potatoes from the other containers into separate china bowls. The stew, which also contained tiny onions and mushrooms, was almost black, and although I'd had *coq au vin* before in the States, even at the famous Pavillon in New York, and indeed in simple Paris bistros, I knew the second I took my first bite of this robustly rich, smooth, incredibly sapid chicken that I'd really never eaten *coq au vin*. What I was also certain of was that while I ate, the same pudgy man in the white uniform would crack open the kitchen door and glance in my direction.

For maybe forty-five minutes, I slowly relished my meal, at once aware that this had to be what genuine French cuisine was all about and, as the alcohol asserted its authority, slightly depressed that I had no one with whom to share this special moment. In years to come, life would be such that I'd learn to appreciate dining alone and actually prefer solitude to inordinate conviviality, but when you're in the flush of youth, and accustomed to family security and the fellowship of friends, and blindly in love, nothing can be so dispiriting—especially far away in a foreign land—as finding yourself truly enjoying something like a great meal with nobody else to partake in the experience.

Just when I had begun feeling a little sorry for myself and wondering whether I could afford at least a cup of wonderful filtered coffee, the waiter appeared again, this time with a glistening apricot tart and bowl of *crème fraîche*. *"Avec les compliments du chef,"* he pronounced proudly before asking if I wouldn't also like a cup of coffee. I was dumbfounded. Who was this chef sending out food I hadn't ordered, and why? Had I perhaps been mistaken for another customer? Cutting into the luscious tart, the second question was answered when I suddenly realized that, except for an extremely well-tailored man with a striking woman who looked remarkably like Princess Grace, I was the only person left in the restaurant and that it was almost three o'clock.

After the coffee had been delivered, I'd no sooner tapped a cigarette from my pack of Winstons than a waiter materialized from nowhere with a heavy gold lighter at the ready. Across the room, the handsome couple finally got up to leave, only to be met at the entrance by both the mysterious chef from the kitchen and the kind lady who'd seated me. There was momentary chitchat, a cordial bowing and shaking of hands, and the customers left. Knowing that I too had to get back on the road, I was about to signal for the check when I noticed the plump chef heading toward my table.

"Did Monsieur enjoy his lunch?" he asked pointedly in rapid but articulate French. His voice was soft but authoritative, his small mustache perfectly trimmed, his fingers short and stubby, and there were heavy bags under the most melancholy brown eyes I'd ever seen. He appeared to be at least in his early sixties.

I assured him it was one of the best meals I'd ever had, then inquired timorously if he'd been the one who sent out the appetizer and dessert.

"And what did you think of Dumaine's terrine?" he diverted my question, a smile on his comfortable, lined face.

"What kind of terrine?" I almost stammered, figuring he was either using another term for *gibier* or referring to some abstruse moniker like those I'd seen attached to so many French dishes on menus.

"*La terrine Dumaine,*" he repeated proudly, his expression lighting up even more. "*My* terrine. My *terrine de gibier.*"

I finally understood and said it was extraordinary, like nothing I'd ever tasted—though I couldn't begin to identify the seasonings.

"Ah, that's the most important aspect," he continued, withdrawing a rumpled pack of Gauloises from a pant pocket and lighting one with a match. "Are you English?"

"American."

"*Ah, américain.* Well, *jeune homme,* for an American, you have curiosity—I can tell. And you speak French well. This must be your first time here."

"Actually, it's my first trip to France," I clarified, wondering whether I should ask him to sit down. "I'm a student—a Fulbright scholar—and I'm going to study at the University of Grenoble."

He didn't seem at all impressed. "Ah, my wife and Madame Bonino were right. A student, though my headwaitress had the impression you were English or German or Scandinavian. We get lots of Americans here, lots—especially in summer. I like the Americans. Without the Americans during the war, we wouldn't be here talking now, and I don't forget that. I remember. And the Americans love good cuisine. They're not critical enough, in my opinion, and most believe that great cuisine must be complicated and rich, but yes, the Americans generally appreciate good food."

After that rapid and slightly intimidating lecture, I pointed to the other chair and asked if he'd like to sit down. He ignored the question, as if he hadn't heard it or didn't understand my French, simply tapping an ash into the crystal ashtray.

"Would Monsieur like a cognac?" he offered.

I shook my head with the legitimate excuse that it might make me sleepy and I had a long drive ahead of me.

"And the *coq au vin*. Did Monsieur enjoy the *coq au vin*?"

I'd learned the delightful French gesture of kissing the tips of my fingers. "Monsieur Dumaine, that has to be one of the most delicious, most memorable dishes I've ever eaten," I exclaimed truthfully. "But one question: Why is the stew so dark?"

"Blood," he almost boomed. "Chicken blood—plus pureed livers. It's the only way."

I wasn't about to let him detect my squeamish astonishment.

"*Ah, le coq au vin*," he then almost sang. "There's still nothing like a real *coq au vin* when it's made correctly with a fat rooster that's cooked slowly for a long time." He seemed to be almost in a trance, his sad eyes again sparkling. "*Ecoutez*, I've been preparing *coq au vin* for over forty years, and I think I'm only now finally getting it right."

The man was intriguing me—his forthrightness, and honesty, and . . . passion for food. But skeptic that I already was, I wondered even more why he was being so attentive to a total stranger.

"The flavor of that chicken!" I continued with equal enthusiasm. "How can any chicken have that much flavor? I live in the South in America, and we make wonderful fried chicken, but never, Monsieur, have I tasted chicken with this amount of flavor."

Still standing and smoking, he raised a hand in the air and shrugged the way only the French do. "But Monsieur, that was a mature *poularde de Bresse*, the finest chicken in all the world. You've never before eaten *poularde de Bresse*?"

Of course, I'd not only never eaten a Bresse chicken, I'd never heard of it and had no idea even what or where Bresse was.

Opening his eyes wide, he appeared actually shocked. "*Ah, jeune homme*, you'll pass by the Bresse region on your way to Grenoble, and I can tell you . . . *écoutez* . . . there'd be no Burgundian cuisine without our great *poulardes aux pattes bleues*."

Pattes bleues? The expression threw me.

Old-Fashioned Coq au Vin with Blood Sauce

Serves 6

It's not easy to find chicken blood in the U.S. unless you have access to a poultry farm that slaughters its own birds. Although this dish is richer and thicker when blood is used, it's still delicious without it. Simply substitute a few tablespoons of red wine for the blood when pureeing the reserved liver.

3 cups red burgundy wine

1 medium onion, chopped

2 garlic cloves — 1 chopped, 1 cut in half

1 celery rib, chopped

6 peppercorns

2 tablespoons olive oil

Bouquet garni (celery leaves, sprigs of fresh thyme and parsley, and a bay leaf tied in cheesecloth)

One 6-pound rooster or stewing hen, cut into 8 pieces and liver reserved

Salt and freshly ground pepper

3 tablespoons flour

¼ pound lean salt pork, cut into small cubes

½ cup chicken stock

6 tablespoons (¾ stick) butter

½ pound mushrooms, quartered

15 to 18 tiny whole onions, peeled

¼ cup chicken blood

1 tablespoon red wine vinegar

Olive oil and butter for frying

12 thin squares of white bread

In a saucepan, combine the wine, chopped onion and garlic, celery, peppercorns, olive oil, and bouquet garni. Bring to a boil, reduce the heat to low, simmer 5 minutes, and let the marinade cool. Arrange the chicken pieces in a glass baking dish, pour the marinade over the top, cover with plastic wrap, and refrigerate 12 hours, turning the pieces from time to time.

Transfer the chicken to a plate, pat dry with paper towels, and reserve the marinade. Salt and pepper the chicken to taste and sprinkle the pieces with flour. In a heavy casserole, fry the salt pork over moderate heat till the fat is rendered, about 10 minutes. Add the chicken pieces and brown on all sides. Add the marinade and stock, bring to a boil, reduce the heat, cover, and simmer 1 hour.

Melt 2 tablespoons of the butter in a medium-size skillet. Add the mushrooms, sauté over moderate heat 5 minutes, and add to the casserole. Add 2 more tablespoons of the butter to the skillet, add the whole onions, sauté about 15 minutes or till evenly browned, and transfer to the casserole. Continue simmering the chicken about 30 to 40 minutes, or till very tender, adding a little more stock if necessary to keep the chicken mostly covered.

Meanwhile, cut the chicken liver into small pieces, melt the remaining butter in a small skillet, sauté the liver over moderate heat 2 minutes, and scrape into a blender. Add the chicken blood and vinegar, puree the mixture, and set aside.

In a large skillet over moderately high heat, combine enough oil and butter to cover the bottom, add the bread squares in a single layer, and brown them quickly on both sides. Drain on paper towels, rub each *croûte* lightly with the cut garlic clove, and set aside.

When the chicken is tender, transfer it with a slotted spoon to a heated serving dish and discard the bouquet garni. Gradually add the chicken-blood mixture to the cooking liquid in the casserole, whisking constantly over moderate heat till the sauce is thickened and smooth. Taste carefully for salt and pepper, pour the sauce over the chicken, and serve with the *croûtes*.

"*Pattes . . . vous savez, les pieds,*" he clarified knowingly. "*Elles ont des pieds bleus.*"

Blue-footed chickens. I thought I'd heard everything, but blue-footed chickens?

He seemed surprised that I was surprised, but this only inspired him to begin a short discourse on how these unique blue-footed chickens are bred, their special diet of corn and dairy products, how their breasts are larger than those of ordinary chickens, and why they must be killed at exactly the right age. At one point during his fervid declamation, I once again signaled for him to take a seat, but again he refused, just as he rejected my offer of a Winston with another wave of the hand and the curt comment, "No taste." Across the peaceful room so devoid of artifice, a waiter stood in almost military silence, and I also observed that, from time to time, the dark-haired lady whom I took to be Madame Bonino would appear at the entrance as if she needed to speak with him. He took no notice of either.

He lit up another Gauloise, then hesitated again as if puzzled by something. "You mentioned *le poulet frit* in America. What is fried chicken? I've never heard of chicken being fried. It sounds horrible. You must mean sautéed chicken."

I assured him that I did indeed mean fried chicken, battered and fried in oil like *pommes frites*, and that it was one of the great specialties of the South—especially when my mother first soaked it in . . . I didn't know the word for buttermilk so began scrambling words.

"*Ah, babeurre,*" he finally determined with more interest. "But your chickens. I understand that American chickens are all commercial, and killed too young, and have no flavor, so . . ." He frowned as if truly disgusted, ". . . how could any chicken dish be good without good chicken to start with?"

Although I remembered as a child in North Carolina eating chickens that were farm-raised and how much better they tasted than those bought in supermarkets, I had to admit it was a subject to which I'd never given much thought. To Monsieur Dumaine, such irreverence was nothing less than a cardinal sin.

"*Ecoutez*," he almost bolted, "nothing matters more in cooking than the quality of ingredients. Without superlative ingredients, even the most brilliant chef can produce only second-rate cuisine. My sole comes all the way from Boulogne. I use only butter from the salt marshes of Normandy. And just right here in my own region, we have Charolais beef around Mâcon, and fat pigs from over in the Morvan, and, of course, the Bresse chickens used to make dishes like your *coq au vin*. Ah, *non, Monsieur*, there's no great cuisine without great ingredients, and I use only the best—no matter the cost." His puzzled expression returned. "Buttermilk fried chicken, you say?"

That he was proffering this astonishing culinary edification to a young intruder who had only scant knowledge of what he was talking about impressed but also daunted me, such that I felt compelled— especially since he insisted on remaining standing—to suggest that I was taking up too much of his precious time and really should be leaving. Nonsense, he said, basically. He could tell that I was interested in food, and he loved nothing more than discussing *la grande cuisine* with someone eager to learn more about it, and he felt he had . . . a mission, a duty . . .

All at once he reached up, opened one of the frosted windows, and shut it again. "The rain is worse than ever, and you should not be driving," he declared as if addressing a son or telling one of his kitchen helpers not to cut a piece of meat in so-and-so manner. "Why don't you stay in the hotel tonight? Our rooms are not expensive, and we've had so many cancellations. Ah, then you could have a nap, and Dumaine would prepare for you maybe a simple *omelette aux fines herbes* this evening since you've had a large lunch, and . . . you're interested in *les poulardes de Bresse*, are you not?"

I uttered a nervous "*Oui, Monsieur*," my brain reeling.

"*Eh bien*," he continued, "I'm due to see my chicken woman early tomorrow morning—I haven't been too happy recently with the size of her chickens—so after a nice breakfast of fresh brioches and apricot preserves, you'll follow me in your car down to the farm and I'll show you our special chickens—the finest in the world. It's on your way to Grenoble, not far off the main highway."

Now my head was really spinning. I knew I had exactly four days to find an apartment in Grenoble and get settled before class registration. I knew there would be other Fulbrights to meet, and that in three days there was a scheduled conference with our local adviser, and that Professor Cellier was expecting me. Exactly what would a night in this hotel cost me? Was breakfast included in the price? And could I really afford another meal in the restaurant? On the other hand, I reasoned, I'd have to pay for a hotel in Grenoble plus dinner, and it was stupid trying to drive at least another 150 miles in the pouring rain, and . . . when would I get another chance to see those blue-footed chickens?

PARIS, OCTOBER 1961—

To cheese shop called Androuët with Monique and Jimmy, then lunch in Luxembourg Garden—just cheese, wonderful bread and Normandy butter, and red wine. Never knew that many natural cheeses existed. One, called Vacherin, so soft and runny we had to eat with a spoon. God, never tasted anything like it. Why in hell can't we have cheeses like this in U.S.?

Southerner that I was, I'd already led something of an impatient, rebellious life, so it didn't take too much further self-debate before I found myself being led by Madame Dumaine up the narrow stairs of the hotel to a room that was plain but neat. I did indeed take a good nap before soaking in a hot tub and returning to the dining room at precisely eight o'clock ("The only thing my husband demands and expects is punctuality," Madame had warned) for a soft, golden, creamy omelette. And what I remember most was hearing the faint clanging of pans in the kitchen after I returned to the room and leaning out the window far enough to watch a busy pastry chef go about making bread and croissants and brioches for the next day. At least for the time being, my apprehension over what lay ahead for me abated, and the loneliness of being away from those I missed was relieved by the consoling reality of a few kind people who seemed to care about me, amazing food and comfortable lodging in a quaint country inn, and the ubiquitous sounds of a language that I loved and was now being forced to speak at every encounter.

Remembering what Madame had said about punctuality, the next morning I was packed and in the lobby checking out at 7:45, ready for my 8:00 date with Monsieur Dumaine. Except for the stunning lady who looked like Grace Kelly sitting in a deep chair reading a magazine, the area was empty and quiet. My entire handwritten bill, including the lunch, dinner, and room, came to all of thirty-nine francs (about eight dollars), and I noticed I'd not been charged for the extras at lunch or for breakfast. What I perceived as special attention and generosity continued to mystify me, the only logical explanation being pity for an indigent, naive student on the threshold of calamity.

"I must come back here someday," I informed Madame Dumaine as she carefully folded the bill and tucked it into an envelope. "You have been so nice to me."

"It's been our pleasure, Monsieur," she assured in her quietly formal tone, handing me a hotel card. "But Monsieur must remember next time to call for a table reservation—at least a few days in advance. We can be very busy. Now you go with my husband to Bresse." She cracked a smile. "You're lucky he's still in a good mood."

Scanning the pictures and memorabilia covering the walls while waiting for Monsieur Dumaine to appear, my eye caught an interesting framed sign addressed to "Cher Client" that listed dishes the chef would prepare with 24-hour notice. There was *Un Pâté de Pigionneaux Rabelaisien, Un Feuilleté Léger de Queues d'Ecrevisses, Une Chartreuse de Perdreaux, Un Lièvre à la Royale, Un Porcelet Rôti Farci de Boudins Blancs et Noirs,* plus many others with words that meant little to me.

"*Ah, Bonjour, jeune homme,*" I heard from behind as Monsieur Dumaine caught me studying the plaque. It was exactly eight o'clock; he was dressed in badly wrinkled corduroy trousers, a heavy flannel shirt, and a well-worn car coat, and he appeared a little restless. "The next time you come, Dumaine will prepare something special for you." He nodded discreetly at the lady in the chair. "Did you notice Princess Grace over there? Such a refined lady, and she knows good food. But the chickens await us. *Allons-y.*"

Outside the sun was brilliant after the torrential rains, the fall temperature invigorating, and after my guide told me simply to follow him, I watched as he virtually stuffed himself behind the wheel of a small, white Simca and zipped out onto the busy highway, the ever-present Gauloise dangling from his lips. At Chalon, we turned east and continued on a narrow, bumpy, rural road, slowing down only when, approaching a small farmhouse with a fenced-in area on one side, Monsieur Dumaine stuck his arm out the window and signaled me to pull up behind him on the grass. Extracting his bulk from behind the wheel, he motioned for me to join him at the fence and pointed down to the largest, filthiest cream-colored hogs I'd ever seen, all wallowing around nervously in the rain-soaked mud as if they hadn't yet been fed. The stench in the air was potent.

"*Voilà quelques-uns de mes cochons,*" he announced gleefully, staring at the feculent beasts with pride in his eyes. "We have no time to stop, but I wanted you at least to see some of the pigs I use. They're fed only dairy products and potatoes." He continued to admire the oinking swine. "Beautiful, aren't they? Beautiful as those over in the Morvan. The best pork in all of France."

After viewing the pigs, we drove maybe fifteen minutes longer, passing a large herd of Charolais cattle with their characteristic white bangs of hair and eventually pulling up to another large farmhouse, this one flanked by a smaller, wooden, multidoored construction surrounded by a vine-covered wire fence inside which were pecking at the ground perhaps a hundred of the whitest, biggest chickens with red combs I'd ever seen. And yes, their feet were indeed a purplish blue.

"*Et voilà, Monsieur, les nobles poulardes de Bresse,*" Monsieur Dumaine boasted in his gentle voice just as a woman almost as stout as himself bolted from the house into the yard. The two shook hands, and he introduced me simply as an "American Monsieur" who was interested in chickens. After the two exchanged a few serious words I couldn't catch, she opened the gate to the pen, sending the chickens clucking to the opposite side while we began clomping through innumerable small piles of chicken dung. Then, holding out both arms and moving steadily toward the convulsive white flock, she finally managed, with one quick thrust, to grab the wing of an enraged rooster and secure him in both hands. As I stood there, the soles and tips of my shiny brown loafers already covered with muck, Monsieur Dumaine poked at the angry chicken's breast, asking the woman one question after another and often sounding as piqued as the rooster. Once they'd finished their heated dialogue and both appeared satisfied, he directed me to caress the bird's ample breast to feel how supple yet compact it was—certainly like no scrawny commercial chicken. Without warning, the flapping brute suddenly pecked my hand savagely, leaving a tiny wound just on the verge of bleeding. Monsieur Dumaine and his chicken lady merely chuckled, and she tossed the vicious creature back on the ground.

After the two talked further and apparently settled whatever it was that troubled Monsieur Dumaine about the chickens, he led me back to Route 9, again pulling over to the side and unmolding himself slowly from the small car as I tried to wipe the crap off my shoes with paper napkins.

"Beautiful chickens, were they not?" he said excitedly after I opened the door.

"A rare experience for me, Monsieur Dumaine," I assured.

"I respect my chickens," he went on. "We must respect all food, for it is life itself. And that's why I do everything within my power as a cook to produce the best dishes possible. When you come next, *jeune homme*"—he seemed to take my return for granted—"Dumaine will prepare for you a simple roasted chicken with truffles . . . or maybe a chicken stuffed with ham mousse . . . or, yes, my *pot-au-feu* of chicken." His dolorous eyes again brightened as they always did when he was talking about food. "And I'm going to look into this fried chicken you mentioned. Yes, I'll do a little research on that."

I thanked him again for everything, we shook hands French-style with a single, quick jerk (a gesture I was gradually getting used to), and for the first time, Monsieur Dumaine cracked a real smile as he waved me on, repeating several times, *"Faites attention et bonne chance!"* Heading in the direction of Lyon, my spirits were revived after my exceptional encounter in Saulieu and the visits to the pig and chicken farms with this strange but remarkable chef. No doubt it had been a unique adventure, but little did I realize at the time to what extent such an unexpected and casual occurrence would inspire my love of France and the French and eventually affect my entire future.

The headiness, however, didn't last, for almost from the moment I checked into the Hôtel d'Angleterre on Place Victor Hugo, walked the vicinity and drove around the city, and then was informed in the middle of the night that already my car had been vandalized, I knew that I'd never really like Grenoble. To be sure, the snow-covered Alps looming in all directions were spectacular, but the city itself was drab, the architecture ruefully antiquated and nondescript, the weather bitter, and the overall provencialism as stifling as that described by Stendhal, a native son, in the early nineteenth century. There were no beautiful parks and squares like those in Paris and Lyon; the university had no trace of a campus to enhance the hideous classroom buildings marred by decades of grime and neglect; attractive shops, public theaters, and concert halls virtually did not exist; and there couldn't have been more than a half-dozen serious restaurants in the entire city. Efforts would be made later on to invigorate Grenoble for its winter Olympics, but in the early sixties, I viewed it as a dead town, from which eventual escape was the only hope.

After living in one seedy hotel after the next for two miserable weeks, I found a room in an apartment to be shared with two French female students on rue Marcel Porte for about thirty-five dollars a month, its only merit being a splendid view of the soaring Alps. Since the place had no heating, it would become routine every month to lug home a huge steel canister of gas from some distributor to feed a flame heater positioned in the middle of the floor, a setup that induced a permanent headache from the fumes. Also once a month, I had the privilege of collecting a set of fresh sheets and towels from my landlady, the availability of a laundromat anywhere in town being totally out of the question. And while there was a tub in the communal bathroom, unless I planned to be home between four and six in the afternoon when hot water was bestowed by the thrifty gorgon of a concierge, my American obsession with bathing would be rewarded only by chattering teeth and the constant risk of pneumonia. My sagging bed was more like a stationary hammock, but even if the mattress had been the equivalent of Serta, the nightly explosions of *plastiques* from all directions symbolic of the raging Algerian conflict would have precluded more than three or four hours of sound sleep.

At the university, I hit it off well with Professor Cellier and, at least in the beginning, attended a number of interesting courses on French Romanticism, the only problem being the overwhelming pungency of body odor that permeated the classrooms and forced me to carry at all times a handkerchief doused with eau de cologne. To economize and meet French friends, I tried earnestly to take most meals at the student restaurants located in what resembled a war bunker, but it didn't take long to realize that I could never tolerate dining on execrable slop with savages more interested in Communist proselytism than the Flaubertian style of prose. Soon I, like the other four American Fulbrights in Grenoble, basically stopped going to classes altogether (attendance was in no way obligatory) and determined simply to show up at my weekly conference with Professor Cellier, travel in the region as much as possible, get to know the French locals, familiarize myself with the culture, and, as my letter from the Fulbright commission had urged, "increase good will and understanding" between two nations.

To nourish myself, I took to eating mostly in cafés and cheap bistros, which is how I happened to meet Pam and Philippe one evening at a modest place called Au Bon Petit Coin, where the limited three-course, prix-fixe menu with a half-carafe of wine was all of seven francs.

"You're American," she asserted boldly in English not thirty seconds after the two had been seated at the adjoining table wedged hard against mine.

"Is it that obvious?" I reacted with some embarrassment while studying the short menu and sipping my standard Pernod.

"The Winstons," she laughed, glancing at the pack on the table. "And the houndstooth jacket, and button-down shirt, and short haircut. . . . We don't see many Americans in Grenoble." She extended a hand. "My name is Pam, I'm Canadian, and . . ." She immediately switched to impeccable French. "This is Philippe, from Chambéry."

Pam was cute, with bouncy auburn hair, delightfully eccentric, and wearing an exquisite light-brown sweater that had to be cashmere. Philippe, with blue eyes and coal black hair that fell sensually in back over the top of a white turtleneck sweater, was staggeringly handsome, like the film idol Alain Delon. As I would learn, Pam was evidently from a prosperous, high-class family in Montreal and had come to Grenoble the previous year to indulge her passion for skiing—nothing more, nothing less. Philippe, on the other hand, was obviously an earnest law student at the university, a keenly intelligent, ambitious young man who seemed as serious about his future career as he was about this sophisticated but free-spirited girl across the table. In the weeks and months ahead, Pam and Philippe would become two of my best friends and see me through more than one episode of frustration and despair; but that first night all I could gather was that she had remained in Grenoble mainly to be with him and that the one obsession they shared, the bonding subject that monopolized their conversations and around which revolved most of their social activities, was dining in restaurants. At the time, I chose not to guess which one probably picked up most of the tabs for this capricious hobby.

"Oh, forget Grenoble itself," Pam snarled after deciding to order *coq au vin.* "The Rabelais has a good *blanquette de veau,* Le Bec Fin does a credible *gratin* and *bourride,* and this place is fine for *bourguignonne* or *pochouse,* but beyond that, Grenoble's a wasteland."

I pretended to follow her commentary, which Philippe interrupted to ask if I'd been to Rostang over in Sassenage or to any of the *bouchons* or *"mère"* restaurants in Lyon. When I confessed utter ignorance, the two looked stunned, almost hurt, as if they were confronted with a real clod. What saved me was Pam's *coq au vin*, which the old waitress placed in front of her.

"That *coq au vin*'s not right," I declared bravely just as she took her first bite. "It's too light, too thin—and it shouldn't have carrots in it."

The two appeared perplexed.

"What do you mean?" Philippe asked, looking up from his *goujonettes* of sole. "That's classic *coq au vin*, like my mother makes and like we eat everywhere.

"Not dark enough," I persisted. "It should be almost black and thickened with the chicken's blood—at least that's what this chef up in Saulieu told me. May I taste it?"

Willingly, Pam placed a morsel of thigh on my plate next to the veal scallop in mustard sauce, then the two glanced at each other with obvious curiosity.

"Did you say Saulieu?" Pam almost gasped.

"Yes, there's this charming little hotel up there where I stopped for lunch driving down, and let me tell you, the chef there prepared a *coq au vin* made with Bresse chicken that you wouldn't believe—it's almost black as ink and smooth as satin and with no carrots. Have you heard about these *poulardes de Bresse*? The chef actually took me to see some. They have blue feet. Can you believe—blue feet!"

Philippe's face lit up. "Certainly, but more important, do you by chance remember if the chef's name is Dumaine?"

Now it was my turn to gasp. "Yes, that's his name exactly—Monsieur Dumaine. How in God's name would you know that?"

The two again looked at each other, then began laughing quietly as if they shared a big secret.

"Jim," Pam began excited, "did you really not know where you were eating in Saulieu and who Alexandre Dumaine was?"

Just the tone of the question was intimidating. "All I know is that it's a delightful little hotel run by Monsieur Dumaine and his sweet wife, and that the cuisine there is unbelievably good."

"And you just showed up with no reservation?" she gulped.

I nodded yes, then explained about the rain.

Philippe reached over and touched my arm. "*Mon ami,* where you had lunch was the Hôtel de la Côte d'Or, and Alexandre Dumaine happens to be recognized as the greatest chef in France—if not the world."

"Three stars in Michelin," Pam added, unaware that my knowledge of Michelin was limited to tires and road maps. "Everywhere in France, he's called Alexandre le Grand. Philippe and I have been trying for months to get a weekend dinner reservation up there."

Pam and Philippe in no way intended to make me feel foolish, apparently perceiving that food simply didn't play that major a role in the life of this vaulting American scholar more disposed to intellectual disputation than to gustatory euphoria. Slowly and patiently they explained to me all about the star system and the power of Michelin in France, why Lyon—just an hour away—was considered to be the country's culinary capital, the differences between *la haute cuisine* and *la cuisine bourgeoise,* and so many other disparate facts pertaining to France's gastronomic heritage and eminence that somehow are never emphasized (if even touched upon) in all those exalted college courses on European civilization. Yes, I, like any other nitwit, certainly knew about the reputation of French food in general before coming to France and had not exactly been denied exposure to certain dishes, but it was only after that simple but exciting three-hour dinner with Pam and Philippe that my interest was really sparked, that I began to construe why Dumaine's restaurant had been so special, and that I determined to explore more fully what was going into my belly. Immediately after breakfast the following morning, I went into a bookshop in the center of town and bought my first red Michelin guide.

It would not be correct to say that I altogether abandoned my academic pursuits while trying to survive in Grenoble, but it is true that throughout most of the winter I concentrated considerably more attention on satisfying my ever-swelling appetite for French food and wines than on elucidating the esoteric symbolism in Nerval's poetry. The second my monthly check would arrive, I'd automatically put aside funds for dining out, and when it became obvious that these would not be sufficient to cover my gustatory needs, I shamefully pleaded abject destitution to my worried parents, which usually resulted in extra cash enclosed in weekly letters.

And the adventure was exhilarating: first visits with Pam and Philippe to La Pyramide in Vienne and Pic in Valence; discovering the lauded haunts of Lyon with two palmy and ravenous friends from Annecy; and an excursion to Père Bise at Talloires for sumptuous crawfish *gratin* and that indigenous, glorious fish called *ombre chevalier*. We even made an overnight jaunt over treacherous alpine roads down to Aix-en-Provence to taste roast suckling lamb raised on lavender and small almond cakes called *calissons*.

No doubt I was savoring both humble and august dishes almost as quickly as my belt notches disappeared in the wrong direction. Each experience taught me something new, each dish revealed still another dimension of French cooking; yet amidst all the ebullience, there still remained no more anticipated and sublime ritual than my periodic meals at the Côte d'Or. Each was carefully planned to coincide with my frequent trips to Paris, and if ever I adjusted my limited budget to accommodate my gourmandism, it was when I knew I'd again be seeing Alexandre and Jeanne Dumaine.

By this time, of course, I was well aware that the restaurant was a mecca for such swells as Dalí, Stravinsky, Horowitz, the soon-to-be married Burtons, a few kings and queens, and dedicated food lovers the world over who ordered expensive wines and left inscriptions of praise and respect in a large, leather-bound *livre d'or* guarded carefully behind the front desk. Somehow I never let this faze me, nor did my menial status ever seem to alter the gracious way I was always welcomed or the close rapport that developed between Monsieur Dumaine and me. At one point I learned that the Dumaines had no children and wondered capriciously if perhaps he was simply trying to share his overwrought enthusiasm with one of many surrogate sons eager to learn all about the master's craft. Could it also have been that Monsieur Dumaine, like so many great chefs I would later get to know, was basically a lonely man desperate to communicate his philosophy and dreams to virtually anyone willing to listen? Whatever the reason, as the months passed our relationship intensified, a teacher-student affinity that would prove to be as deep as that in any university.

Perhaps I was just naive and unwitting at the time, but even after I learned that La Côte d'Or was one of France's distinguished three-star restaurants and Monsieur Dumaine the premier champion of *la grande cuisine*, never once was I made to feel that I was dining in some sacred temple where the chef, with special innovative and mystical powers, was out to prove something to an overawed, dazzled audience.

"I don't really create anything new since only God creates," I remember Monsieur Dumaine declaring one day when I accompanied him to a vegetable market. "French cooking has been evolving for centuries according to nature's laws, and a chef's only job, his only duty, is to interpret and strive to perfect what he knows best. In serious cooking, there's essentially nothing left to create."

Of course, today such a heretical philosophy would bring on apoplexy in headstrong superstar chefs determined to reinvent the culinary wheel; but then, how many chefs today would even attempt to reproduce Dumaine's complex pâté known as *l'oreiller de la belle Aurore*, or the indescribably sapid truffled chicken steamed over an aromatic *pot-au-feu* that still haunts me? And how many could effect his transformation of the peasant dish *saupiquet* into a simple but elegant *jambon de Morvan à la crème gratiné* that he spent an hour one night after dinner explaining to me in the presence of an up-and-coming chef from Lyon by the name of Paul Bocuse? "There's a good deal more to great cooking than ingredients, imagination, and talent," this chunky little man also warned nearly forty years ago, "and you find it out only after many years of careful search and hard work."

"My husband is preparing something *très spécial* for you," Madame Dumaine informed me when I called early one cold February morning to reconfirm my one o'clock lunch reservation. "Be sure, Monsieur, to be right on time."

On this trip, Pam had asked to accompany me, not only because she wanted to see friends and shop in Paris, but because it promised a dining experience that had so far eluded her. Obviously jealous, Philippe was not too happy having to remain in Grenoble to take law exams, nor was I exactly happy when Pam delayed our departure almost thirty minutes by deciding curiously at the last minute that a rather racy miniskirt outfit would be more appropriate than the tame beige pants suit she was wearing. I tried to convince her otherwise, but I'd already learned that once this strong-minded gal made a resolution, debate was out of the question.

Consequently, from the moment we left the city, I maintained a heavy foot on the gas, partly because I didn't dare risk being late for our reservation and partly because most of the time I was excitedly distracted telling Pam what she might expect for lunch. Everything went fine till, just after zooming through Chalon on the N. 6, I heard a shrill, spasmodic siren and saw flickering blue lights in the rear-view mirror. "*Merde*," I cursed, pulling nervously over and watching as the officer got out of his tiny car and approached me on the side. Just as I was scrambling in the glove compartment for my international driver's license, Pam suddenly threw open her door and scooted in her miniskirt around the car before I could even begin fabricating excuses.

"*Bonjour, Monsieur l'agent*," she greeted with poise, standing on one foot so that the other knee was cocked and placing her hands on both hips in such manner that her impressive breasts were revealed in full measure beneath the tight sweater. "We're rushing to have lunch at the Côte d'Or in Saulieu. Do you know the Côte d'Or, Monsieur?"

It was hard to tell whether the middle-aged officer was studying my license or Pam more closely, but once he'd returned the paper to me and informed me that I'd been driving over 80 kilometers an hour through town, he uttered, *"Hôtel de la Côte d'Or? Oui, Madame . . ."*

"Mademoiselle," she corrected cunningly but politely.

"Oh, excusez-moi, Mademoiselle," he apologized. His wandering eyes fixed on Pam as he seemed to be debating whether to write out a ticket. "But of course I know the Hôtel de la Côte d'Or. Everyone knows the Côte d'Or. Three stars. And I've eaten there once."

"Ah, then, Monsieur," she continued fearlessly, "you can understand why we're rushing so as not to be late for our one o'clock reservation. The traffic in Lyon was *affreuse* . . . and there's construction all around Tournus . . . and as you must know, Monsieur, if we're late at the Côte d'Or, we could lose our table." She assumed a mournful expression. "My friend's American, and I'm Canadian, and it's our first visit there, Monsieur."

The officer hesitated another moment, then, prying his eyes off Pam, he gave me a stern look. "Since you're foreigners, consider this a warning, Monsieur," he puffed. "Next time I won't be so understanding." He immediately turned back to Pam, his eyes still roving. "By the way, Mademoiselle, I highly recommend the *quenelles de brochet* at the Côte d'Or. *Délicieux. Bon appétit.*"

"You're shameless!" I whooped as we drove off.

Pam quickly lit a cigarette. "My dear, you just have to know how to handle the French," she quipped, obviously proud of her outrageous performance. "I just saved you big francs."

Even with the delay, we still pulled up at the hotel ten minutes early, and though there were a few glittering luxury cars scattered amongst the Renaults and Peugeots, Pam couldn't get over the unpretentious, almost rustic simplicity of the place—especially after having been in such regal surroundings as those at La Pyramide in Vienne. Madame Dumaine congratulated me, as always, for being on time, perused Pam's outfit suspiciously, then seated us at my favorite table next to the window. By now most of the dining room staff and I knew each other by name, which impressed Pam to no end and made me feel comfortable. As expected, she was overwhelmed by the menu, and, typically, she didn't blink at the prices.

"I should inform you that the chef has taken the liberty today of preparing your main course—*très spécial,*" Madame Bonino whispered as we studied the menu.

Since she had her heart set on ordering the black *coq au vin* I'd raved so about, Pam appeared let down, but when I said that Monsieur Dumaine had done this before, that we really had no option, then guaranteed she wouldn't be disappointed, we proceeded to order artichoke hearts with crawfish sauce for

> SASSENAGE, FRANCE, JANUARY 1962—
> *Dinner with Pam at Jo Rostang's restaurant where I ordered my first genuine gratin dauphinois made with local yellow mountain potatoes and farm-fresh cream and baked 2½ hours. How can I ever eat ordinary "scalloped potatoes" again?*

her, *les oeufs au jambon à la gêlée* for me, and a moderately priced bottle of chablis. One bite of her appetizer, a bite of mine, and her eyes rolled back in her head in ecstasy.

Then the anticipated moment came when Jean, Madame Bonino's son, arrived, presented on a platter what looked like medium-size, oblong, golden fish cakes, and quietly announced, *"La Poularde Frite en Marinade pour Monsieur et Mademoiselle."*

"Did he say fried chicken?" Pam gasped in English after the waiter turned and began preparing the plates.

"He did," I vented in equal astonishment, mentioning the conversation I'd had with Dumaine my first night. "But what in hell could they mean by *'en marinade'*?"

"We come to a three-star French restaurant to eat fried chicken?" she almost growled.

I reached over and patted her lovingly on the arm. "Trust me, honey. Or rather, trust Monsieur Dumaine."

And my instincts were right, for what we were served were boned, delicate, moist pieces of chicken that had been gently fried till crisp and partly surrounded by a light, mysterious sauce and that virtually exploded with flavor like none we'd ever experienced.

"God, this can't be true," Pam swooned, dipping another bite into the sauce and commenting on the phenomenal contrast of crunch and smoothness.

"Well, all I can say," I added jestfully, obsessed with the sauce, "is that it's a far cry from Southern fried chicken. Dumaine's a genius."

As expected, the man himself appeared at the table after we'd finished sharing a sublime fresh orange tart and most of the other customers had left. He had a proud glint in his eyes.

"So what did you think of Dumaine's fried chicken?" he asked with typical enthusiasm, standing with a Gauloise between his fingers. "It's light, isn't it?"

"How, Monsieur, did you ever create that?" was my excited response.

He glared intently at me. "I created nothing—nothing. After our talk about your mother's fried chicken, I simply started thinking, and eventually I began reading and searching, and then, one night there it was in one of my old recipe books from the last century: *la poularde frite en marinade.* Wine, vinegar, olive oil, herbs and spices, citrus rinds, garlic and onions—you soak the chicken in the marinade, then flour and batter and fry it briefly in oil, and make a sauce with the marinade plus a little *babeurre.*" He smiled. "No buttermilk in the original recipe—you, *jeune homme,* gave me that idea." He took a long puff, then looked at us both. "Ah, but as I discovered, fried chicken is a very old French dish that was popular a hundred years ago. Like I've said, there's really nothing to create. It's all in the old books, and only a fool thinks he's inventing something new." He smiled again. "*Ecoutez,* that chicken is good, is it not? Of course it was *poularde de Bresse.*"

Pam and I both caught our breath after this discourse on how fried chicken is actually French, and no doubt she would have sat there till dark had Monsieur Dumaine not abruptly apologized that he was working on a special pheasant Souvaroff for a dinner guest and had to get back into the kitchen. She had to catch her breath again when we split the modest bill and she noticed that we hadn't been charged for the French fried chicken.

The only time I recall not talking with Monsieur Dumaine about food and cooking was one night when he and I were seated in the lobby and he thoughtfully asked me about Grenoble and how my studies were progressing.

"To be honest, I haven't cared much for Grenoble from the start," I informed him. "I'm basically bored."

"Then leave," he pronounced bluntly, as if dismissing one of his chefs who was not happy.

"It's not that easy. I'm there on a student grant, as you know."

"There's a way, there's always a way," he assured me, his kind eyes betraying the rebel in him. "I wasn't satisfied living in Vichy, or in North Africa, or even in Paris while working at the Elysée palace, so I left. People told me I was crazy, but I still left—and I haven't had a bad career." He sipped his cognac and puffed on a cigarette. "Tell me: Are you doing what you really want to do?"

The question startled me, and I remained silent for a while.

"I don't know," I finally stammered.

"Ah, well, what do you think you'd like to do with your life?"

I hesitated again awkwardly, impressed that he cared.

"Write. If I were truly free to do anything and didn't have to worry about making a living, what I'd really like to do is become a writer."

Again he fixed his intense gaze on me. "Then, *jeune homme*, you must start writing as soon as possible—before it's too late." He tapped his nubby, gnarled fingers on the arm of the chair, and I noticed that his nails were as messy as ever from cooking. "*Ecoutez*, all that matters is that you love what you're doing. Myself, I had no real education, but I decided at a very early age that what I wanted to do was cook—and cook well. *Ah, oui*, life is short, so we must set out doing what we love to do—

and with real passion and dedication and . . . hard work. There's no other way, no other way." He looked down into the snifter cupped in his fleshy hand. "And we must never stop dreaming."

Suffice it that about a month and a half after that moving conversation, I received notification from the Fulbright Commission that my request (corroborated by Professor Cellier) for a transfer to Paris to pursue my Nerval research had been approved. I was ecstatic. For almost six months, I, unlike two other disillusioned Fulbrights, had survived the monotonous, stolid provencialism of a city I'd never care to visit again. Not that the experience didn't have its merits. Living in Grenoble, I'd been privileged to study with one of France's most distinguished scholars, whose influence would continue to affect my academic career. I'd met some wonderful people who would remain friends for years to come. I'd traveled extensively throughout an entire region of France, come to know a people and culture that would impact my future in ways unimagined at the time, and acquired reasonable fluency in a language I loved more each day. Grenoble matured me spiritually and emotionally, taught me the value of solitude and self-dependence, and made me fully aware of an innate melancholy and stoicism that would eventually serve me well as a defense against disappointment and adversity. Grenoble was a necessary expedient to psychological growth, but when the opportunity to live in Paris finally materialized, I couldn't load up the VW fast enough.

Although life changed radically once I moved back to Paris, I continued to make periodic excursions down to Saulieu not only to eat, but simply to visit the couple whom I now considered wistfully to be my French family. There was always a table for me no matter how booked the restaurant was, my small room was usually available if I decided to spend the night, I was finally permitted to glimpse—but only glimpse—the postage stamp-size kitchen where the master and four helpers turned out culinary masterpieces, and Monsieur Dumaine was never without his surprises. Apparently frustrated by my parsimonious but necessary drinking habits, for example, he appeared at the table in a huff late one evening carrying an opened bottle of '53 La Tâche and two glasses, and when I tasted the rare, glorious burgundy for the first time and was forced to profess total ignorance of its provenance, nothing would do the next morning but for the two of us to cram into the Simca and drive over to the renowned Côte d'Or area itself so I could meet the winemaker and sample a few other vintages.

Over the next months, I was also introduced to Monsieur Dumaine's potato and asparagus grower, his melon lady, and the old man who supplied the tiny, luscious wild strawberries known as *fraises de bois*. All these excursions were fascinating and instructive, but it was not till I accompanied my famous mentor to a farm that produced his favorite version of Burgundy's greatest cheese, *époisse*, that he revealed a side of his personality that few others ever saw—or would believe.

"I'm starving," he grumbled, typically slamming on the brakes when he spotted a café in the village we were passing through at about nine o'clock in the morning. "Let's stop and have a hot dog and beer."

At first I thought I'd misunderstood when he said *saucisse chaude*, but sure enough, after he and the barman had shaken hands and exchanged a few words, Monsieur Dumaine pointed to a contraption with two long, round metal spikes on the back counter and held up two fingers. His friend then reached for two small baguettes, rammed them lengthwise down the heated spikes, and let them stand a few moments. Next, he filled the holes with generous slatherings of spicy Dijon mustard, poked two steaming, fat frankfurters inside of each, wrapped the hot dogs in paper napkins, and handed them to us before drawing two *demis* of Kronenburg beer.

"*C'est bon*," Monsieur Dumaine approved hungrily, consuming a third of the baguette in a single bite and chewing with the same concentration he might apply to tasting an elaborate pâté. "These are good *saucisses*—the best quality, made with our superior pork." He washed down the bite with a slug of beer. "I love a good hot dog—simplicity itself. *Ecoutez:* There's more to good eating than *foie gras.*"

In the fall of 1962, I sailed home aboard the magnificent new S.S. *France*, a more sophisticated young man still determined to pursue an academic career and make my mark the best way I knew how. I never saw Alexandre Dumaine again. In 1963 (the same year, ironically, that Julia Child made her first TV appearance and virtually introduced Americans to the glories of French cuisine), the newspapers all over France announced that he and his wife had sold the Hôtel de la Côte d'Or to a young Burgundian protégé by the name of François Minot, who had vowed to uphold Dumaine's classic tradition. As is the policy when any starred restaurant owner abdicates or dies, Michelin automatically stripped the Côte d'Or of a star, and when Minot later sold out to twenty-three-year-old Bernard Loiseau, the restaurant was dropped from the guide altogether. (A proponent of the reckless *nouvelle cuisine* movement and creator of something weird called *cuisine à l'eau*—water cooking—Loiseau eventually did transform the charming inn into a plush, expensive hotel and, much to my surprise and horror, recaptured the restaurant's three stars.)

After numerous inquiries, I learned that France's greatest chef and his wife had returned to his small hometown of Digoin, not far from Saulieu, and retired there as quietly as they'd operated the legendary restaurant for more than thirty years. While completing my studies, I wrote him a couple of letters in care of the Côte d'Or that went curiously unanswered, and when I finally got back to France in the late sixties, the urge to make further attempts to contact Monsieur Dumaine was checked by my better instincts. Monsieur Dumaine died in June 1974, just one year shy of his eightieth birthday. I was having dinner in Paris at Au Pactole with the expatriot American food author Richard Olney when the restaurant's owner, Jacques Manière, whispered the news. We sat solemnly for a few moments, then Richard uttered sadly, "That's the end of an era."

Unlike Michel Guérard, Roger Vergé, the Troisgros brothers, Paul Bocuse, Alain Ducasse, and so many other ambitious Turks whom I'd come to know and who would strive to revolutionize French cuisine while becoming world superstars, Alexandre Dumaine never wrote a flashy cookbook; he never turned his tiny, archaic—almost medieval—kitchen into a fashionable training arena for visiting young chefs; he never strutted around the dining room soliciting praise; and he never traveled much outside his beloved Burgundy to promote himself. Dumaine's only rebellion was against novelty for the sake of novelty, and he had little patience with egotistical dilettantes eager to reform overnight a sacred culinary tradition that had taken centuries to develop. His major legacy was his inimitable professionalism, his humility, and his profound humanity.

Today, only informed French chefs and food historians recognize Alexandre Dumaine's name as one in the same pantheon with Vatel, Carème, Escoffier, and Point; to the fickle public and most food journalists, he is forgotten. To be sure, Dumaine was an extraordinary chef, but at least to me, he was also a big-hearted, dedicated giant amongst men who once fostered and tolerated a forlorn American student grasping for purpose and inspiration. I long ago abandoned fatuous belief in any form of afterlife; but if by chance there is some magical kingdom looming in the spheres, I'm certain that Monsieur Dumaine is there still trying to perfect his *coq au vin*, munching on spicy French hot dogs, and tending a huge flock of blue-footed chickens.

Aboard the Leonardo da Vinci, 1976.

Julia Child, who acted as my second cooking teacher after Mother, via her classic *The French Chef* television program, 1967. Courtesy AP Wide World.

The annual awards of *Holiday* magazine, which offered me my first stab at restaurant reviewing.

Holiday's choice of American restaurants

Fifty-Five New York Restaurants of Special Interest to Visitors

CHAPTER TWO

HUNGRY FOR NEW HORIZONS

ITH TWO UNIVERSITY DEGREES and a Fulbright under my belt after leaving France in 1962, I was given the enviable option of pursuing a Ph.D. on a teaching fellowship at either the University of Illinois, the University of Wisconsin, Yale, or North Carolina. Following the blind throbbing of my naive heart, I chose to return to my alma mater, invest in an amorous relationship that would peter out within months and open my eyes partly to reality, and fulfill the scholastic requirements leading to a professorial career while teaching beginning courses in French language and literature to undergraduates.

Chapel Hill in the early sixties (with Duke University almost next door) was not only an eminently intellectual community, but one of the very rare areas of North Carolina (indeed, of the entire South) that boasted a high tolerance of homosexuality at least a decade before the movement toward gay liberation. Elsewhere in the state, queens were still literally being sent to mental wards and the state penitentiary for "crimes against nature," whereas Chapel Hill was virtually a latter-day Gomorrah, a sequestered haven where the lifestyle of most gay students was basically ignored and where even faculty members could set up house discreetly with a lover without fearing disastrous consequences.

As in my case, it was not unusual for gay graduate students to socialize in private with certain professors under whom they were actually studying, a potentially touchy relation that had to be predicated firmly on mutual respect and could prove to be as enriching to one's academic development as the most stimulating seminar on Baudelaire. I loved Chapel Hill, I had wonderful friends and teachers there during my four years as a doctoral candidate in Romance languages and comparative literature, and while, admittedly, I led a wildly promiscuous life in my free time, I, like the majority of those with whom I associated, was a serious student and instructor who never allowed social shenanigans to interfere with my studies, teaching responsibilities, or professional ambitions.

Unlike gays of the present generation, caught up in their multiple causes, we at Chapel Hill never seemed to take our sexuality all that seriously back in the sixties. This was due, maybe, to the fortunate influence of older, seasoned, well-adjusted acquaintances who, by example, taught us not only how to deal with society's bigotry, but actually how to benefit from our quiddity. Always utterly secure in my sexual fabrication, I perceived being gay as a normal and felicitous quirk of nature, an engaging circumstance that set me apart from the herd, and an excuse to indulge freely in high camp (a lost art) and have lots of outrageous fun and frolic. I rarely analyzed the pros and cons of my plight, and to this day I still consider solemn deliberations on homosexuality to be almost as boring as listening to women talk about failed marriages and having babies.

If Chapel Hill was an intellectual and libidinous paradise, it was also a gastronomic desert, where liquor and wine by the glass in bars and restaurants were still forbidden by state law and where nourishing oneself on a daily basis generally meant eating in dull cafeterias and coffee shops, venturing out to a rowdy steak house or barbecue joint, or convening in some destitute graduate student's derelict apartment for the predictable mystery casserole made with canned soup. One queen in the English department, for instance, who would go on eventually to be appointed dean at a major Texas university, could always be counted on to produce a bizarre baked confusion of leathery pork chops, soggy rice, raisins, and condensed milk as fodder for a louche Saturday night drag party attended by a few of the most respected faculty members of the university. Another friend, a brilliant pianist destined to join the faculty at the Juilliard School of Music in New York, prided himself on the most disgusting brussels sprouts quiche imaginable, reason enough for my everlasting aversion to the vegetable. And how could I forget Marcie, a ravishing nymphomaniac from South Carolina

> GLENDALE SPRINGS, NORTH CAROLINA, JUNE 1967—
> *Drove today with Mother and Daddy up to Clayton Long's farm to buy two real country hams. I wondered if the vicious dog snarling at the gate was there to protect a little moonshining on the side or frighten those damn state inspectors who Clayton says are about to put him and every other ham producer out of business with the ridiculous new regulations.*

who, characteristically, was writing a complex doctoral dissertation on Tennessee Williams; who, by her own confession, had seduced three out of the four married, tenured Italian professors in the Romance Language department; and whose culinary specialty was a concoction of Campbell's baked beans, bacon slices, orange juice, and marshmallows glazed to crusted perfection in the oven and served with a congealed canned fruit salad. As for myself, thanks to my talented mother's early teachings, I could already turn out reasonably good fried chicken, Brunswick stew, and buttermilk biscuits, but beyond the standard Southern repertory I was almost as green in the kitchen as my crazy classmates.

Partial salvation did emerge in 1963 when my fellow Fulbright, Jimmy, called excited early one evening to say that I had to drive over to his small house to watch a segment of some phenomenal new cooking series (I still didn't own a television). The show, of course, was *The*

French Chef. The star was a large, slightly daft woman named Julia Child, and although the program was in black and white, we sat absolutely transfixed as she demonstrated for unsophisticated America the glorious cuisine we both had so relished during our year in France. In no time we and two other Francophiles rushed out to buy *Mastering the Art of French Cooking*, and watching Julia every Wednesday night with cookbooks in hand became a veritable ritual.

Soon we all owned Le Creuset pots and sauté pans, Sabatier knives, and an assortment of whisks, sieves, mortars, and fancy measuring cups, most of which had to be ordered from the Bazaar de France in New York. Watching and reading Julia, we learned how to make stocks and clarify butter, fold proper omelettes, gratiné vegetables and seafood, compose savory pâtés and stews, mount elegant sauces, and glaze fruit tarts. When time allowed, Jimmy and I would spend afternoons together trying to make aspics, bone fowl, carve tiny tomatoes and carrots and mushrooms into fancy intricate shapes, and even approximate authentic French *petits pains*. Of course, in those days we had no access to delicate milk-fed veal or crème fraîche or even genuine Dijon mustard, but we learned by instinct to substitute young Kentucky Wonder green beans for the thin French variety, spring onions for shallots, and our superior slab bacon for lardons. Eventually, all of this interest and effort would be manifested in our Friday night "Julia Dinners," the idea being that once a month each of us four would take turns preparing a different French meal based exclusively on recipes from our culinary bible. This exciting venture lasted over two years, the experience changed our lives forever, and even dear Marcie eventually joined the club. Between trysts with Tennessee Williams's dramas and her inamorati, she actually managed to produce a very credible carbonnade, which made a welcome change from her standard baked-bean atrocity.

I was also very lucky to have a rather eccentric half-Greek, half-Swedish father, born in New York City, whose passion was fine dining and who, for as long as I could remember, had exposed Mother, my sister, and me to some of the country's greatest restaurants on a regular basis.

Daddy couldn't fry bacon, but he not only knew good food, he made it his mission to become acquainted with renowned restaurateurs in New York, Chicago, San Francisco, New Orleans, and any other city he deemed worth a gastronomic visit. As a result, at a still tender age I'd already been introduced to Ella and Adelaide Brennan in New Orleans, to Maude and Dave Chasen in Los Angeles, to Phil Brody at the Pump Room in Chicago, and to the legendary Henri Soulé at Le Pavillon in New York. In the early days, I'd hardly really cared about or fully appreciated my father's efforts to turn his yokel son into a worldly gourmet, but by the time I'd entered college, Daddy's pilgrimages had begun to take on new importance: there was more wonder and excitement about eating French, German, and Italian dishes, and at least I'd developed some critical sense of what refined cuisine was all about.

In preparing for our eating trips, my father's reliable and sacred guide was the annual *Holiday* restaurant awards, whose recipients were selected scrupulously by the travel magazine's food and restaurant editor, Silas Spitzer. Throughout the sixties, the *Holiday* awards were the closest thing America had to a comprehensive dining survey, a compilation of over 150 critical reviews that appeared in the magazine's July issue and that Daddy (and soon I) studied with a fine-tooth comb. Typically, he would analyze the awards for a given city, plan a trip, and after determining the restaurants on which Spitzer had bestowed the highest accolades, call to book both lunch and dinner reservations for every sybaritic day of our stay. New York, of course, was the major venue, and while I was in Chapel Hill and well after, it became routine for Daddy, Mother, and me to meet up at the Hotel Astor or the Waldorf two or three times a year, visit our Greek and Swedish relatives, return to restaurants we loved, and check out new ones recommended in *Holiday*. Lüchow's, Café Chauveron, Saito, Gripsholm, Lindy's, and Parthenon were perennial favorites. But it was during a particular dinner in 1965 at Daddy's beloved San Marino on East Fifty-third Street that an incident occurred which was to have a monumental impact on me and my future.

San Marino was, in both *Holiday*'s and my father's opinion, the best Italian restaurant in New York if not the entire country, and after repeated visits, he'd come to know the owner, Tony Gugnoni, on a friendly, informal basis. On the evening in question, Daddy, in his typical fashion, was debating with Tony what dishes we should order, only to have the savvy, colorful proprietor lean down discreetly, nod in the direction of a well-dressed couple a few tables away, and whisper, "Mr. Spitzer has high praise tonight for the osso buco."

His eyes blinking rapidly, Daddy remained silent for a few seconds, then asked quietly, "Spitzer? Do you mean Silas Spitzer of *Holiday* magazine?"

Tony confirmed that it was, adding that he now knew Mr. Spitzer well and that he and his wife came frequently to the restaurant just to eat and relax like any other customers.

If my father was impeccably well mannered in most social matters, he was also bold in the Greek manner, meaning it didn't faze him to ask Tony to convey to Mr. Spitzer that there was a gentleman who greatly admired his work and would like to say hello when the couple had finished dining. And sure enough, once they'd had coffee and were waiting for the bill, the stout, serious-looking man did come over to the table to thank Daddy for the compliment and ask how long he'd been reading *Holiday*. Mother and I were introduced, there ensued further animated talk about various restaurants and dishes around the country that the two men liked and disliked, and by the time Spitzer finally shook my hand a second time and returned to his wife, it was as if we'd made a new friend. Little did I suspect that in the future I'd run into Spitzer again under similar circumstances.

The following year, I received my doctorate at Carolina, accepted a professorship at the University of Missouri, and began the drive out to Columbia one beautiful June morning in my snazzy Mustang convertible. My excuse for leaving the South was the then hefty salary of nine thousand dollars I'd been offered at MU; but the truth was that I, unlike most of my peers, was finally fleeing the nest in search of more distant

Osso Buco San Marino

SERVES 4 TO 6

3 pounds veal shanks, sawed into 6 to 8 pieces 2 inches thick

All-purpose flour

Salt and pepper to taste

3 tablespoons butter

3 tablespoons olive oil

1 medium onion, finely chopped

1 celery rib, finely chopped

1 small carrot, finely chopped

2 garlic cloves, minced

1 teaspoon crumbled dry rosemary

1 cup dry white wine

2 ripe medium tomatoes, peeled, seeded, and chopped (juices included)

Grated rind of ½ lemon

2 anchovy fillets, minced

Dredge the shank pieces in flour seasoned with salt and pepper. In a large, heavy casserole, heat the butter and olive oil over moderate heat, add the shanks, and brown on all sides.

Add the onion, celery, carrot, and garlic and stir till the onion softens. Add the wine, tomatoes, lemon rind, and anchovies, stir, and bring to a low boil. Reduce the heat to low, cover, and simmer slowly till the meat is almost falling off the bones, about 2½ hours.

Transfer the shanks and sauce to a large platter and serve immediately.

horizons, new challenges, and an altogether different cultural climate. No doubt my roots would forever remain as Southern as my drawl, but somehow I knew when I left Chapel Hill that I'd never return to the region that had formed and nurtured me. What I didn't realize at the time was that I was also leaving behind an optimism and happiness that would never be recovered, and that I was embarking on a venture of discovery destined to afford as much disillusionment as reward.

My three years at MU were gratifying, due partly to an affable, helpful contingent of unpretentious colleagues who shared my intellectual interests; partly to eager, bright students still basically unaffected by the crazed political insanity erupting at universities in most large American cities; and partly to a number of beefy, amorous affairs that kept my frisky libido intact. Unlike one brilliant but overzealous professor and friend who, in states of late-night alcoholic frenzy, made a habit of raiding fraternity houses and was eventually run out of town in disgrace, I conducted my extracurricular activities with discretion, either in the privacy of my simple apartment or in the fleshpots of Kansas City and Saint Louis. I also took my job and responsibilities very seriously, thus earning the respect of my colleagues and students and qualifying myself by the second year for a summer research grant to Paris that would not only launch a book project, but subject me to the tumultuous final days of the 1968 student revolution that rocked France as much as the one in Chicago stunned the U.S.

Although Columbia, Missouri, was almost as desolate as Chapel Hill when it came to good restaurants, I did get to know a few eccentric faculty members and graduate students who were as keen as I on throwing rather ambitious dinner parties and who, viewing themselves as disciples of Escoffier, displayed an almost frightening sense of adventure about cooking. For two in particular, literally nothing within the realm of culinary feasibility was beyond exploitation. The first, a portly, rather pompous but likeable professor of art history, was actually quite proficient in the kitchen and could turn out anything from delectable game pâtés to sauerbraten to exemplary seafood brunch soufflés. Once, researching the history of English late-Gothic miniatures, Edzard became obsessed with some of the Elizabethan cookery portrayed in the paintings and determined to reproduce an authentic dinner for five discerning friends. The ceremonial meal began with a highly herbed fowl soup thickened with almond paste; proceeded to a breast of veal boiled (if memory serves) in salted water and vinegar with herbs, sugar, and grated orange rind and served with a paste of capers and hard-boiled eggs; and ended with a creamy "foole" made with stale bread crumbs, eggs, rosewater, currants, sherry, and God knows what else. With it all we drank something he'd concocted called cinnamon wine. Guests did not linger long after the "foole."

Edzard's Elizabethan repast was exotic and . . . interesting, but it paled next to an Italian Renaissance feast prepared and served to the music of Monteverdi by a colleague engaged in a very scholarly book on entertainment at the court of Cosimo di Medici. Although Wickum originally hailed from western Texas and was weaned on chicken-fried steak and roasted goat, his illusions about his cooking expertise were almost as grand as those pertaining to the damsels about campus whom he never stopped trying to woo. More than once his stuffed veal birds, Turkish-fried mussels, and curried lamb balls had sent me racing home for the Alka-Seltzer; had he invited the university's administrative top brass to his Medici extravaganza, no doubt the school would have had to close down the following day.

To whet the appetites of seven select guests, there was first prosciutto poached in wine with grape pulp, capers, and spices, followed by a chilled, rock-hard chopped meat pie in a weird aspic that had liquified all over the platter. We were treated next to some species of nut (maybe almonds) baked with milk curds in vine leaves; but the pièce de resistance, the challenge for which he'd carried out impeccable research and slaved prepping over a period of three days, was a spectacular bevy of tiny marinated quails stuffed into a small capon that was, in turn, stuffed into a huge turkey and roasted. (Never mind that turkeys were unknown in Renaissance Italy and that Wickum was unable to obtain a more legitimate swan.) The complex assemblage was presented very dramatically at table, and all were duly impressed till our host, struggling to wrench the capon from the larger bird's cavity, devastated the entire turkey carcass only to reveal that the interior fowl were half-raw and bloody. Not one to admit defeat in the kitchen, Wickum simply pronounced that this was surely the way the dish would have been best appreciated at Cosimo's court and proceeded to hack away at the pathetic creatures as we looked on with trembling interest, wondering what we could and could not safely ingest.

Thanks to my exposure to Saint Julia and, subsequently, to other equally learned exponents of *la grande cuisine*, in Columbia I produced my share of exotica and considered my tongue pâté, tripe niçoise, and grilled pig's trotters to be exemplary. I experienced my own humiliating moment of infamy, however, the time I decided to serve a horse-meat loaf to a very liberal-minded female instructor in the university's famous journalism school and to none other than my departmental chairman and his wife, both of whom had proved to be good sports when it came to trying new dishes. The inspiration for the loaf couldn't have been more simple and sound. While studying in France, I'd learned to love the distinctive, sweet flavor of horsemeat (*la chevaline*), found widely in butcher shops and inexpensive restaurants (the chopped steak topped with a fried egg—"à *cheval*"—at Aux Assassins in Paris was a particular favorite), and ever since I'd regretted and loudly denounced America's squeamish aversion to eating the meat. When, therefore, a graduate student whose father operated a slaughter house and meat-packing plant up in Saint Joseph informed me that he could get me some federally inspected frozen horsemeat, I determined then and there to prepare a delightful Sunday night surprise for my colleagues, telling them only to come over for an unusual meatloaf.

During the afternoon I ran the reddish, lean meat twice through my proud state-of-the-art grinder, chopped any number of additional ingredients, mixed everything with the appropriate seasonings, and packed the mound carefully into a loaf pan with strips of bacon over the top, just the way I would with a standard meatloaf. Shortly before my guests were due to arrive, I placed the pan in the oven, fed my beagle, and went about other business. After about fifteen minutes, I noticed a faint, strange odor, which became increasingly offensive. I ignored it.

"God, what's that smell?" growled Martin in his typically outspoken manner the second he entered the apartment, his nostrils flaring as he headed for the bar.

The two ladies were initially more chary, but after a while even they began to sniff the air with tortured expressions.

"Dear, are you sure the dog didn't have an accident somewhere in the house?" the instructor friend finally bolted, fanning her face.

Fully aware that the source of the vile stench was the oven, I had no alternative but to explain that it was very scarce horsemeat I was cooking, that it was considered a certain delicacy all over France (untrue), and that I couldn't imagine why its odor was so repulsive. Normally I would have been insulted by the looks of horror and disgust that greeted my revelation, but when I actually opened the oven and thought I might faint, I was the first to open every window in the apartment, cram the stinking loaf down the disposal, and beg even the dog to forgive me. Suffice it to say that I never discovered why the horsemeat was so wretched, that I've been unable to eat the stuff again till this day, and that once the four of us had at least partly recovered, I swallowed my embarrassed pride and drove everybody to a Pizza Hut down the road.

More important than my salient cooking successes and disasters was my discovery of the restaurants of Kansas City and Saint Louis and the friends I gradually made in both metropolises. Columbia was exactly equidistant between the two cities, and rare was the weekend that I didn't pile one friend or paramour into the blue Mustang, take off east or west on Interstate 70 for the four-hour drive over and back, and indulge in still another eating spree. In Kansas City, it was Savoy Grill for shrimp de Jonghe and giant fresh lobsters, Jasper's for impeccable northern Italian fare, La Méditérranée on the Country

Club Plaza for French cuisine that reminded me of Paris, and the Golden Ox at the stockyards for prime beef, which simply didn't exist outside the region. The seafood at Nantucket Cove in Saint Louis was equal to any I'd had back East, the small, romantic Malmaison served an incredible *gigot* with flageolets that's still as vivid in memory today as over thirty years ago, and the toothy pastas and fritto misto at Tony's were on a par with those at San Marino in New York. No doubt Kansas City and Saint Louis were considered by haughty Easterners to be the culinary boondocks, and perhaps my budding palate was still absurdly defective. All I know is that in Kansas City I relished a great deal more than steak and Arthur Bryant's overrated barbecue, and that dining out regularly in both cities contributed a whole new dimension to my gustatory education.

With a full undergraduate and graduate teaching load, not to mention a book and a number of scholarly articles I was ambitiously turning out to enhance my standing in the academic world, I still somehow found time in 1967 and 1968 to try my hand at writing articles about food and restaurants. I would promptly and confidently mail my efforts off to major magazines, and while every single piece was returned with a polite rejection slip, there was one proposal on the restaurants of Kansas City sent directly to the editor in chief of *Holiday* magazine, Caskie Stinnett, that was to have unforeseen repercussions. I had sung the praises of Silas Spitzer and the *Holiday* awards, but I had also boldly questioned not only the exclusion of Kansas City in the annual roundup, but also the overall cursory nature of the restaurant critiques.

"As I see it," I explained, "what is really needed is a series of articles (or, say, an article every two or three months) devoted to truly comprehensive coverage of the major restaurants in various U.S. cities. Not just listings accompanied by a sentence or two, but evaluative discussions. I am a college professor, but I, for one, would be happy and enthused to contribute what I could to such a project." Since Mr. Stinnett never responded to my earthshaking suggestions, I assumed that they had been dismissed and that my services would not be needed.

Not long after that disappointment in 1968, I decided to attend the December Modern Language Association convention in Chicago, not so much to listen to highbrow lectures on the mystical symbolism in Yeats's poetry and Cervantes's use of sexual metaphor as to visit a restaurant called the Bakery that I'd heard a great deal about. Owned and operated by an extremely erudite, controversial, and slightly mad Hungarian by the name of Louis Szathmáry, the restaurant was known for its eclectic menu, and word had spread that Chef Louis's potted duck, turkey chowder, stuffed walleyed pike, goulashes, and banana éclairs were extraordinary creations not to be missed. Since dinner reservations were at a premium, I booked well in advance and showed up exactly on time, accompanied by my latest heartthrob, whose breathtaking beauty more than made up for his stolid intelligence (traits that seemed to characterize all my flames in those wanton days).

Led through a warren of rooms by an attractive Asian lady toward our assigned table, I was observing the rather outlandish decor and the crowd when I thought I recognized an elderly, corpulent man sitting at a table for four with an equally well-nourished lady, he swirling a glass of wine and she still studying the short menu. I looked again, told the hostess and my beau to continue on, and brazenly approached the couple.

"Mr. Spitzer?" I greeted as cordially as I could.

He looked up, then rose graciously from his chair. "Yes?"

I introduced myself, shaking his large hand and reminding him that we'd met with my parents a couple of years back at San Marino in New York.

"Oh yes, of course I remember," he assured me, a smile breaking over his seasoned face. "Osso buco." He acknowledged his wife, Helen, whose hand I also shook, then turned back to me. "And I also saw the letter you sent to Caskie Stinnett at *Holiday*. He showed it to me. Very interesting. So you're now a teacher?"

I confirmed that I was, then nervously apologized for interrupting their dinner.

"I wouldn't mind talking with you about Kansas City," he stated with real curiosity in his voice. "That's one town we don't know very well, and as you pointed out, we've never given any awards there. Perhaps we could chat about it over coffee later on—here at the table. This is a pretty good joint. Don't waste your time ordering the potted duck, though—too dry and under-seasoned. But the veal's damn good." He cracked another smile. "Just don't blow my cover if Szathmáry happens to stop by your table."

> SHORT HILLS, NEW JERSEY, MAY 1969—
> *Invited by R. Neas to Jane Englehart's palatial digs for dinner with duke and duchess of Windsor. Duchess (not too friendly—or attractive) was one hr. late, ate only salad, and talked about dogs. The duke nibbled at beef tenderloin, mumbled something to me about Oxford, and left before dessert. He looks 100. Dieu . . . my one brush with true royalty.*

Joe and I had what we thought was a delicious meal, and sure enough, Chef Louis, a hulk of a man with a bushy handlebar moustache, paid his regards the way he did with all the customers (and I had no doubt whatever that this shrewd professional knew exactly who Silas Spitzer was). Some years later, I'd get to know him well, browse through his amazing eighteen-thousand-volume culinary library upstairs, and write about him; but on this cold December evening, what I cared about most was the prospect of establishing a relationship with Spitzer, the gastronome I admired above all others.

No doubt the couple viewed with some suspicion a college professor dining with a ravishing younger man who had little to say about anything, but that didn't seem to affect Spitzer's interest in my ideas. For a few minutes, we chatted about Alexandre Dumaine in France, Henri Soulé in New York, and Ella Brennan in New Orleans, and I think the much-older man was impressed that such a young American was actually acquainted with these legendary personalities whom we both so revered. Then he wanted to know how often I dined out in Kansas City. Was there good variety in the restaurants, and how many exceptional ones would I peg? Were the posh places truly sophisticated or phony?

How did the clientele dress in the more refined locations, and was wine taken seriously? Where could he find the best prime Midwestern steak, the best country ham and barbecue, the best simple French and Italian cooking? He asked me to describe decors, name specific dishes, and comment on service. I felt as if I were being subjected to another harrowing doctoral oral exam, but Spitzer's enthusiasm and intelligence about food and restaurants were so compelling that I sat there conversing in utter awe.

He then explained that, although he alone supervised the annual selection of and edited all the *Holiday* awards, he also depended on anonymous regional "eaters" whose abilities and taste he trusted to contribute their input to the procedure. Would I, therefore, be interested in sending him critiques of a few Kansas City restaurants with the bare facts, detailed descriptions of the food, decor, and service, and whatever other objective observations I might care to proffer? Of course, food quality and preparation were the main considerations, but reception, atmosphere, service, and any unusual, distinctive aspects of a place were also important. There would be no fee, and the cost of any test meals could not be reimbursed, but if I'd like to undertake the project on a trial basis as with his other scouts, it could possibly lead to future assignments.

That I was virtually being solicited for slave labor with no prospect of financial reward or public recognition was a thought that never entered my mind at the time. All that mattered was that Silas Spitzer had expressed an interest in my hobby and me and that, in some small way, I might be involved in the mechanism behind the country's most prestigious restaurant awards. I considered it a privilege, to say the least, and wasted no time first calling my father (who was fully impressed but, being the ever-practical Greek, needled that my efforts would not be remunerated), then setting out to fulfill the task. Eventually I submitted four reports to Spitzer, who seemed to like what I wrote, and while I had no way of knowing if and how my work would be checked, the following year two of the Kansas City restaurants I'd recommended were accorded their first *Holiday* awards.

Spitzer and I did communicate from time to time in 1969, and no doubt I would have pursued my new undercover "vocation" more aggressively that year had I not been debating whether to accept an offer to teach at Rutgers University in New Jersey. "You won't be happy till you're smack in the middle of New York City with all those fancy restaurants," chided a close and perceptive friend, "so if you're determined to be at the heart of it all, I suppose that Rutgers is a sensible first step."

He was right, of course. Missouri had been an enriching, often exciting experience, but after three years in the Midwest, I was restless to return East, and yes, as near to Manhattan as I could get. As it turned out, I loathed my job at Rutgers; the hippie students were almost as reactionary and dull as my colleagues were pompous, and New Brunswick had to be the most depressingly drab city I'd known since Grenoble. Only my constant forays into Manhattan to hit the gay bars, hear great music, and dine out with new friends protected my sanity.

As a result, I began to neglect my classes and had little inspiration to write further books or scholarly articles. When the opportunity to move into the city and teach at Hunter College materialized (thanks to the influence of an old professor at Carolina), I quickly submitted my resignation at Rutgers (before I most likely would have been fired). Hunter was even worse; the student aptitude level was even lower than that at Rutgers. One evening at the end of the first semester an ambulance had to be called to haul away a thuggish student who keeled over in class from a drug overdose, and I determined then and there, still in my early thirties, to end my teaching days forever. After 1972, I never again set foot in a classroom.

Not that my few years at Rutgers and Hunter were without carnal and gastronomic adventures. It's true that not long after I would abandon the futile demands of the flesh as readily as I'd abandoned a successful but unfulfilling academic career, but if this facet of my life began to assume less and less import, my passion for cooking, dining out in all sorts of restaurants, and writing about food and drink virtu-

ally exploded. I remember saying at the time that my vocational interests had shifted dramatically from the brain to the belly, a theory that
played itself out in the plush culinary citadels and humble bistros of
Manhattan, on the many eating trips about the globe I continued to
take with my parents, in the way I devoured cookbooks and classic volumes about food, and, to be sure, in the production of one unsolicited
(and rejected) article after another. How I would continue to support
myself in New York City with no steady job was the sobering question
that still, in recollection, generates shivers.

Throughout these volatile and insecure times, the one figure who
never ceased to loom in the background of my development and whose
food articles I studied scrupulously was Silas Spitzer. Periodically I'd
send him reports on restaurants where my parents or friends and I had
dined, as well as a couple of full-fledged stories on food topics that interested me. Fully respectful of Spitzer's role as *Holiday*'s one and only official contributor on food and restaurant matters, I never once tried to
coerce him (or his superiors) into publishing a piece of mine, and never
did he suggest the possibility. I was well aware that I was still a tiny fish in
a big pond, but I was also greatly encouraged when my mentor would
write or call from his home in Westhampton Beach on Long Island to
compliment me on something I'd written and offer advice.

It was only then that I began to assimilate Spitzer's biography and
disparate credentials: his early career in advertising and movie pub-
licity, his partnership in the operation of New York's famous
Hapsburg House restaurant during the thirties, his membership in
various distinguished dining clubs and societies over the years, his
writing for *Holiday* shortly after World War II, and his eventual creation of the magazine's first restaurant awards in 1952. And the more
the seventy-six-year-old man's mystery unraveled, the more I
admired him.

Once I'd moved to New York, Si and I became relatively good
friends as he took me more and more under his wing, steered me in the
right directions, and introduced me to a few important press contacts

and restaurateurs. An intensely private man who literally lived to eat well, he often spoke like a gangster but always dressed and conducted himself in public like the consummate gentleman. It was Si who, when I was debating whether to take the dangerous plunge from teaching to writing, advised in his candid and gruff way, "Just get the hell out if you're unhappy and while you're still young." It was Si who, upon reading a piece I'd done on Southern cooking, criticized my flowery, long-windedness in the lead and showed me how to "get to the goddamn point." And after seeing my first story on ocean liners published in the *New York Times*, it was Spitzer who declared, "Use more of that personal style in your food writing and you'll be in the money."

Si was tough, often ruthless, but he was also as honest and fair toward me as when he judged restaurants. Like all serious professionals, his attitude toward other food authors, cookbooks, chefs, dining trends, and experimental dishes could be dyspeptic if not downright cynical, and I shudder today to imagine what his reaction might be to blueberry martinis, Emeril Lagasse, sneakers and T-shirts in upscale restaurants, and macrobiotic sushi. But at least his mind remained open to sensible culinary, literary, and social changes occurring around the world: his attention focused sharply on any facet of the scenario that might promise the next great meal.

Whatever else I learned from Spitzer, nothing would command more respect or serve me better in the future than his sacred rules for reviewing restaurants professionally. Never, for example, visit any restaurant when you're not feeling well, or in a bad mood, or have little appetite. He also believed strongly that any restaurant can be fairly judged after just two anonymous visits, and that once a place has been deemed a winner, it's the critic's duty to identify himself and spend time at some point interviewing the proprietor and/or chef. An attentive journalist should avoid the shabby practice of taking notes on a pad (even concealed in the lap) and learn to memorize as many details as possible; and while it's preferable to request a menu to take away for later reference, snitching one cleverly as a desperate alternative is often necessary and considered a fine art. Observe carefully the service and food presentation at surrounding tables, particularly if you sense you're recognized and receiving special attention. Passing different dishes around the table for tasting is gauche and attracts unwanted notice; if many dishes need to be sampled, always plan to dine with those whose judgment you respect. Despite your being on an expense account, prices—especially for wines—do matter greatly and should be assessed with the ordinary diner in mind. Spitzer worked according to these and many other principles, but his cardinal doctrine, the tenet that governed all considerations and that I'd never forget, was that a great restaurant, whether it's a blue-chip French shrine or humble hamburger joint, is one that has no false pretensions and does extremely well what it set out to do.

And Si was, if nothing else, a visionary who anticipated the gastronomic revolution in the U.S. some twenty years before it took on real momentum. In 1960, two years before anybody had even heard of Julia Child, for example, he wrote the following in *Great Restaurants of America*, the first major book to provide in-depth coverage of well over one hundred restaurants in this country:

> With rewards such as good and well-run restaurants offer, it is inevitable that intelligent young people will be attracted to seeking them. They will learn about the business end of a restaurant by taking business courses, about running a restaurant by apprenticing themselves to good ones, and about cooking from studying under good chefs. They can learn a great deal about cooking simply by practicing doggedly at home; but they can learn more by spending time in a good restaurant kitchen, by going to one of the few good cooking schools which exist in this country, or by going to the Cordon Bleu in Paris. Studying abroad has become quite the thing for young Americans, and studying at Cordon Bleu or the famous hotel school in Vienna would entitle a student to all the privileges he would receive in any other recognized institute of learning. There are already indications that the restaurant career is about to become, for young people in this country, the fashionable thing it has become for young people in England.

Today such realities are taken for granted, but to forecast forty years ago that one day the restaurant kitchens of this country would, for better or worse, be dominated by American chefs was nothing less than a leap of faith.

Spitzer's world suddenly changed in the early seventies when it was announced that *Holiday* had been sold and that its new publishers were moving the headquarters from New York to Indianapolis. "After all these years, I'm afraid the gig's finally up," he informed me sadly on the phone, referring, of course, to the famous awards. Oh sure, the magazine would no doubt continue to do some sort of listing every year, and something had even been said about his being a "consultant," but for all intents and purposes the eminent and mighty *Holiday* awards as conceived and executed by Spitzer were a dead phenomenon. For awhile, Si made monumental efforts to find another sponsor, but even when Caskie Stinnett became editor in chief of the new *Travel & Leisure* and offered Spitzer the food editorship of that magazine, it was understood that annual awards would not be part of the format.

"It's hard to admit, but it seems the public is less and less interested in what some of us old-timers perceive to be truly fine dining," he lamented gravely, describing a decline that would only worsen as the era of inexperienced, superstar chefs, sloppy dress codes, and contrived "New American" cuisine not only gradually reversed every civilized standard that Spitzer and his vast team of "eaters" had struggled so valiantly to maintain, but ushered in . . . the proletarian Zagat.

The irony of all ironies was that one of my first magazine assignments in early 1973 was to be a profile of Silas Spitzer for *Town & Country*. Si found the idea preposterous but did eventually agree to meet me for a formal lunch interview at his beloved Le Mistral in Manhattan, where he hadn't been in some time. Although he was heavier than ever in his dark vested suit and his face looked tired, his spirits rallied as he greeted the fawning French owner with "Jean, the joint looks really great," studied the setting and menu with his eagle eye, and mounted a quiet attack on both a garlicky *soupe de poissons* and a waiter with dirty fingernails. He described a new way he was preparing four-pound lobsters at his beach house, he told about an article on the best American steak houses he was trying to complete for *Travel & Leisure*, and he expressed a longing to return to the Auberge de l'Ile in Alsace to eat the inimitable salmon soufflé. The old hedonist never made it back to Alsace, for about a month after our memorable lunch, his wife, Helen, called one morning to report that he'd died of a heart attack the day before. His obituary in the *New York Times* was scant and "to the goddamn point," and I always suspected that Si had written it himself.

In the years to come, I would meet and get to know other dynamic individuals whose influence on my gastronomic sophistication and literary development would be profound, but never could I forget that it was Spitzer who really lit the spark that sent me in the right direction. All I needed next was a stroke of good luck.

With Don Erickson, my editor at Esquire, 1973.

The original Town & Country crew at leisure: (left to right) JV, Marylou Doyle, Jean Barkhorn, photographer Slim Aarons, Frank Zachary, Melissa Tardiff, and Kim Waller, 1993.

Frank Zachary, editor in chief of Town & Country, and me, 1993.

CHAPTER THREE

LEARNING TO BREAK THE RULES

ATTRIBUTE IT TO THE GREEK BLOOD that flows with ample sufficiencies of whiskey through my veins, but I've always subscribed to the Hellenic doctrine that Fate (Moira) and only Fate governs every moment and phase of our lives. That might reek of fatuous cliché, but how else can I explain the fortuitous series of events that occurred after I abandoned the academic profession in 1972 and embarked rashly on a career in journalism? Virtually overnight, I finally had two unsolicited food articles accepted simultaneously, by *Gourmet* and *Travel & Leisure*. Then, one day shortly thereafter, while scanning a copy of *Esquire*, my eye caught a small notice written by editor in chief Harold Hayes. It stated candidly that the magazine was looking for a sharp new assistant editor and advised any reader who could find anything radically wrong with the current issue to write him a letter, proffer constructive criticism, and— who knows?—maybe land a top-notch job at the prestigious publication. (Such an eccentric editorial challenge in today's flabby magazine world would be viewed as certifiable madness.)

Flipping the pages, I noticed a piece with no byline called "Frankly, My Dear, If It's Bourbon, I *Do* Give a Damn," illustrated with a dramatic two-page photo of at least a dozen colorful sour-mash cocktails. The problem was, I determined instantly, all but one of the drinks were traditionally made not with bourbon, but with blended whiskey or rye. I informed Mr. Hayes, explained why it mattered in great depth and detail, and ended the letter declaring forthrightly that I'd like the editorial job. I didn't get the job, but I did receive a puzzling handwritten postscript on the rejection stating that Mr. Hayes would like to see me in his office the first possible moment.

Arriving somewhat terrified for my noon appointment on the fourth floor at 488 Madison Avenue, I gave my name to the *Esquire* receptionist, took a seat, and couldn't help but notice across from me a thin, pale man dressed nattily in a three-piece white suit, white shirt with a high, starched collar, and white shoes. He asked about my Southern accent, we chatted for a few minutes, and he introduced himself as Tom Wolfe from Virginia. He appeared understandably startled when I said that I had no idea why I was seeing Mr. Hayes, and just as I was about to try to explain, a secretary came to usher him into somebody's office. Shortly thereafter, another fair maid fetched me for the boss himself.

"Hi," greeted the youthfully middle-aged, ultramacho man with a polka-dot bow tie and a short cigar stuck between his teeth, shaking my hand. "Have a seat."

He started back around the desk, then, glancing at his watch, turned and headed across the office to a small refrigerator concealed beneath a bookcase. "Noontime," he announced gleefully in a slight Southern accent, reaching into the fridge for bottles of Bombay gin and white vermouth, a small frosted pitcher and two stemmed glasses, a tray of ice cubes, and a ramekin of stuffed green olives. "How about a martini—a *gin* martini?"

"Sure," I stuttered, watching as he went about what was obviously a sacred ritual of blending and stirring and pouring.

"So, you were a schoolteacher," he said, throwing one leg over a corner of the desk and taking a slow, purposeful sip of his cocktail.

"Well, a literature professor," I corrected nervously, lighting a cigarette.

"Teacher . . . professor—same thing," he dismissed the topic. "I liked your letter. So how'd you get interested in food and wine and booze?"

Giving him a brief rundown of my background, I happened to mention at one point the prime beef I used to drive more than a hundred miles to eat in Kansas City while teaching at the University of Missouri in Columbia.

"Boy, there's nothing I love better than a great steak," he swooned, puffing on his stogie.

Emboldened by the icy silver bullet in my hand, I looked him straight in the eyes. "Excuse me for saying so, Mr. Hayes, but I doubt seriously you've ever tasted a really perfect steak—a genuine K.C. prime strip sirloin."

He started blinking rapidly. "Whadda you mean?" His eyes now widened as if I'd accused him of not knowing how to edit a magazine. "Everybody knows we get the best damned beef in America right here in New York City."

I assured him that simply wasn't true—it was a myth—and that the finest quality steaks, the truly prime cuts, rarely left the vicinity of the stockyards around Kansas City and Saint Joseph and Omaha. I talked about connective tissues, and gobby kidney fat, and streak marbling, and flat-bone density, and dry aging, and I even named a certain producer over in Kansas City, Kansas, who never shipped one ounce of his beef off the premises and catered only to local consumers.

Captivated, his mouth almost visibly watering, Mr. Hayes gazed silently into space for maybe thirty seconds, then glued his dark eyes back on me.

"Yeah. Okay," he ordered with lofty authority, "I want you to fly out there and bring me back one of those steaks and write an article on the perfect steak. Three thousand words. Seven hundred fifty dollars plus expenses. Think you can handle it?"

I sat stunned. "But, Mr. Hayes . . ."

"Let's cut the crap," he interrupted impatiently. "Everybody around here calls me Harold."

"Well, Harold, I'm flattered, but you've never even read anything I've written."

He waved his cigar in the air. "I read that long letter you wrote, and that's enough for me. You can handle the assignment, and by God, I want to taste one of those steaks."

He looked at his watch and picked up the phone. "Bernadette, what about that reservation?" His face gradually flushed as he listened, thanked the secretary, slammed down the phone, and began poking his finger angrily at the window overlooking Fifty-second Street. "I wish somebody could tell me how to get a table at that goddamn frog pond down there. When even the editor of *Esquire* . . ."

"Do you mean La Grenouille?" I asked.

"Yeah, the frog pond. I've been wanting to taste their chocolate soufflé somebody told me about, and this is the third time they've said they're fully booked. Damn!" He slapped the desk.

"Actually, it's pretty simple," I declared confidently, finishing my martini. "I happen to know that the owner, Charles Masson, loves—is really passionate about—unusual, good-looking neckties. Learned that tidbit of information from my daddy, who loves the place. So you might want to have someone drop off a sensational tie with a note enclosed, and I can almost guarantee you'll have a table anytime you want one."

Now Hayes looked stunned—and impressed. "Well, I'll be god-damned." He walked back over to the bookcase, poured his glass half-full, then poured the remaining potent mixture into mine without asking if I wanted it, his mind obviously buzzing. "Any chance you know a few more tricks like that?"

I assured him I did, reeling off ways I'd learned to beat the system at other restaurants, and a few snazzy hotels, and one private club, and even the small first-class, very exclusive Louisianne dining room aboard the majestic S.S. *France.*

"That's great, really great," he almost yelped. "Okay, okay, I have it. You'll also do a piece on how to get in where you're not wanted. Yeah." He already had composed the title: "How To Get In Where You're Not Wanted." "That's really great. Fifteen hundred words. Five hundred dollars. Think you can handle that one?"

My heart was pounding. *Esquire* in the early seventies was still the unruly, avant-garde, cutting-edge literary magazine it had been throughout the sixties under Hayes's stewardship, the champion of what was being called the New Journalism, the rag that was publishing Gay Talese, Tom Wolfe, Raymond Carver, and Norman Mailer and was the spirit behind Diane Arbus, George Lois, and Jean-Paul Goude. And here, in less than thirty minutes, I'd been given two assignments and offered more money than I would have made teaching for months. I was electrified with excitement, but it all scared the hell out of me.

Hayes grabbed the phone again, and in a matter of seconds there appeared at the door a relatively young man with a short, neat beard and wearing a dapper, plaid-vested suit cut in the English style. He was introduced as Don Erickson, the executive editor, and he, too, was smoking a cigar.

"This guy's going to be doing some writing for us," Hayes informed Erickson casually. He wrinkled his brow suspiciously. "Rhodes scholar, Fulbright, Ph.D.—you brainy lugs should hit it off well together, so get on with it." He tried to wave us out, but there was still something nagging at me.

"Just one more question, Harold: Who in the hell did write that lousy piece on bourbon?"

Smiling wickedly and without blinking, Hayes extended his right hand toward Don. "You just met him. Now, would you guys please get out of here? I have work to do—and I need to call about that goddamned necktie for the frog down the block."

I did indeed trek out to Kansas City and returned with a huge

Styrofoam chest filled with exactly fourteen of the most beautiful fresh prime steaks known to man. As directed, I immediately dropped off the rare treasure at the offices of *Esquire* for Hayes's personal inspection before a scheduled photo session the following day. All the slabs of beef were exceptional, but the real prize of the lot—and the one I told the photographer absolutely must be used for the main double-page, close-up color shot—was a particularly thick, purplish-red, ideally marbled K.C. strip sirloin of utter perfection.

At the studio we began removing the dry ice and unwrapping the exquisite hunks of meat, only to discover to my outright horror that the quintessential steak, the specimen that was to illustrate bovine perfection, couldn't be found. We rummaged through the chest again and again, carefully separating and studying the various cuts. No luck. Then I began counting, and in a matter of seconds determined that, without question, there were only thirteen steaks and the Great One was not among them. I knew that I'd supervised every step of the packaging in Kansas City, that the chest had been checked as luggage on the return flight, that the one and only time it could have been opened before now was . . .

I raced to the phone and put a call through to Don Erickson, but even before I had a chance to describe the pending disaster and ask questions, he said he had good news to report.

"I have to tell you right off, my friend, that you must know what you're talking about. When Harold saw that load of steaks yesterday, he just picked one out, pan-broiled it last night, and said it's the greatest beef he's ever put in his mouth. Good job, Jim."

Suffice it that when the article entitled "This Is the Perfect Steak" appeared and caused such a sensation, the dramatic photo was not of the perfect steak, which had long since been savored and digested by the editor in chief.

About a year later, Harold, after twenty brilliant, trail-blazing years at *Esquire,* was replaced by Erickson in the top position, and thus began one of the most productive, enlightening, and utterly woolly periods of my entire career. From the very beginning, Don and I hit it off well

THE PERFECT PAN-BROILED STEAK

SERVES 1

1 tablespoon lard

One 2-inch-thick prime sirloin strip steak

1 tablespoon butter

¼ cup dry red wine

Salt and freshly ground pepper to taste

In a very heavy skillet, heat the lard till almost smoking, add the steak to the pan, and sear for 1 minute on each side. Reduce the heat to moderate and continue cooking for 7 minutes, turning the steak once.

Transfer the steak to a heated plate and pour off all fat from the skillet. Add the butter, then the wine, deglaze the pan till the wine is slightly reduced, and pour the sauce over the steak. Season with salt and pepper.

together, partly because we shared such passions as Wagner, England and bespoke English clothes, French cuisine, and strong cocktails; partly because we were truly dedicated to hard work and maintaining the magazine's superiority; and partly because we both—to put it genteelly—were instinctively more titillated by Michelangelo's "David" than by Leonardo's "Mona Lisa." While I was still leading in my leisure time a wildly promiscuous existence of gay bars and one random love affair after the next, Don had long ago settled down sensibly, loyally, and happily with the one and only lover of his life—though the two always maintained separate apartments. That he never exactly approved of my lowly lifestyle had no effect on our relationship, but then, to this day I've never known a homosexual who was less interested in his sexual orientation or more bored with the topic in general than Don. To my knowledge, I was the only other fag besides his lover with whom he associated socially, and if he ever perceived his sexuality as a threat to his high standing and importance at *Esquire* (and remember that these were still the bigoted early seventies), I was never aware of it. As for any effect this ever had on his close professional affiliation with ladies' man Harold Hayes, it was only much later that I learned about a certain senior editor who, one night over dinner, asked the head honcho about Erickson's sexuality. "None of your fucking business," Hayes snapped. "And I don't know anyway."

A slightly eccentric gentleman from the Midwest with a staggering intelligence, Don had indeed been a Rhodes scholar at Oxford before assuming his first editorial job at a small magazine in New York and was, on the surface, a manifest disciple of both Hayes and *Esquire*'s jaunty founder, Arnold Gingrich. He lived and breathed *Esquire,* and while nobody could be more relaxed, foxy, and fun when tempered by high quotas of grain spirits and vintage wine, he was also a stern taskmaster who demanded the utmost from writers and tolerated no nonsense from any—myself included. Even after we'd become close friends and would cook together at his country retreat in New York's Columbia County, Don never once allowed friendship to sway his editorial judgment, I still feel a slight shiver when I recall meeting him one evening at the Metropolitan Opera for a performance of *Tannhauser* and asking cheerfully how he liked a fanciful piece on french fries I'd just turned in. "It stinks," he grumbled, looking up from his program. "Rewrite it."

When it came to his writers, Don took everything personally, even to the point of criticizing work of mine he happened to notice in other magazines. "Your Jovan piece is a knock-out, and it's good to see you so deft in conveying character," he once began a letter on a profile I'd done on a famous Chicago restaurateur. "I have to be honest and say that you've written the best words of your descriptive career for some-one else and not for me. They are, of course, 'cushioned tirades.' I wonder if you know how good that is. But you don't get away unscathed. Your editor should have seen that 'individual (kitchen) duties strictly defined' and 'working as a team' are not, as you would have it, two dif-ferent things necessarily. And I think 'nefarious' is the wrong word for the place you've put it." Such frank, unsolicited memos from Don arriving out of the blue became routine, pithy commentaries that he simply felt compelled to write and that, perhaps more than anything else, taught me what a truly dedicated editor and friend are all about.

Although Don was as obsessed as Alexandre Dumaine with classic French cuisine and revered every recipe Julia Child ever composed or demonstrated on TV, this hardly meant that he was not interested in and receptive to any gastronomic topic that might make a substantial impact in the magazine. As a result, over the next few years I produced a slew of articles that were as disparate in subject as they were often controversial in nature. Under Don's weighty influence and guidance, I wrote about making my own wine, working undercover at a fancy French restaurant, the joys of eating raw meat, menu ripoffs in restau-rants, college cafeteria slop, the horrors of yogurt, Carolina pig versus Texas beef barbecue, how stupid government regulations were destroy-ing great country hams, and the evils of the martini.

"Fried chicken!" I remember hearing someone yell in the distance.

Looking across all the roaring traffic to the other side of a busy mid-town street in Manhattan, I spotted Don rushing somewhere with Nora Ephron, his hands cupped at his mouth. "Fried chicken!" he repeated loudly. "Do fried chicken! We'll talk later."

And that's how I was assigned an article that almost brought on a second Civil War and, thanks to Don, was so unorthodox in style that it was eventually anthologized in a number of college textbooks. Obviously, the subject of fried chicken had been mulling in his brain for weeks.

"I'm bored to death with dull, formulaic food writing," he exploded when we sat down to discuss what he wanted. "Let's really break some balls in this piece, take a definitive stand, and present it in a way that keeps the reader guessing what in hell is going on." This, he explained, would mean first setting myself up daringly as the world authority on fried chicken, followed immediately by the in-depth, perfect recipe itself, followed by an intricate analysis of the recipe details, followed finally by a scathing attack on what's wrong with all other fried chick-en. In other words, everything in reverse.

This also meant demonstrating for Don himself the entire cooking procedure, from actually cutting up the chicken to seasoning and bat-tering to frying and draining on paper bags—all before I committed one word to the page. And to pass this initial test, which would prove to him without any doubt that I really knew what I was writing about, nothing would do but for me to show up in his small, nondescript apartment in Greenwich Village at the crack of dawn with three whole chickens, the right heavy cast-iron skillet, the right styles of shortening and flour, the right seasonings and buttermilk, and of course, the exact right paper bags for shaking and draining the chicken. Suffice it that by eight o'clock A.M. in that tiny, unventilated kitchen, I had cooked up some twenty-four pieces of golden, moist, crisp-skinned chicken, three of which Don devoured with approval for breakfast before heading for the office. As for myself, I couldn't face eating fried chicken again for months.

The Quintessential Southern Fried Chicken
(Shortened Version)

Serves 4

One 3½-pound fryer chicken,
  preferably freshly killed

3 teaspoons salt

Freshly ground pepper to taste

3 cups buttermilk

½ lemon, seeds removed

3 cups (1½ pounds) Crisco
  shortening

1½ cups all-purpose flour

¼ cup bacon grease

Cut the chicken into 8 serving pieces, rinse the pieces under cold running water, dry thoroughly with paper towels, and season with 1 teaspoon of the salt plus pepper. Pour the buttermilk into a large bowl and squeeze the lemon into it. Add the chicken pieces to the bowl to soak, cover with plastic wrap, and refrigerate for at least 2 hours.

Remove the chicken from the refrigerator and allow to return to room temperature. While melting the shortening over high heat to measure ½ inch in a large cast-iron skillet (add more shortening if necessary), combine the flour, remaining salt, and more pepper in a heavy brown paper bag. Remove the dark pieces of chicken from the milk, drain each momentarily over the bowl, drop into the bag, and shake vigorously to coat. Add the bacon grease to the skillet and when small bubbles appear on the surface, reduce the heat slightly. Remove the chicken pieces from the bag one by one, shaking off excess flour, and using tongs, lower them gently into the hot fat.

Arrange the pieces of dark chicken in the skillet so they cook evenly, reduce the heat to moderate, and cook for exactly 17 minutes. Reduce the heat slightly, turn the pieces with the tongs, and fry for 17 minutes longer. Quickly repeat all procedures with the white pieces of chicken, adjusting the heat as necessary and frying exactly 15 minutes on each side.

Drain the chicken on a second brown paper bag for at least 5 minutes, transfer to a serving platter *without* reheating in the oven, and serve hot or at room temperature.

Unlike most other editors, who often pigeonhole a writer within the confines of a given subject, Don also urged me to explore interests besides food and drink, an experiment that often produced inordinate consequences. Dining together at the Gloucester House in New York, for example, and utterly smashed after having cocktails at the Plaza hotel with none other than Truman Capote (whose infamous "La Côte Basque—1965" Don would soon publish), I asked what all exciting was coming up on *Esquire*'s agenda. Sipping God knows what number martini of the evening, Don cracked a devilish smile.

"Well, since you asked, there's one project that might be right down your alley: a huge, five-hundred-page issue on . . . sports." He then let out a roaring laugh.

"Oh, God," I moaned in revulsion. "How butch."

"Now, let's see what topic you could cover with great expertise," he slurred facetiously as I swirled the cherry in my manhattan.

We mentioned a few asinine possibilities that broke us both up snickering and cackling; then, in a drunken spirit of triumph, I bolted, "I've got it: the jock strap," which inflamed even more paroxysms of laughter. "A comprehensive piece on the noble jock strap."

"I can see it now," Don almost howled while diners at the next table began to gawk, "a huge jock strap stretched across the cover!"

All of which would have remained a frivolous joke had the phone not rung the next morning with Don's woefully hungover deep voice sounding almost as raspy as my own. "Okay, kiddo, I say let's go with it."

"Go with what?" I croaked.

"The jock strap, that's what."

"You've gotta be kidding," I stammered in disbelief, just barely remembering the banter from the night before.

"I ain't kidding, my friend. It's a great idea, and—excuse the pun— it's something you can sink your teeth into. Trace the whole history of the goddamned thing, interview Joe Namath and Tom Seaver and a few other studs for their opinions, and . . . be bold. You can handle it."

"Don, are you really serious?" I appealed with the same terror and admiration I had experienced that first day with Harold Hayes.

"Dead serious. It's a great idea. When can you get on it?"

The nervy essay that Don titled "A Short History of the Jock Strap—From Soup to Nuts" appeared with the lead sentence "Now for the heart of the matter" and was positioned dead center in the fat issue. It had taken courage to assign such an offbeat piece even after the liberating sixties, and it took even greater courage when Don, along with Gingrich and other editors, fought lawyers and the advertising department to display a taboo jock strap on the cover the same way that bras, panties, and other female underapparel had been featured for years in magazines. In the end, bureaucratic pressures forced them to back down, the only eventual consolation being that about a year after the provocative article was published in *Esquire*, ads by Bike, Jockey, and other manufacturers began to appear all over the place for the first time.

> PARIS, HOTEL RITZ, APRIL 1973—
>
> *Charles Ritz called at crack of dawn to tell me to come down to the dining room to taste season's first purple asparagus. When I took knife & fork, he smacked my hand hard. "Fingers, jeune homme, only the fingers to eat asparagus." Was pretty taken aback.*

After resigning from *Esquire* over a heated dispute with management, Harold Hayes went on to host a program on public television, edit a couple more magazines, and, ever the renegade adventurer, write three compelling books on Africa, including one on Dian Fossey. From time to time we'd meet up in New York, and we even had a couple of lunches at Harold's revered "frog pond," once he'd ingratiated himself with the owner by sending him no less than ten fancy neckties from Sulka. It always shocked Harold that I'd be involved with such "prissy" magazines as *Town & Country* and *Gourmet*, and till the day he died in 1989, he never stopped reminding me that basically I was a red-clay Southern boy and a "beef and bourbon man."

Don Erickson left *Esquire* in the late seventies to create *The Dial* magazine for public television, easily convincing me to tag along to contribute from time to time the same sort of unconventional pieces I'd done for him in the past. Times and public tastes were changing, however; the literary sophistication that had characterized magazines like *Esquire* for two decades was gradually succumbing to a politically correct vapidity and rank mediocrity in publishing that continues to this day. When *The Dial* eventually folded, there wasn't much left for Don but a rather bland job at the *New York Times Magazine,* editing a fatuous weekly column devoted to male ambitions, happiness, and frustrations. He was miserable.

"Well, kiddo, they tell me I have throat cancer," Don announced one day on the phone in his typically dispassionate, stoic way, almost as if he knew that Nature was about to control his plight. "Must have been the frigging cigars. I may make it, maybe not."

I don't think I'd ever been so devastated. Somewhat to my surprise, Don opted ultimately and bravely to undergo the ghastly horrors of surgery, after which he was forced to feed himself a liquid diet by tube. Often I would take him foods and wines I knew he loved, aware that he couldn't swallow anything, but knowing the pleasure he got from just looking at and smelling them. We would talk for hours about *Esquire,* and opera, and London restaurants, and my latest romantic escapades, and of course what articles or book I was working on. Even while reporting regularly to the hospital for treatment, he never missed a day of work at the *Times* or a subscription performance at the Met, and though he couldn't eat or drink, he still enjoyed nothing more on occasion than to meet me and his "chum" at a French restaurant in the Village and, in his hoarse voice, talk mainly about food while the other two of us made our way awkwardly through and critiqued the *navarin d'agneau* and *foie de veau à la moutarde* he always relished. Don didn't make it. When he finally had to be hospitalized, I sat and held the scrawny hand that had slashed and amended and improved so many of my sentences and words, and before he went into a coma, the last words I remember him uttering to me were, "Always remember, kiddo, to break the rules." Realizing one night the end was near, I cowardly whispered goodbye to my cherished editor and friend for the last time and was unable to cry on the subway home. Don was fifty-six when he died, and with his premature death I sensed for the first time the cruel sting of mortality that haunts me to this day.

The same week I met Hayes and Erickson in 1973, Fate dealt still another lucky card in the form of a call from a man who identified himself as Frank Zachary, the new editor in chief of *Town & Country*. He explained that before coming to *T & C*, his final job as art director of *Travel & Leisure* had been to set up the illustrations for my food piece that had been recently accepted, that he liked the article very much, and would I come in to discuss doing something for him. Again I had to take a deep breath and pinch myself.

After I did my first story, on cognac and cigars, Zachary summoned me again.

"Who is this French guy Bocuse from Lyon?" he asked blankly. "I hear he's coming to visit New York."

"One of the greatest chefs in France, whom I met some years ago," I informed him. "He now has three stars in Michelin."

Wiping his hand repeatedly over his mouth while contemplating, he finally decided we should do something on Bocuse and wondered what I thought. I suggested naively maybe a long interview for an in-depth profile. Nervously, Zachary resumed stroking his mouth and bushy eyebrows. "No, no, no, I don't think so. Everybody will be doing that," he muttered, obviously not too excited.

Getting up from behind his desk, he began pacing the floor and looking out the soaring window overlooking Fifth Avenue. Then he turned and snapped in half the pencil in his hand. "I mean, how can we actually cook with this guy, and taste his food, and let the readers share the experience. Not in any goddamn restaurant, but . . . Hey, any chance we could talk him into cooking . . . convince him to prepare a whole meal in someone's home the way he would in his own? Yeah, Bocuse at home. Now that would be different, wouldn't you say?"

It took time, and stamina, and lots of clout, but eventually, sure enough, Paul Bocuse was persuaded to prepare a full lunch for a dozen swells in a Manhattan town house. I followed him through the markets early in the morning, helped him in the kitchen and watched him work, and supervised the great Arnold Newman's photography. Then I sat down with the other guests to savor the luscious dishes, got the recipes, and though half the time I really didn't realize what was happening or know exactly what I was doing, somehow it all came together in a highly dramatic and unusual piece that apparently bowled Zachary over.

It was I, however, who was really bowled over the next time I met with him and heard him announce, "What I'd like, James, is for you to be *Town & Country*'s food and wine editor"—just like that.

"Good God, Frank," I gasped, almost out of control, "that's insanity—really crazy. Listen, as you know, I'm green as a gourd in this business, and have so little experience, and . . ."

"That's exactly what I want," he assured me rather cryptically, adjusting his bow tie. "Somebody fresh and willing to learn. You've got a good head on your shoulders, and are obviously willing to work hard, and don't worry, I'll be here to advise and help. I have big plans for this magazine, so what say we give it a try?"

I did, indeed, agree to give the job a try—an experiment that lasted till Frank retired some twenty years later and one that would change my life forever. The unusual deal was that while I would be listed on the masthead of *T & C* as Food and Wine Editor, my only actual responsibility would be to come up with original food, beverage, and other ideas and produce articles on a steady basis. Period. I would not have an office at the magazine, and since technically I would not be part of the regular staff and thus not salaried, I, like other such recruits, would work as a freelancer, paid a fee per article that I deemed appropriate and fair, be given a liberal expense account, and, in this gentlemen's agreement, not even have to bother with such unnecessary trivialities as assignment contracts, which Zachary had no use for. It was further understood that I would be totally free to write for other magazines. That this unorthodox, privileged, downright wacky professional arrangement bucked every convention in the publishing world was a fact I'd appreciate only later, but then how could I know at the time that I was working for a unique iconoclast, whose irreverent disregard for the rules made even that of Hayes and Erickson pale by comparison.

In his late fifties when Hearst brought him to *Town & Country*, Zachary had already not only created a number of highly innovative art magazines, but served in every capacity from copywriter to managing editor to managing director to art director at such August publications as *Holiday, Modern Photography*, and *Travel & Leisure*. Over the years, he'd dealt with Faulkner, James Jones, John O'Hara, and Jack Kerouac, but it was primarily in the realm of magazine photography and graphic design that Zachary had made his most indelible mark by exploiting the exceptional talents of men like Arnold Newman, Slim Aarons, Ronald Searle, and Edward Gorey and developing his revolutionary concepts of cinematic imagery and environmental portraiture. The idea had been to not merely represent but interpret people, places, and events through pictures, to give the artist the freedom to study the components of an entity and create an image that would tell the whole story. Today, such a method might seem commonplace at certain magazines, but back in the fifties and sixties it was startling.

When Frank arrived at *T & C* in 1972 and hired me shortly thereafter, his vision was to take a bland, fatuous society magazine with a circulation of only 117,000 and transform it into a vibrant, fresh, intelligent publication that not only reflected the diverse nature and interests of the affluent, but focused on a new social conscience concerned with drug problems, education, the fine arts, financial markets, gastronomy, and the like. To implement his goal, he assembled around him a relatively small staff of editors and freelance writers and photographers from whom he expected little more than staunch loyalty and lots of hard work. In almost no time, we became a close-knit family that would remain together for many years.

While nobody who worked for Frank ever doubted for one second who masterminded the magazine, fomented the best ideas, and called the ultimate shots, we also knew that his office door was never, ever closed; that we had the independence to develop our own creative senses and spend huge sums of money to get a good story; and that, so tolerant and understanding and human was our boss, we would always be protected against most lapses in efficiency and any personal adversity in our private lives. Never once can I recall Frank losing his temper or bellowing or threatening to fire someone the way more power-hungry editors did at other magazines. He would constantly roam the halls mumbling repeatedly to himself, "Goddamn, son-of-a-bitch" when something unannounced troubled him, but for Frank to take out his worries and frustrations and wrath on his staff was gallantly inconceivable. Being the old-fashioned, politically incorrect gent he was, he thought nothing of huddling in his open-door office with some of his male cronies and, even in my presence, howling over one lascivious girlie or fag story after the next, while docile young secretaries and assistants simply took it in stride. In reality, however, no man ever existed who idolized, respected, and fought for the rights of women like Frank Zachary, and pity the dolt who might ever have made a truly disparaging remark to him about the homosexuality of one of his trusted editors, authors, or photographers. As for the way Frank always attracted the opposite sex, I can remember a rosy female editor at another magazine once proclaiming him "the sexiest man in New York"—this when he was in his seventies.

NEW YORK, DECEMBER 1973—

Tasting of four caviars at Roger Yaseen's town house with Joe Baum, Jim Beard, Jean Troisgros, et al. Then dinner prepared by J. T. Wines: Dom Pérignon, '53 Lafite Rothschild, '55 Pétrus, '61 Haut Brion Blanc, '61 La Tâche (with brie). Memorable.

As circulation graduated to almost half a million readers and revenues swelled steadily, the public image of *Town & Country* as the country's most glamorous magazine, of Frank Zachary as the ultimate man about town, and of me as the sophisticated gastronomic globetrotter rose accordingly throughout the seventies and eighties, all of which amused Frank and me to no end. "I'm sure that most people who come up here for an appointment expect to find me perched in a goddamn velvet armchair, wearing white tie and tails," he would jest. And no doubt visitors must have been slightly startled to encounter a man whose frayed Brooks Brothers shirt collars, wrinkled madras jackets, and ancient Gucci loafers would have been rejected by Goodwill, who could often be seen on his knees in the art department studying layouts scattered all over the floor, and who would wander down the office corridors absentmindedly darting a handful of push pins at the ceiling while discussing serious business.

Unlike other top magazine editors whose idea of success and fame was to be recognized almost daily at any one of New York's tonier restaurants, Frank rarely went to lunch with anyone but his few close friends. Nor did he attend many receptions, or charity dinners, or other such events deemed de rigueur by the publishing establishment. Nor did he travel much—and certainly never on the Concorde. An intensely private individual deeply devoted to his family, he loathed social show and pretense almost as much as he disliked featuring celebrities in the magazine, preferring simply to show up at the office as early as seven o'clock in the morning or meet colleagues at some coffee shop for a business breakfast, put in a hard day of work, and have a quiet dinner with his wife in some neighborhood bistro. Although Frank didn't get around the city on a motor scooter the way Harold Hayes did, or fight the subways like Don Erickson, I never once saw him in a limousine and was more likely to run into him walking miles to work. "It's good for the old ticker," he'd say—especially after his first bypass operation—"and besides, that's when I have plenty of time to come up with ideas for the magazine."

And if Frank was nothing else, he was an ideas man—original ideas, creative ideas, daring ideas, ideas that nobody else could conceivably engender and would come only from someone who, having had very little formal education in his hometown of Pittsburgh, devoured books the way some consumed french fries. Frank's curiosity was endless, his knowledge multifarious, his intelligence daunting. Having digested maybe two dozen books and magazines over a weekend, he would show up at editorial meetings with questions and ideas and proposals that would stagger those around the table. He wondered, Who might own the most land in the U.S., or Mexico, or Thailand? What company in America markets the best Christmas trees? Who is this family in the midwest who produces great fireworks, and who are the modern-day descendants of the Peruvian conquistadors? What about a short history of canned sardines, and which are the premium brands? There's a small, private girls' school in the Swiss Alps, and a blind wine maker in Napa Valley, and several new vaccines for hepatitis. Should we pursue?

In my own specialized area of food and beverages, working with Frank was never without challenge. Typically, about twice a year I would draw up a list of proposed topics, outline them in detail, then schedule a long meeting with him to discuss the pros and cons. And typically, no sooner had we begun the debating than Frank, who always suffered from a prostate problem he ignored, would announce, "Come on, James, let's go take a leak." For what seemed like hours, there he would stand at the urinal, weighing the merits and weaknesses of articles on wild game, white fruit brandies, Barcelona restaurants, and risotto while I paced the floor talking and endured constant interruptions by female editors banging on the door with questions for Frank that needed immediate answers. We'd then return to the office, only for Frank to experience the urge again in twenty or thirty minutes and repeat the scenario. Some of Frank's and my most productive conversations took place in that damned bathroom, leading me to declare more than once to close friends and colleagues that *T & C*'s food department consisted of two urinals, three stalls, and a lavatory.

Where *Esquire* and *Town & Country* were similar was the way my proposals were approved by the editor in chief and him alone, the practice of soliciting opinions and comments from a disparate network of staff having been determined too time-consuming and often counterproductive given the highly subjective nature of my field. Not that Frank in any way considered himself more informed on food and wine than his talented team of editors, or that he didn't respect others' ability to deal intelligently with recipes, restaurant reviews, and the art of wine making and spirits distillation. Like Hayes and Erickson at *Esquire*, he had tenacious convictions about which gastronomic topics were generally right and wrong for *T & C*, but once decisions had been made, he simply trusted me to execute the ideas in my best professional way and to work closely with the assigned editor.

During my twenty-year tenure at *T & C* under Zachary, we published more than two hundred articles on every subject from hash to pink champagne to international cooking schools to the restaurants of Lyon, and we prided ourselves enormously on being the first to cover such emerging phenomena as American caviar and farmhouse cheeses, the boutique wineries of California, exotic wild mushrooms, America's new women chefs, and premium vodkas. I traveled the globe eating and drinking, often in the company of our cute and eclectic art director, Melissa Tardiff, and sometimes even with a photographer. Unlike so many other food writers, forbidden by their paranoid editors to take exploratory press trips or accept free hotels and airline tickets for fear of some unlikely backlash, I tolerated boring companions, enraged aggressive hosts and companies by never guaranteeing coverage of their "product" till I was certain of its merits and feasibility, and benefited enormously from invaluable exposure while saving the magazine thousands of dollars that could be put to better use scouting restaurants on my own. Far from finding anything unethical about freebies so long as intentions were kept above the table, Frank viewed rejecting such obvious advantages as both unprofessional and downright stupid.

If, on the other hand, there were large bills to be paid, it was just not Frank's style to question even the most outrageous expense, forever convinced—correctly—that I was not out to bilk the magazine, but simply determined to "get the story" at any cost. No doubt there were times when I should have flown economy instead of sailing first class on the *QE2* to Europe (a story?), when ordering a noble bottle of Riesling Clos Ste. Hune (a story?) at the Auberge de l'Ile in Alsace was unnecessary, and when pasta in Milan would have tasted almost as good without a flurry of exorbitantly priced fresh white truffles (a story?). "I don't give a damn about the money," Frank would bark, uttering a phrase that would have curdled other editors' blood. "Just get a great story."

Of course, getting a great story often involved biting off almost more than I could chew, as when I once proposed to Frank that we track down the origins of tiramisu—a creamy, sinfully rich Italian dessert that was about to take America by storm—and come up with the authentic recipe. Told by a so-called expert that the coffee-enriched confection made with custardy mascarpone cheese and ladyfingers was first concocted in Venice in the late eighteenth century, off I went to La Serenissima, only to be informed by another expert that, no, tiramisu was actually a Tuscan dish made with Florentine chocolate and ricotta cheese and created in the nineteenth century.

"Better get over to Florence and check it out," Frank advised when I called with the news from my comfortable room at the Cipriani.

Then in Florence, a reputed food authority (from Turin) insisted that, without question, the first tiramisu, made not with ladyfingers but leftover yeast cake, was Piedmontese in origin—from a small bakery in Alessandria.

"Rent a car and see what you can find up there," Frank next directed, as if telling me to drive from midtown Manhattan to Greenwich Village. "Just stick with it, James."

"That's absurd," scowled none other than Marcella Hazan. "Mascarpone is a unique Lombardian cheese, so it makes sense that the source of genuine tiramisu is Lombardia."

And so the chase continued as Frank urged me to follow any and every lead, and the expenses became ridiculous. Down to a farmhouse in Emilia-Romagna, back up to an inn in Friuli, and, finally and infuriatingly, back to Venice when the ever-savvy managing director of the Cipriani, Natale Rusconi, calmly said on the phone, "But why didn't you tell me last week you were here for tiramisu? It was created only about thirty years ago just north of here at my old friend Alfredo Beltrame's restaurant in Treviso. He has it all documented."

Once I was convinced that this was indeed the real McCoy and watched the pastry chef assemble the decadent dessert, Frank sent the famous photographer Slim Aarons straight over to compose just the right "environmental" picture, after which I finally returned home to labor over the bloody article. Frank read the manuscript enthusiastically in a matter of minutes standing in the middle of his office, made a few changes with a pencil, pronounced it "a great story," and proceeded down the hall to give it to the assigned editor. Although he exclaimed about that article for years to come, he never so much as glanced at the edited version, and knowing Frank, I'm sure he never read the piece again when it was published. He trusted me, he trusted the editor, he trusted the story, and that was simply the way he worked.

While I was eating, drinking, and smoking myself into an early grave, Frank, a recovered alcoholic actively involved in AA, was generally the paragon of dietary self-discipline and restraint—except when it came to desserts. Anytime I'd do a piece that included recipes for a tempting confection, I could almost plan on receiving one of Frank's 8:00 A.M. calls to inquire sheepishly if, by chance, there might be a few leftovers from the testing that I could bring up to the office—innocent requests that usually produced some cookies or morsels of cake or slivers of pie he and other staff members would relish with the excitement of children.

Then the lemon meringue pie episode occurred, a near disaster that, for once, deprived *T & C* of its editor in chief's services for two entire days. It all began when I submitted the recipe for my mother's glorious lemon meringue pie, only to discover that of all Frank's sweet-tooth passions, none was so intense as the one for this particular pie.

FRANK'S LEMON MERINGUE PIE

SERVES 6

For the pie shell:

1½ cups all-purpose flour

½ teaspoon salt

½ cup Crisco shortening

4 to 5 tablespoons ice water

For the filling:

1 cup plus 6 tablespoons
   granulated sugar

¼ cup cornstarch

¼ teaspoon salt

1½ cups boiling water

2 teaspoons grated lemon rind

⅓ cup fresh lemon juice

3 large eggs, separated

2 tablespoons butter

To make the pie shell, combine the flour and salt in a large mixing bowl. Cut in the shortening with a pastry cutter or two knives till the mixture resembles coarse meal. Stirring with a wooden spoon, gradually add the water till a ball of dough is formed. Wrap the dough in plastic wrap and chill till ready to use.

To bake the pie shell, preheat the oven to 425° F. Grease a 9-inch pie plate and set aside.

Place the chilled dough on a lightly floured surface and roll it out from the center with a lightly floured rolling pin to a 1/8-inch thickness. Carefully fold the pastry in half, lay the fold across the center of the prepared plate, unfold it, and press it loosely into the bottom and sides of the plate. Prick the bottom and sides with a fork, trim and crimp the edges, and place on a heavy baking sheet. Bake till the shell browns slightly, about 12 minutes. Allow the shell to cool completely on a wire rack.

Reduce the oven to 325° F. To make the filling, in a medium-size heavy nonreactive saucepan, combine 1 cup of the sugar, cornstarch, and salt; mix till well blended. Gradually add the boiling water, stirring constantly, and cook, still stirring, over moderate heat till the mixture thickens. Stir in the lemon rind and juice. In a small bowl, beat the egg yolks till foamy, add a small amount of the hot lemon mixture to them, stirring constantly, and then pour the egg mixture into the lemon mixture in the saucepan, stirring. Add the butter and continue cooking, stirring, till the mixture is very thick. Let cool slightly, then pour into the prepared pie shell.

In a medium-size mixing bowl, beat the egg whites with an electric mixer till thickened. Gradually add the remaining 6 tablespoons of sugar and beat till stiff peaks form. With a rubber spatula, cover the pie with the meringue, being careful to seal all the edges. With a spoon, make a few peaks in the meringue. Bake just till the top has browned slightly, about 10 minutes. Cool completely before serving.

"I'm just going to make him a whole fresh pie," announced Mother, who happened to be visiting me at my house in East Hampton when I handed in the article. "Then he can share it with everybody at the magazine or with his family."

I delivered the golden, fluffy, zesty pie, and Frank's eyes beamed as he studied it carefully. Then, not volunteering to place it on the hall table as usual for all to taste, he closed the box and placed it almost out of sight on a bookshelf. When, the next morning, he still hadn't appeared at the office by ten o'clock, his worried secretary finally decided to call his apartment.

"Frank's not feeling at all well today," his wife reported, more in exasperation than apprehension. "Can you believe that he came home yesterday and, without a word to anybody, sat down by himself and devoured an entire lemon meringue pie someone brought him? He was sick as a dog all night—and deserves it."

Nearing eighty and having warned repeatedly that he was going to retire, Frank, despite the begging and pleading of Hearst management, finally carried out his threat in 1992, agreeing only to remain as a consultant in the company on special publishing projects and magazine development. Against his better advice, I stuck around a few more years to witness three editors in succession gradually fire most of the old staff, unravel many of the standards we'd all worked so hard to establish, change *T & C*'s unique personality and direction by sucking up to advertisers and the celebrity culture in ways Frank had always refused to do, and revert the magazine to the fluff publication it was back in the sixties and remains today. After Frank, there was no more fun, no new horizons, no real challenges, and no brilliant architect to maintain and steadily improve the monument's proud image. "Just sour grapes," one of my many detractors has accused, and maybe he's partly right.

Unlike Harold Hayes and Don Erickson, both of whom died at relatively young ages, Frank Zachary survives and thrives alone at the healthy and energetic age of eighty-eight. He still reports to his office every morning at an ungodly early hour, submits proposals to Hearst for innovative new magazines, and lunches with his old buddies. Routinely, he travels to Virginia to visit his wife in a nursing home, and to Canada to spend holidays with one of his beloved daughters. Roughly half of his original staff and he are close, loyal friends, and we jump at any chance to get together socially and kid him about his same pathetic madras jacket and faded bow ties. I dine frequently with the man to whom I owe so much and still depend on him like none other for advice on my manuscripts and my life. Today, he rarely reads *Town & Country*.

At cooking school in Paris, 1991:

Boning a saddle of lamb.

Trimming strawberries, with John Mariani (at right).

Listening to Chef.

CHAPTER FOUR

LOST IN PUFF PASTRY

T O BE A FOOD WRITER in the 1970s was to participate in a stage of
gastronomic history that was nothing less than explosive, and as
Town & Country's budding food and wine editor and a freelance contributor to a number of other magazines, I dived headfirst into the
action. Since the dominant influence on culinary trends in America
was, of course, the untamed nouvelle cuisine of France that eventually,
for better and worse, would change or radically modify cooking and
eating habits everywhere, I wasted no time returning to my adopted
homeland. There I met Michel Guérard, the Troisgros brothers, Alain
Chapel, and most other major practitioners to learn what all the fuss
was about. At the same time, I was one of the first to hasten to
California to explore the blossoming wine industry in Napa Valley, to
pursue rumors about a putative innovator named Alice Waters who was
creating an offbeat new "California cuisine" at a place called Chez
Panisse in Berkeley, and to check out the goofy glitziness of carnation-
lapeled Patrick Terrail's Ma Maison, in Los Angeles.

In New Orleans to cover the restaurant scene, I was the one who told Ella Brennan about an enormous, unemployed, brilliant Cajun cook by the name of Paul Prudhomme, only to have her call some weeks later to say she'd just hired him as head chef at Commander's Palace. Curious about whether the swill served in college cafeterias was any better than when I was a struggling scholar, I convinced *Esquire* to let me tour a number of our more exalted institutions of higher learning, which resulted in my being admitted to a hospital in Houston with acute food poisoning. And when I told my editor at *Town & Country* that I'd like to shed a few pounds by indulging in a self-styled, rather eccentric fresh caviar diet for five straight days in first class aboard the *QE2*, scores of letters from irate readers howling about my immoral extravagance flowed in.

NEW YORK, APRIL 1974—

Le Cirque just opened and everybody there—Julia, Craig, Jim B—the whole gang. I predict it'll be the Pavillon of the 70s, maybe the 80s. Sirio Maccioni mad as a hatter, but the same pro Soulé was. Incredible bollito misto—but crème brûlée not crusted enough.

It was during the unbridled seventies that I dined with the duke and duchess of Windsor at a palatial home in New Jersey shortly before the duke's death. At a party at the Gotham Book Mart in Manhattan, I was approached by a soused Tennessee Williams and asked gallantly if I'd care to have a quiet dinner at La Caravelle "with an elderly gentleman who enjoyed nice companionship" (a proposition that inspired a warm and often reckless friendship with the great playwright and would have future professional consequences of an hilarious nature). And on an eating spree aboard the S.S. *France*, I shared a corner table with Salvador Dalí and his pet ocelot, Babou. Being the food and wine editor of *Town & Country* and a writer at other magazines opened doors magically to all sorts of privileged venues and people, but the position also made me painfully aware that if I was to pursue my career with any degree of real expertise, there were certain practical gaps in my sophistication that simply had to be addressed.

Although I never had either the ambition or ability to become an accomplished chef, I nonetheless did determine early on that it was almost the duty of any aspiring food writer and restaurant critic first to spend at least a little time at a good cooking school, and second to work in a first-class restaurant to get some idea of what really goes on behind the scenes. To this day, I still firmly believe that no pundit should be allowed to pontificate about cooking and dining out without a modicum of first-hand exposure on the professional level.

It wasn't that I didn't already consider myself to be a fairly instinctive, competent cook capable of turning out numerous classic American dishes and reproducing all sorts of exotic fare found in the books of Julia Child, Marcella Hazan, Diana Kennedy, and even Madhur Jaffrey. No, siree. Actually, I was cocky as hell about my culinary skills and convinced that all I needed was to round off a few rough edges. And so I soon found myself enrolled for one week in an advance-level course at Paris's famous La Varenne cooking school.

"*Vous êtes en retard, jeune homme,*" roars Chef Ferdinand Chambrette, glancing up from his work just long enough to comment on the fact that I'm exactly six minutes late to class. Having learned that no excuse is better than a feeble one as far as this particular French chef is concerned, I opt not to explain how the Paris Métro was late this morning and simply proceed to tie a long white apron around my distended gut, collect my personal set of knives, and hasten to join the chef-teacher and my fellow American students in the small kitchen.

Already my compatriots are gathered around the large wooden table: two males, six females, the same familiar faces I've been studying about six hours a day for the past week. As I join the group, Chef is opening a long cylindrical can. Removing the lid, he turns the tin upside down, punctures a small hole in the other end, and blows forcefully through the aperture, releasing onto a marble slab one huge luscious block of fresh truffled foie gras. We all gasp at the sight, then gasp even louder as Chef slits the hunk of pure matter lengthwise, removes the fat truffles from the center, and casually tosses the precious goose liver onto a wire screen stretched across a mixing bowl.

"Work it through the sieve," he directs in French, handing Moyna a large wooden pestle, "every morsel of it." While she pursues this act of desecration, I begin my fifth puff pastry of the week (so far all unsuccessful), while others go about their assigned duties, carefully following the printed recipes we've received. Helene and Kathy tear the skin off chicken breasts and imitate Chef's method of deboning the meat. Sammy chops mushrooms for *duxelles*. Gloria makes Chantilly by beating sugar and kirsch with heavy cream. Cynthia cleans red snappers. Herb prepares the dough to make fresh noodles. Isabelle stands over a simmering stockpot, inwardly praying that her consommé will jell properly when later stirred over ice.

This was my last day at La Varenne, and my feet were killing me. Others had been around for three, four, six weeks and were fully acclimated to the strenuous schedules and the hard floor. Still others would remain in residence three months or more, and in all likelihood they would leave as expert chefs. At times I felt like a dunce and wished I could take it slower and easier with the intermediate group upstairs. Then my soufflé would rise perfectly, or my terrine would come out with a beautiful texture, or my sauce wouldn't separate. At those proud moments, I was glad I'd decided to take the full plunge into *la haute cuisine française* like that I remembered from years ago at Alexandre Dumaine's mecca in Saulieu. Furthermore, I was now convinced that anybody could do it who loved to cook and was willing to work hard and learn. But my feet . . . my swelling feet!

Moyna's foie gras arm is exhausted; so, at the risk of suffering recriminations from Chef, who for more than thirty years has reigned over the kitchen in one of Paris's most distinguished restaurants, she lets up momentarily. Rolling out my dough and placing it in the refrigerator for the first of six fifteen-minute intervals, I glance about the room. Helene and Kathy are sisters from Long Island—young, energetic, both married, and both simply eager to master French cooking so they can entertain more lavishly when they return home to their families and friends. Sammy, in his twenties, never has much to say but hopes one day to open a restaurant back in Oregon. Cynthia, from Pittsburgh, will tell you in no uncertain terms that she's been cooking for a large family for more than twenty years, that she's "done all this," and that there are a few things she could show Chef. So far Cynthia has broken specks of egg yolk in her whites, stuffed a fish from the wrong side, and destroyed an entire main course by confusing fish and beef stock. But we all love Cynthia, and we're jealous of her flawless soufflés. Isabelle is a Chinese girl from Indiana who's much more at ease in front of a copper mixing bowl than a wok. Herb was brought up in Georgia perfecting Brunswick stew; now he considers himself an authority on *filet de boeuf en croûte à la périgordine*. And dear Gloria. Nobody is quite sure exactly where Gloria is from since she's been wandering the European continent with her diplomat husband for years and for some reason, doesn't care to discuss the last time she visited the States. Not one member of the class appears underfed, but Gloria, who apparently buys her stunning if rather snug cooking outfits at Dior and who is never without a few sapphires and a wedge of French bread coated with fresh butter, does undoubtedly have a slight weight problem. Everybody speaks fluent French, and in all, it's a good group.

"*Au travail!*" Chef blasts in my direction, noticing my idleness. I grab a few endives and begin washing the leaves for a salad. "*Moyna, au travail!*" he repeats, staring at her with his piercing eyes.

"But Chef, my arm's about to fall off," she protests. "This is worse than beating egg whites, and besides, it seems it'll take forever to work all this foie gras through the wire. Surely there's an easier way."

"*Non, ma chérie,*" he snaps, "this is the only method, and I suggest you develop a little patience. *La bonne cuisine: c'est l'école de la patience,*" he continues, adding still another colorful aphorism to his repertory.

Today, like every day, we are preparing our own lunch—a hedonistic affair that in many respects could match the fare at Taillevent. To begin, there's mousse of foie gras in aspic. Then red snapper with *dux-*

elles en papillote, followed by ground boned chicken breast *Pojarski* in cream sauce, fresh noodles, watercress and endive salad, and, for dessert, my *tarte aux fraises.* Sound simple? It's not. Chef assigns everyone a certain duty. The recipes we follow are not only in English and French, but also in U.S. standard measures as well as in the metric system (although we work solely by the latter), and if we're lucky, our 9:30 A.M. class will end over lunch about 1:30. Then it's back upstairs at 2:30 for a two-hour demonstration of methods that will be practiced in class the following session. And finally, for those with fortitude, there are often wine tastings or kitchen tours in the late afternoon, visits to pastry shops, cheese shops, or the market out at Rungis, and in the evening, special meals in special restaurants. Those lucky few who have the time and money and energy to complete all three twelve-week levels will not only walk away with 1,100 mastered recipes, but will also be virtual human encyclopedias on anything pertaining to the art of French cooking and eating. I find it all slightly more than humbling.

Isabelle is worried about her brown aspic, which is to be chilled and used in molds for the foie gras mousse. Yesterday she began her stock, full of vegetables, gelatin, Madeira, and two egg whites for clarification (yes, we've learned how to clarify liquids with egg whites). Now she checks the hot broth. It's still not adequately clear, so she separates an egg and is just about to add another white.

"Stop!" shouts Chef. "It's too late. That'll do absolutely no good, and all you'll end up with is a stringy mess. We'll have to make do with what you have."

"But Chef," she tries to reason, "if we cook down the stock, why wouldn't the extra egg white help the clarification?"

ABOARD S.S. *FRANCE,* JULY 1974—

Dining in Chambord with Salvador Dalí and his pet ocelot, Babou, who tonight lunged at the pot-au-feu and dragged every dish and glass on the table to the floor with his chain. Waiters barely flinched. It's all utter madness.

"It just won't, and that's that. One of the mysterious laws of nature. All you could do is start again from scratch, and we don't have time for that. Besides, one of the important challenges in cooking is trying to work with imperfection when necessary in hopes of attaining perfection. Here, let me see what I can do."

With that he begins dipping spoonfuls of aspic from the stockpot into a small metal container. "*Des glaçons!*" he directs Gloria. "Stop eating all that butter—which is going to destroy your liver—and fill a large bowl with ice cubes. And, Sammy, did you put those molds in the freezer? Good. Bring me one."

Everyone jumps except Cynthia, who's busy counting the folds of baking paper being wrapped airtight around a *duxelles*-covered red snapper.

"*Non, ma chérie,*" he says to arm-aching Moyna, "don't stop working that foie gras while you watch me! And, Kathy, that chicken's not ground fine enough. Run it through again, then beat it thoroughly with a wooden spoon till it's smooth."

All this time Chef is gently stirring the aspic over ice, glancing down from time to time to see if it's setting properly while simultaneously searching for unwanted particles that might surface when chilled. His massive hands, toughened and scarred from years of exposure to hot pans, stubborn dough, and misdirected knives, tend to conceal the innate delicacy of his technique and the refinement of his professional skill. But he studies the aspic with the love and intensity of a sculptor analyzing the first states of a stone coming to life. His keen eyes seem to lose focus as he stares momentarily into the hypnotic golden liquid, waiting, just as the alchemist does, for that moment when the transformation of confusion into order begins. Chef is a craftsman, and he is also an artist.

When the aspic starts to congeal, Chef spoons a little into the mold, then slowly turns and twists the mold in hopes that the aspic will adhere to the base and sides. It works (almost mysteriously), so he lets us coat the other molds.

"*Les truffes,*" he utters. Dead silence. "*Les truffes!* Where *are* the chopped truffles?" We freeze. "*Dieu,*" he swears, "don't tell me no one took the initiative to chop the truffles! Now everybody here has studied the recipe, everybody knows the mousse calls for specks of truffle, so why hasn't someone taken ten seconds to chop those truffles! Time wasted is the worst enemy of great cooking."

Two or three people grab knives, Gloria drops hers within one precarious inch of my foot, Chef glares, and by the time she's regained her composure, the cutting board is covered with black nuggets. Chef directs everyone to sprinkle the specks evenly around the molds, then explains how the molds must be refrigerated before a second coating of aspic can be applied.

Down the stairs comes an attractive middle-aged lady from the beginners' class carrying in her arms an enormous casserole full of *coq au vin blanc*. She explains in half-French, half-English that their refrigerator is full and asks if she can put the pot in ours for a while.

"*Oui, oui,*" he responds, throwing a hand in the air in mild irritation. "But pay attention to that *pâte feuilleté.*"

My God, my puff pastry! I should have rolled it the third time ten minutes ago, so I race to the refrigerator, grab the butter-stuffed dough, sling flour on the ice-cold marble, and begin rolling and folding in thirds.

"*Non, jeune homme,*" Chef exclaims, springing from the main worktable over to my marble counter. "Look, you can see the butter through the dough, and if you don't close up those ends, you're going to lose half your butter in the baking." I stare closely, and sure enough, there are faint yellow patches on top, and the ends are loose. Hmmm, I think, maybe that's why my puff pastry has been heavy as lard every day. I cover the patches with flour, roll out, then seal the ends very carefully with the rolling pin. But how in God's name did Chef notice that from across the room?

As soon as I give up the marble, Herb takes over, rolls out the dough for fresh noodles, and sets up the pasta machine. Back at the worktable, others are busy preparing the foie gras mousse and chicken mixture for the Pojarski. Anyone obsessed with calories and cholesterol would suffer cardiac arrest over the huge slabs of fresh butter, cartons of crème fraîche, and tubs of heavy cream being added from all sides. (And not ten minutes ago, Chef, with typical French sagacity, explained that the trouble with Belgian cuisine is that it's too heavy with butter and cream.)

Helene blends the ground chicken and cream with a large spoon, then stops when Chef moves in forcefully, expresses exasperation with a *"Mon Dieu,"* crams his thick hands down into the bowl, and in ten seconds, finishes mixing the ingredients with his fingers.

"Ma chérie," he sighs, "you must learn to use your hands whenever possible—for mixing, tasting, scraping, stirring, almost everything. Oh, I know they consider this unsanitary in America, but believe me, no Frenchman has ever died yet from mixing his steak tartare or green salad by hand. There's very little a spoon can do that two hands can't do better." He licks the feathery-light raw chicken from one finger as thoughts of salmonella sting our brains. "Salt, it needs more salt."

> NAPA VALLEY, CALIFORNIA, MAY 1974—
> *Here to see if there's any truth about this handful of winemakers producing superior American wines. So far very impressed by Stony Hill's and Mondavi's chardonnay, Beaulieu's spicy pinot noir, and Joe Heitz's remarkable "Martha's Vineyard" cab. These guys could have a big future, but I've yet to taste a champagne or riesling that can come close to the French. And why can't they use American names? Want to keep an eye on Simi in Sonoma now that Tchelitcheff is consultant.*

Clunk! We all turn in horror, only to discover Gloria and Herb kneeling on the floor over a pile of sticky ribbon noodles.

"I told Herb we shouldn't have tried to dry the noodles like this," she explains to the group, "but he insisted we suspend that steel oven rack between that nail and this can opener, and now just look."

"Stop complaining, Gloria," Chef says sympathetically, "and learn to deal with the problem. All that matters is the results. *Ce n'est pas grave.* After all, those wet noodles aren't going to break, so you two simply restring them, attach the rack more sensibly, and get on about your work." It doesn't faze Chef that the noodles have been all over the floor.

He now takes a pastry bag, fills it with handfuls of cream-enriched foie gras mousse, calls for the aspic- and truffle-lined molds, squeezes the bag till a little mousse flows (which he casually licks off), and artistically fills the first mold faster than the eye can follow. Everyone takes a turn, but nobody's mousse looks quite so exquisite as Chef's. *"Il faut de l'expérience,"* he quips. A few more truffles on top of each, more aspic, and the glistening molds are returned to the refrigerator to chill.

ABOARD *MICHELANGELO* TO CANNES, OCTOBER 1974—

Dining with Hermione Gingold and Richard Olney. She drinks Shirley Temples and spits food as she talks. He is obsessed with wine and chain smokes. Both delightful companions.

Tension builds as the clock moves past noon, and once again we're made aware of what it's like in the kitchen of a great French restaurant or large home, trying to complete complex preparations on time. Chicken cutlets are formed, dusted lightly with flour, and sautéed slowly in butter before being flamed with brandy. The small red snappers, covered with *duxelles* and cloaked airtight, are made ready for the oven, where they'll bake in their own steam and retain every ounce of their succulent natural flavor. A large pot of water is put on to boil the noodles. Mushrooms are quickly sautéed, transferred to a bowl, and along with lemon juice, white wine, and cream, positioned so there'll be no time lost when the moment comes to finish off the chicken *Pojarski*. Isabelle beats a vinaigrette for the salad, Helene checks the fresh strawberries for flaws, Kathy carefully stirs the delicate pastry cream she's prepared for my *tarte aux fraises*, and I remain squatted at an oven door, peering through the small window and praying my puff pastry will rise to fluffy heights. Out comes the foie gras from the refrigerator for unmolding, and just as Sammy is about to plunge the bottom of one mold into hot water, Chef screams for the last time, *"Non, jeune homme!* What do you want? Dribblings of hot water in your mousse?" And with that he takes a heavy dish towel, saturates it in the water, wraps it around the mold, and waits a few seconds. Out slides a masterpiece, smooth, firm, and glowing in black-speckled golden radiance.

CHICKEN POJARSKI

1 large egg

1 teaspoon vegetable oil

1 teaspoon water

1/2 pound plus 4 tablespoons (2 1/2 sticks) butter

2 pounds chicken cutlets

10 thin slices of white bread, crusts removed

1/2 cup heavy cream

1 teaspoon salt

1/4 teaspoon freshly ground white pepper

Unbleached all-purpose flour

1 1/2 cups fresh bread crumbs

1/2 cup canola or sunflower oil

Fresh lemon juice

In a small bowl, whisk together the egg, vegetable oil, and water; set the egg wash aside. In a small heavy saucepan, whisk 4 tablespoons of the butter over moderate heat till the color turns a russet brown, strain into another small saucepan, and keep the browned butter warm.

With a heavy chef's knife, cut the chicken into very small pieces, then chop it rapidly into a fine paste. Tear the bread into pieces and soak in the cream.

In a large mixing bowl, cream about 1 1/2 sticks of the remaining butter with an electric mixer; then, with the mixer still running, add the chicken 3 tablespoons at a time till well blended. Gradually add the soaked bread, then the salt and pepper, and continue beating till the mixture is homogeneous.

With the hands, shape the mixture into 12 cutlets 1/2 inch thick and 2 inches long. Dust each cutlet in the flour, brush each with the egg wash, and coat lightly with the bread crumbs.

In a large, heavy skillet, heat the remaining butter plus the oil over moderate heat. Add the cutlets and cook about 5 minutes on each side or till golden. Transfer to a serving platter, season with additional salt and pepper, and drizzle the browned butter and a little lemon juice over the tops. Serve immediately.

Twelve-thirty, and we have cleared the long wooden table, set it with china, flatware, and crystal worthy of the sybaritic feast we've prepared, opened three bottles of vintage Corton-Charlemagne (there's no *sou*-pinching at La Varenne), and begun devouring the luscious *mousse de foie gras en gelée.* At appropriate intervals, students get up to serve dishes for which they're mainly responsible: Cynthia and Sammy, the snapper; Helene and Kathy, *Pojarski;* Herb, the noodles; Isabelle, the salad; and Gloria—well, Gloria helps everybody with everything. Chef doesn't budge from his seat, content in carrying on his profound discourses about everything from how to truss a partridge to the philosophy of Voltaire to the current political happenings in France—all subjects on which he's a self-acclaimed authority.

My feet sting so badly I can hardly enjoy the sensuous fare, but while Gloria cleans away the cheese and salad and opens a little more champagne, I struggle up to serve my *tarte aux fraises.* It looks exquisite—a long, golden, beautifully risen, cream-filled pastry cradling giant fresh strawberries glistening with apricot glaze. Perfection. I wait for all to cut their first bites. Polite silence. Chef tastes and sits and stares at me. Then everyone glares, even Gloria. I taste. Something's wrong. But it can't be wrong, for the tart looks perfect, and I'm proud I finally got my pastry to rise properly. "Salt," mumbles Moyna, breaking the deadening silence, "you left out the salt!" "Yes, salt," everyone chimes in, "there's not one grain of salt in this pastry. It's too bland, it needs at least a half teaspoon of salt, it . . ."

Okay, I say to myself, so I forgot the goddamn salt. But what about the absolutely marvelous way my pastry rose?

"Jeune homme," Chef interjects, "no doubt you've finally learned the trick to making puff pastry, but no matter how beautiful a dish looks, if the taste is not perfect, the dish is a failure. You didn't recheck the recipe and therefore forgot something so seemingly unimportant as salt. An accomplished chef can't afford to forget anything. It's all right to make mistakes as long as the end result is satisfactory. Maybe you've learned an important lesson."

Chef and the others did end up being sympathetic, but as I dragged my swollen feet out the door and into the cool, sunlit streets of Paris, humiliation turned to fury. Damn it, I'll show them, I raged to myself. I'll simply prolong my stay in Paris, arrange to remain enrolled at the school one more day, and come Monday I'll prepare puff pastry the likes of which would put even Paul Bocuse to shame. Yes, decided! And with that I marched back to the hotel, obtained permission to keep my room, put my feet to soak, and resolved then and there never again to ridicule any chef anywhere under any circumstances without damn good reason.

Undercover as table captain at Le Perroquet in Chicago, 1977. Photo: Rudolph Janu

Menu from Le Perroquet

JAMBON DE BAYONNE
LES SURPRISES
MELON AU PORTO
POTAGE DU JOUR
MOUSSE DE SAUMON, SAUCE VERTE
PÂTÉS ASSORTIS
CAVIAR MALOSSOL (14.00)
LA TRUFFE EN FEUILLETAGE (6.00)
TOURTE AUX CHAMPIGNONS
MOULES NORMANDE
SAUMON FUMÉ (2.50)
GAZPACHO ANDALOU
BISQUE DE HOMARD

LES POISSONS FRAIS
ST. JACQUES GRILLÉS
MIXED GRILL À L'ANGLAISE
NOS PLATS DU JOUR
SOUFFLÉ DU JOUR
L'ESCALOPINES DE VEAU AU CITRON
ENTRECÔTE MINUTE
CONFIT D'OIE, POMMES SARLADAISE
TRIPES BASQUAISE
ROGNONS DE VEAU DIJONNAISE
BOEUF À LA FICELLE (2 PERS.)

FROMAGES
OU
PATISSERIES AU CHOIX
MOUSSE AU CHOCOLAT ET MOKA
LES FRUITS DE SAISON
CRÊPES SUZETTE (TWO PERS. 6.00)
SORBETS ET GLACES MAISON

CAFÉ   ESPRESSO   SANKA   THÉ   IRISH COFFEE (3.00)

LE DÉJEUNER 10.50

5/77

Jovan Trboyevic, owner of Le Perroquet, with Paula Wolfert, Ruth Reichl, and his wife, Maggie Abbott, at the Hôtel Plaza Athenée in Paris.

CHAPTER FIVE

BORN TO SERVE

AFTER MY GIG AT LA VARENNE, my next mission was to somehow work undercover in a deluxe, expensive restaurant, not only to discover exactly what was going on behind the scenes, but to experience what it might be like serving much the same public that was reading my articles and reviews. Of course, setting up the project involved every obstacle imaginable, but in the end, even my most skeptical friends and colleagues had to admit that the plan was ingenious.

Since there was always the chance that my face might be recognized in New York, I finally made contact in Chicago with Jovan Trboyevic, owner of the city's most renowned and respected restaurant, Le Perroquet, and the only maverick willing to accept the challenge and cooperate. Now, it so happened that one of Jovan's old buddies in the business had recently opened a new luxury restaurant in New York; our story was that the friend was sending this promising waiter by the name of Jim Anderson (my alias) out to Chicago to receive initial training as a table captain by Jovan and his veteran staff. Jovan agreed to all the terms: Nobody but he himself was to have an inkling as to what I was about (with the polite but firm understanding that if I suspected betrayal, I'd discontinue the venture on the spot). I would stay at a hotel, but there would be a fake address and phone drop elsewhere in case someone wanted to contact me. I would work both lunch and dinner, keeping the same hours as the others. I would be treated by Jovan exactly like any other employee, even nastily if necessary, and I would eventually turn all tips over to the other captains to be included in the normal distribution, since after all, I was there only for the experience. Suffice it to say that the boys bought the story hook, line, and sinker and were convinced from the start that this Anderson guy was no more than a New York hashhouse waiter with a sloppy Southern accent who was aspiring to the restaurant big time. How did I happen to know French? By slaving with a bunch of frogs for a year in some French dive on New York's West Side, that's how.

Now, imagine that you're seated in a very fancy French restaurant. The last thing on your mind is what the captains and waiters and busboys are saying about you. Right? Well, after my week at Le Perroquet, I can tell you right off exactly what is said. For instance:

"Forget the goddamn coffee refill on nineteen, my dear," directs Paul, another captain who's saucing a rack of veal at the serving table. "And how about cutting me a wagon for the chick on fourteen. For God's sake, don't do anything to raw 'em off. Dig the rock on that fat paw. Her old man's a mark if I ever saw one—good for maybe twenty-five percent."

I'm worried that the customers might hear the crude, indiscreet language we tend to use among ourselves, possibly as a reaction to all the elegance and display we have to affect for the job. I'm also worried about the coffee for the couple at table nineteen.

"Forget 'em for now," Paul says. "All he cares about is snowing the broad, and besides, you can tell by the wine they're drinking he's no more than a fifteen percenter. Come on, for God's sake, step on it please with that tenderloin . . . Quick, Jim, behind you on twenty."

I snap around just in time to pull out the table for the lady who is getting up, heading most likely for the john.

"Captain!" This is from table nineteen. "How about a little more coffee over here and a few more of those chocolate things."

I nod, back off, and go across the room to get a busboy to take care of the coffee and chocolate truffles. Then I make tracks for the silver trolley and begin carving three slices of beef. No sooner have I ladled on a bit of Bordelaise sauce and started to wipe dribbles from the edges of the hot plate than Jean-Pierre, the handsome, suave maitre d', passes by taking a new party to their table. He glances down at my handiwork, and, never for an instant losing pace with the two couples, he murmurs, "*Les bouts, n'oublie pas les bouts.*" I still haven't gotten it through my thick skull to cover the ends of the meat with sauce.

"Quick, Paul, I need vegetables," I say.

"Yeah, I know, but the bastards didn't send out enough. See if you can grab a kitchen man and . . . no, forget it . . . why don't you just run back to the kitchen yourself while I finish up the veal, and I'll try to find a cover for the tenderloin. And Jim, while you're back there, for God's sake do something about that . . . tacky sauce on your jacket."

As I broke my way through the busy waiters and busboys and pantrymen snitching food, slid across the glop in the dishwashing area, grabbed a wet towel to wipe the Bordelaise off my dinner jacket, and stood puffing frantically on a cigarette while waiting for a chef to spoon out the neglected vegetables, I once again had the feeling I couldn't make it through the evening. The blood blisters on my left foot, the excruciating pain in my lower back, the dizziness from lack of anything to eat since the cheeseburger in midafternoon. So far I'd managed to survive this self-inflicted ordeal, and no doubt I was convinced more than ever that the project was both noble and constructive. To my knowledge, none of us highfalutin, omnipotent, forever-complaining restaurant critics had ever made any effort to experience firsthand the actual running of a great restaurant, and by God, I was now smack in the midst of it.

Okay, I know. The customer is shelling out plenty of hard cash, and he shouldn't be expected to understand why a place happens to flop miserably on any given occasion. Correct? For years, that was my way of thinking too, until, that is, I began to wonder, really wonder if there weren't a few hidden facts behind the scenes that could reveal ways whereby I and everybody else just might get better food and service. So I did it, and I learned a lot. Things like this:

— You should expect a maitre d', captain, or waiter in any first-class restaurant to be able to do anything to enhance your pleasure, but like it or not, no matter who you are or how fat your wallet, if you don't make some small effort yourself, you'll have a very ordinary, maybe lousy experience. You should dress decently, preferably a jacket and tie for men, a nice dress for women, and leave the jeans and T-shirt and sneakers at home. Despite what you hear and read, deluxe restaurants have little use for clods, even in these relaxed times. You should ask the captain or waiter his name when he arrives at the table—formally and with no hint of chitchat. You should smile from time to time at the people serving you, and for heaven's sake, you should say thank you when they do something special. You're even better off if you can show an intelligent interest in the menu and wine list.

— It seriously upsets captains and wine stewards to see guests pouring their own wine. If your glass needs refilling and everyone on the staff is busy, try to be patient a few minutes till someone has time to pour. You shouldn't go thirsty, however, and if you must pour after a short wait, go ahead. But understand that the staff will take this as a complaint. If it's deserved, make it. Wine stewards respect customers who know and ask questions about wines; they loathe those who simply try to show off and impress others.

— Nobody on a restaurant staff is overly fond of couples (deuces), for the simple reason that they require virtually the same amount of time that it takes to serve four, and for half the tips or less. Singles are never loved, contrary to what anybody says. Quite often a maitre d' will turn down dozens of same-day requests for deuces in order to hold space for parties of four, six, or eight. As for pulling that old stunt of booking a table for three when you know you'll be only two, it might work once, but the restaurant will be on its guard the next time you call.

— Since those working the floor receive hardly any salary to speak of (union or no union), tips matter more to them than anything else in life. Almost everywhere (except in New York City), tips are pooled and distributed after lunch and dinner among either the entire floor staff (as at my restaurant) or those working their separate stations: generally a full cut for captains, waiters, and wine stewards; a three-quarters cut for kitchen men; and a half-cut for busboys. Although this means you're really tipping many for a job performed by one or two, don't try to take out your wrath on the system (unless, of course, you found the service rotten). If you automatically stiff the bill, thinking the tip is basically impersonal and meaningless, remember you're only decreasing the cut (i.e., livelihood) collected by those who served you well. (Even if you palm a captain, he's expected to contribute that tip to the pool— except in New York City.) Also don't forget that knowledge of your stinginess filters down quickly among the staff, and this could have a disastrous effect on your next visit, no matter who waits on you. Often the bottle of wine a guest orders is indicative of what the tip will be, but we prayed for 25 percent, were thankful for 20, and said ugly things about those who left only 15. Nor did we have much use for customers who ordered wine by the glass.

— The best way to tip? Most people simply add a percentage to the credit card slip (either in one lump sum or, say, 15 percent for the waiters and 5 percent for the captain), but nobody impressed us more than those who made the rare gesture of personally handing us the tips while expressing thanks. Does palming a maitre d' or captain a ten or twenty before you sit down guarantee special attention and possibly better food? You're damn right it does!

— Nothing irritates a staff so much or causes a greater disruption of service than when customers jump up and leave the table for one reason or another, especially while the main courses are being served. If you must pee, do it while a course is being cleared from the table.

— It hurts when an obviously satisfied customer who's leaving doesn't even have the decency and graciousness to thank those who've provided good service—palmed tip or no palmed tip. This discourtesy is never forgotten.

From the moment I showed up for my first lunch, it was pretty obvious I was working in a first-class restaurant, one of the best in the country. On the surface, Le Perroquet manifested just about what you would expect (and more) of a luxury restaurant: muted mustard and light-green murals, red velvet banquettes with appliquéd cushions, starched linen tablecloths, fine etched crystal, silver flatware, small individual table lamps, Lalique flower vases, silver ice buckets, bottles of mineral water on every table, fancy complimentary hors d'oeuvres and chocolate candies, and so forth. Like at Le Cirque in New York or Taillevent in Paris, it was all very high class, to say the least, but what was to amaze me continuously during my week there was the assemblage of experts who made the place function so beautifully: three young Americans holding down the important jobs of head chef, pastry chef, and wine steward; a perfectionist Mexican bartender who had no patience with staffers who didn't follow his directions on how to place drink orders; a French maitre d' who could detect (and reject) a slob after ten seconds on the phone; a brigade of American, French, Syrian, Mexican, and Spanish waiters and busboys who didn't seem to need to speak much English in order to communicate; and, of course, the ever-present, dynamic force of Jovan himself. He was an elegant, proud, brutally demanding, often melancholy Yugoslav who proclaimed himself a philosophical anarchist in his never-ending struggle against mediocrity and boredom. He didn't think twice about throwing out customers who caused unnecessary problems and embarrassment. And unbeknownst to his staff, he was secretly courting the petite lady who delivered and arranged the flowers every day and would one day become his wife.

So there I was that first miserable day, determined to make a go of this thing yet frightened stiff that somebody on the staff—not to mention the customers—would decide there was just something too weird about me. Even the most illiterate, inexperienced greasy-spoon waiter knows how to carry a full tray of drinks, write down an order, and serve food without dumping it in someone's lap. I didn't, and in case you suffer under the illusion (as I always had) that a captain does no more than smile, take orders, carve an occasional

> PIEDMONT, ITALY, NOVEMBER 1975—
>
> *My first fresh white truffles—shaved over fonduta at Ristorante Cambio in Turin. Smelled just like dirty socks, but, my God what flavor—like nothing I've ever tasted. This morning at market in Albi, Signore Mo bought me a golf ball–size truffle in jar filled with rice from one of his shady cohorts. $100, I figure. I ate it driving to Lombardy—died and gone to heaven!*

duck, and grab for tips, let me clue you in. In addition to having to execute the most menial tasks, I (like everyone else in Jovan's employ) was expected to be able to cup ashtrays deftly when emptying them, hold lamp wires up with my foot while pulling out tables, pour wine across three bodies when a wall made it impossible to pass behind a customer, gracefully pick up a plate of food and place a clean napkin over a spill without drawing too much attention to the customer's sloppiness, and, of course, prepare and sauce in a matter of seconds an array of exquisite dishes on a flaming-hot serving table not much bigger than a TV set.

No task, I was to learn quickly, is too demeaning for any captain who wants things to run smoothly, no matter how proud or experienced he may be. By the same token, it's understood in a great restaurant that regardless of whether you wear a tuxedo or a waiter's white jacket or a kitchen man's lowly black uniform, success (i.e., satisfying customers, keeping your job, and above all, raking in as much money as possible from the split on tips) is determined by unrelenting teamwork. If a captain sees a dirty dish on a table, he doesn't wait for a busboy to pick it up. If a patron takes a cigarette out, a waiter doesn't hesitate to rush over and light it. And it's nothing extraordinary for a wine steward to fetch a quick pot of coffee, slice a side of smoked salmon, or help a hurried captain dish out at the serving table. As a result of this interchange, a remarkable sense of togetherness develops behind the scenes, an understanding on the part of everyone that if you expect to make a decent livelihood, you'd sure as hell better respect and help the next guy. Being straight or gay makes no difference whatsoever, and while a number of the staff with whom I worked were openly gay, we all knew there was no time or place for much hanky panky—at least not while on the job.

By the third day, I had the basics pretty well under control, thanks mainly to the sympathetic help of everybody on the staff. I had grasped the technique of referring to tables and customers by number and writing down orders accordingly—horseradish flan for number 2 on table 14, for instance. I reeled off all the specialties with their exotic descriptions, encouraging customers to sample these extraordinary (and money-making) dishes instead of the more standard preparations listed on the menu. I learned how to decant fine red wines at the table and handle dishes and silver and crystal without so much as a tingle. I mastered the delicate art of "pushing" soufflés by telling customers how delicious and special they were and reminding them that, of course, these must be ordered in advance. I'd even begun to develop that inimitable look of self-confidence and authority I'd always admired in a good captain. What did once throw me off a bit was a bejeweled, middle-aged lady who, fluttering her long eye lashes, kept patting the banquette and encouraging me to sit down next to her while reciting the specials. I simply pretended I didn't understand. Nor did I respond one night to a young, nice-looking gentleman who, in his cups with two friends, made overtures about my dropping by the hotel later on for a nightcap, though I must admit, that proposal was tempting.

Horseradish Flan with Fennel Sauce

Serves 4 to 6

3 large eggs

1 ½ cups heavy cream

¼ teaspoon salt

⅛ teaspoon ground white pepper

Pinch of grated nutmeg

2 tablespoons fresh grated horseradish

½ cup thinly sliced fennel bulb

⅓ stem fennel, including a few leaves, roughly chopped

3 tablespoons coarsely chopped onion

3 tablespoons coarsely chopped mushrooms

3 tablespoons dry white wine

¾ cup chicken stock or broth

1 to 2 tablespoons butter

3 drops of Pernod

Fennel leaves for garnish

Preheat the oven to 325° F.

In a large mixing bowl, whisk the eggs lightly. Add the cream, stir, and strain through a fine sieve into another bowl. Add the salt, pepper, nutmeg, and horseradish and stir till the batter is well blended.

Ladle equal amounts of batter into 4 to 6 buttered ramekins, stirring the batter before each ladling. Place the ramekins in a baking pan and add enough water to come halfway up sides of the ramekins. Bake 15 minutes or till slightly puffed, remove the pan from the oven, and let the ramekins sit in the water to keep warm.

Place the fennel bulb and stem, onion, and mushrooms in a medium skillet, add a little water, cover, and steam over moderate heat 5 minutes. Add the wine and reduce the liquid slightly, uncovered. Add the chicken stock and cook about 5 minutes longer. When the vegetables are tender, transfer them to a blender or food processor, reduce to a puree, and strain into a clean skillet. Add the butter and Pernod, and blend well.

Roll a film of puree around the bottoms of 4 to 6 warmed plates and unmold the flans into the centers. Garnish the sides with fennel leaves.

And, of course, there were outright disasters, like when I poured '70 Haut Brion into a glass containing humble beaujolais (the customers were given a new bottle of the hideously expensive juice, and I received a blast from Jovan), or when, not having any idea what to do when a slimy crème caramel slid off the plate onto a lady's dress, I frantically picked it up from her lap with my fingers, dropped it in a napkin, and inspired something close to hysteria on the part of Madame and staff members alike. I also had to be told constantly by a particularly concerned and cute Mexican waiter (who sometimes discreetly pinched my butt) always to stand erect when taking orders and never, but never, to touch the table while talking with a customer. The maitre d' had to remind me time and again to be sure to clear away extra place settings, to stand by a table so as not to turn my back to customers, and never, heaven forbid, to serve any dish if the customer happened to be away from the table. These things seemed to work themselves out, however, and I felt that generally I was making fairly good progress.

I gradually became accustomed to much of the same way of life the other guys knew forty-nine weeks out of the year, every day except Saturday lunch and Sunday. The routine, which was no doubt generally like that in any good restaurant, was deadly and never varied. Around 10:30 in the morning you show up to analyze the reservations with Jovan and Jean-Pierre, study the special dishes to be offered at lunch, deal with the fresh linen and setting of tables, see that the cold dishes are properly displayed and the sherbet containers spotless, answer the blasting phone and take reservations and make clever excuses when necessary, and on and on, one thing after another. If the laundry isn't delivered, you're sunk and can only pray there's still enough new stock in supply for those tables you can't fake with last night's linen. If a waiter calls in sick, you have to rechart stations and figure out who can best cover for him. If the crayfish pâté looks or tastes wrong, an equally exotic dish must be decided on and prepared in split-second time back in the kitchen. Shortly before noon you change from ratty garb to tux or uniform, exposing holes in T-shirts, pale white skin that's rarely exposed to the sun, a gut bloated from too much wee-hours beer and wine swiped in the pantry, feet forever swollen from pacing the job some twelve to thirteen hours a day. Soon you hear the first voices of customers, and the bowing and scraping and sweeping of arms begins as the mechanics of still another lunchtime are put into motion.

You continue till 3:00, 3:15, 3:30, or till the last guests finally decide to leave. You're anxious to collect your cut of the tips (distributed after every meal around the bar or back in the pantry), and you've had nothing to eat except snitched bits off plates, and you're a bit pooped. Instead of sticking around to take chances on what some of the guys who never leave the place are served at 4:30, you head out for a cheeseburger and fries, dash home, and maybe watch a little TV or soak in a hot tub before heading back to the restaurant around 5:15.

Friday night is booked solid, and since there is no reasonable way to turn down anybody who reserved two weeks in advance, you're stuck with far too many deuces to make the evening truly profitable in the way of tips. "Seventy-five, maybe eighty apiece for the captains," guesses Paul, who is gay, "but then you never know. See those two fags on four? They're weekend regulars and actually pretty nice and generous. Give 'em plenty of attention—if you know what I mean—and they'll leave a good twenty-five percent. The couple on six is also around about once a week, but remember, the one thing that infuriates that guy is having the menus pushed on him till he asks for them. And the two on twelve—well, I heard those Southern accents when they arrived, and if they're like most Southerners, they can't count past fifteen. No offense to you, my dear, but Southerners are rotten tippers, the worst."

Enter Tennessee Williams and party of three. The great man himself is a regular when in town, and Jovan suggests privately I take on the table in hopes of reaping an interesting scenario. I explain in a whisper that I've met the playwright, and he might recognize me even in the dark room. Jovan reminds me that Williams is not only virtually blind in his right eye but usually drunk, so I should simply stay to his right and stand as far back as possible when speaking. Besides, he'll never suspect in a thousand years. ("But he gets no better treatment than any other customer in this restaurant," barks the owner.) Williams does not recognize me but smiles, says there'll be no cocktails, and asks what nice dry white wine I'd recommend.

"Sir, would you care to see the wine list?" I answer, trying to modify my voice.

"Naw, naw, I don't feel up to having to wrestle with a long wine list tonight," he drawls, "but you seem like the type of captain who'll choose something that's very appropriate for the occasion—hee, hee."

Of course I have no idea what occasion he's talking about or why the giggle, but I nevertheless discuss it with Alain, a wine steward, and together we decide on a fairly rare but reasonably priced Pavillon Blanc du Château Margaux.

"This is superrrb," cries Williams tipsily after checking the nose like the old pro he is and taking a huge gulp. "I think I can tell you right now that we'll just have to have two bottles, young man, and I'll have an explanation of where you happen to be from with that marrrvelous accent. Now don't tell me. It's Georgia, or maybe South Carolina, but it's *not* Mississippi."

Nervous, I hold my head at an angle; then, suddenly, I notice the man at the next table reaching for his bottle of wine in the ice bucket. Relieved to leave Williams's question dangling, I excuse myself momentarily and pour the wine in a flash. No sooner have I placed the bottle back on ice than a waiter who's looking deathly pale asks if I could cover his station and handle serving the soufflés on twelve while he goes to the bathroom. Action is at its peak throughout the restaurant, with not one captain, waiter, or busboy to spare. Held prisoner by two raspberry soufflés that must be spooned out immediately, I'm unable to help poor, dear Roberto, who is struggling with both the pastry wagon and sherbet trolley for the dessert orders on sixteen. Dirty dishes should be cleaned off twenty, but it seems all the busboys are back in the pantry preparing espresso—and besides, though I know my attitude is wrong,

I've really lost all desire to try to make things nice for two dolts who've nursed martinis throughout an entire glorious meal and kept business papers spread out in every direction on the table.

"Hey, captain," I hear behind me, as I feel a hand being placed around my shoulders. "See that cute little thing sitting over there? Well, I got a big favor to ask of you. See, it's her birthday tonight, and I was just wondering if maybe the restaurant had a little special cake or something. And I was also wondering if later on you could come by and, you know, just give her a little kiss on the cheek and wish her a surprise happy birthday. Really would give her a bit of a thrill, and don't worry, I'll make it worth your time—ya know what I mean?"

"Not in this restaurant you don't!" Jovan booms at me. "You inform the guy this place is no playground." Suffice it to say I did a little hand-kissing, then watched the oaf walk out without so much as a fare-thee-well.

As I pass by twenty to check on the wine glasses, I notice the attractive party of three—one lady, two gentlemen—is still seriously involved in their comparative tasting of two first-growth Bordeaux and two fine California cabernets. Like many of the customers, they ordered their food intelligently, asked me the details of each preparation, and in general have conducted themselves in such a delightful manner that I find waiting on them an absolute joy. Although Le Perroquet has an exquisite selection of cheeses included in the price of dinner, I've learned not to waste my breath suggesting this course to those who obviously couldn't care less. But for the party at this table, I don't even ask, but make the special effort to present the wicker tray, discuss which cheeses I feel would go nicely with the wines, and, although not doubting the ability of the waiter to cut the cheeses properly, choose to serve them myself. And as I suspected, these sensible souls order no more than a little fresh sherbet for dessert, espresso, and a bit of cognac. More than likely they'll tip me an extra twenty-in-hand (which it so happens they eventually do), but even if they didn't, I would still consider it a privilege to have served them.

"Jim, do you think you can handle that scene on twenty-one?" whispers Alain.

Rushing up to Williams's table, I see that the drooping head of the guest sitting in front of the playwright is practically touching his salmon steak.

"Excuse me, captain," says Williams calmly, now well through the second bottle of wine, "but they suspect that my companion has a brain tumor, and it appears that he's been stricken by an attack of acute vertigo necessitating an immediate cup of strong black coffee." (I jotted down that line the second I got back to the pantry.) Strangely enough, the other two guests never stop their conversation or so much as glance over to see if this guy is alive, and even Tennessee seems too accustomed to his friend's soused condition to become in any way alarmed.

It's 12:30 A.M. With only one couple still lingering over coffee, Jean-Pierre and I stand in the small area behind Gino's bar, where throughout the evening we've left cigarettes smoldering in a filthy ashtray. Although I know some of the boys are back in the pantry pilfering more food from the cooler and finishing up whatever was left on the trolleys and even on plates, I'm too exhausted to be hungry. All I want now is to go out and get drunk and cruise gay bars. Returning to check the dining room, I see Dan, Roberto, Alain, Paul, Zigi, all standing and waiting and praying it won't be too much longer before they can finish up, collect their tips, and leave. The sight of this saddens me, and I know I'll remember it the rest of my life.

Finally, the time came for Jovan to reveal my cover-up to the staff—I didn't have the guts to do it myself. All the guests had left, Paul had just announced that a certain party had tipped exactly $7 on a $410 bill, and a group of us were standing at the bar bemoaning the outcome of the evening's sacred tip sheets. "I'm falling apart," Jovan declared, then directed Gino to pour him a straight vodka on the rocks.

"And just what do you think of all this, Monsieur Villas?" he bolted, putting his hand on my shoulder.

No reaction from anybody—anybody!

"Gentlemen, look here," he continued. "What would you say if I told you we've got a phony creep in the group whose name is not Anderson?"

The Staff   23 September 1977
Le Perroquet Restaurant
70 Walton Place
Chicago, Illinois 60611

Dear Gentlemen:

One week ago I truly wondered if I'd survive still another evening working at a job for which I'd had not one day of training and which produced the type of burning feet and aching back that you're all either accustomed to or have long forgotten about. To say the least it was an altogether new and different experience for me, and now I want to thank each of you personally for all your help, incredible patience, and, above all, understanding once you learned what was happening. It disturbed me deeply—especially after getting to know you so well—having to deceive you and play the fake. But this was a very important project to me, and I think if you'd been in my shoes you would have agreed it was the only way to carry it out if I were to really get the feeling of what it's like working in a great restaurant.

I suppose what I really want to say is that you taught me so much more than what it's like to be a captain and serve the public. In so many ways you taught me what it's like to have a true sense of pride and devotion to an idea. No doubt you probably realize you're working in one of the finest (if not the finest) restaurants in the country, just as I'm sure you realize that Jovan is the type of rare individual none of us will run across many times during our lives. I now know what it feels like trying to do one's best job day in and day out, night in and night out, just as I now know what it feels like to be unappreciated by an indifferent public, a mere object who's expected on the surface to do no more than serve perfectly, smile when it's difficult to smile, and perform each and every duty without ever asking a question.

So thank you, Jean-Pierre and Hal, for not neglecting me; thank you, Bill and Roberto and Alain and Dan for tolerating my stupidities; and to you all, thanks for the encouragements and friendship. It was indeed a rare privilege working with you all.

Best wishes,

James Villas (alias Anderson)
Food and Wine Editor

Jean-Pierre raised his eyes, glanced at Jovan, then at me, then back to Jovan. As the explanation continued, a formidable silence came over the rather frightened men as they all glared at me in disbelief. Feeling more and more rotten, I could find nothing to say but "I'm sorry," and I was sorry, for the noble project now seemed a little distasteful. These guys had become my friends. Then Gino smiled politely for the first time, and Paul offered to light my cigarette, and nobody reminded me it would be my turn to buy the beer after work. I did wink at Roberto, but I knew a unique experience was over.

So the week came to an end. Physically, I ached and had lost five pounds; spiritually, I'd gained invaluable insight into the special world I was writing about. Perhaps the most objective lesson I learned at Le Perroquet is that the public is dealing with pros who, if treated right, can and will move mountains to make people feel special, but what hit home most was the utter humanity of these men, these moving shadows who struggle to survive the best way they know how and are generally ignored by the public.

And my experience in Chicago made me even less tolerant of those in the business who're quite obviously out to con every customer who walks through the door. Shortly after my arrival back in New York, for instance, I had occasion to dine for the first time in one of the city's most fashionable restaurants. At the very beginning, I attempted to establish a rapport with the captain by asking his name, soliciting his opinions on the menu, taking his wine recommendation, and generally making him feel we needed and trusted him. Nothing worked. The food was mediocre, the service shoddy, and the captain totally indifferent. He never supervised anything we were served, he allowed us to pour our own wine throughout the meal, he stood chatting casually with the haughty maitre d' while I motioned for him. When I finally managed to wave him over to complain that my companion's calf's liver was tough as leather, he merely shrugged and suggested that perhaps she just didn't like liver. He was hopeless and should have been jobless. When time came to pay the bill, naturally he was there, hovering, pampering, eyeing. To the amount of the bill I begrudgingly added 10 percent for the incompetent waiter only because he might have been inexperienced or sick or in love.

"Did Monsieur not enjoy his meal?" questioned the captain as the lady and I brushed by, still hoping I'd palm him a bill.

"No, Monsieur did not enjoy his meal," I snapped, "and I'd like to add that the service was inexcusable."

"But, Monsieur, you don't understand. Tonight was exceptionally busy, and if you could put yourself in my place, having to take care of this many people, maybe you'd understand better."

MEXICO CITY, MAY 1980—

Thanks to Diana Kennedy, I'm getting some idea of what authentic Mexican food is all about—and most glorious: the moles, chiles en nogada, Mayan pork tamale pie, amazing white cheeses, and this hideous-looking but delectable corn fungus called huitlacoche. Diana's passion for this food is uncontrolled and catching. So much for Tex-Mex crap.

Staring him straight in the eye, I was almost tempted. Then I turned, took the lady's arm, and walked out.

*Mary Frances
Kennedy Fisher, 1984.
Photo: Janet Fries.*

*A note from M.F.K. Fisher.
By permission.*

Bouverie Ranch
13935 Sonoma Highway
Glen Ellen
California 95442

December 1, 1978

Dear Jim:

Yes, I do think your interview came off very well, and I've had really favorable comments about it. Thank you again for all the trouble you took...

I do think you should insist on galleys from any magazine you write for...

I still feel sad to remember how awful you felt, that day...really, I don't see how you could stand to describe lunch, for instance.

Your stay in France sounds heavenly...and then coming back on an honest-to-god ship! It appals me to realize that most probably I shan't ever sail again. And unfortunately I must agree with you that the other ways to travel become less agreeable every minute. Ho hum.

Norah and I had a fine time, as always, in Aix...stayed at a small inn outside the town, and were in Marseille quite a bit. Then in October we spent about 16 days in Japan, mostly in Osaka with our friend Shizuo Tsuji at his culinary school...hard work, but fascinating. I was halfway through work on an introduction for Tsuji's next book when I had to dash to the hospital...emergency gut-ache, but all is well, and now I'm home again and gradually getting back to work again.

When are you coming to San Francisco? I trust you to let me know. Meanwhile, all my best wishes for a very fine new year.

Mary Frances

M.F.K. Fisher

to

James Villas, Esq.
Town & Country
717 Fifth Avenue
New York, N.Y. 10022

CHAPTER SIX

HOW TO TAME A WOLF

THE FIRST TIME I HEARD THE NAME M.F.K. FISHER was during a memorable meal in 1961 with Lucius Beebe (creator of Café Society, notorious journalist, and bon vivant extraordinaire) at New York's Le Pavillon when the favorite topic of oysters came up.

"Nobody has ever written as eloquently about the mollusk as M.F.K. Fisher," the magnifico pronounced at one point.

"Who is he?" I asked innocently.

Raising his head imperiously as if he were about to impart the secret of the Philosopher's Stone, he sounded a deep, unexpected chuckle.

"Not he, my friend, but she," he corrected with a bit of resentment now in his voice. "I once made the same embarrassing mistake when I assumed that the 'M.F.K.' had to be some wispy Oxford don, and felt betrayed to learn that this phenomenal food author was actually an American of the female sex."

Mary Frances Kennedy Fisher remained a mystery to me till the mid seventies, when after years of being disgracefully out of print, her most important writings were republished under a single title, *The Art of Eating*. (Since I'd read Brillat-Savarin's *La phsysiologie du goût* in French, I was even unaware of Fisher's brilliant translation.) Seeing the thick volume in a bookshop, I immediately recognized the initials from the conversation long before with Mr. Beebe, bought the book, and spent an entire day and most of a night engrossed in tales and ideas and sentences and a literary style that would have an explosive effect on my own developing approach to food writing and on my life. Like many others, I was inspired by all the aphorisms that would become almost clichés to a later generation of admirers: breaking bread and drinking wine being a communion of much more than our bodies; the desire for food being but one of many great hungers of the world; dining alone being the ultimate test of character; and our most compulsive urge being the need to civilize our innate savagery, to tame the wolf inside. This was toothy, passionate thinking and writing, but what I would remember most vividly in years to come, and what would define for me personally the refined art of M.F.K. Fisher, was the poetic manner in which she could translate some of her life's most difficult challenges into revelations of spiritual and sensuous enlightenment. Witness in *The Gastronomical Me*, for example, a heartbreaking invocation of a beloved husband slowly dying of cancer during a voyage on the *Normandie*:

> We got up late, and went after bathings and shavings to the Lounge, where we sat in soft chairs by the glass wall and looked out past the people sunning themselves to the blue water. We drank Champagne or sometimes beer, slowly, and talked and talked to each other because there was so much to say and so little time to say it.
>
> Even when New York loomed near us, we felt outward bound. I bit gently at my numb fingers. I seemed beautiful, witty, truly loved . . . the most fortunate of all women, past sea change and with her hungers fed.

Or read the departing words of an admirer when, not having his amorous affections requited by the stunningly attractive Fisher during a final lunch of fondue in a Swiss train station, he rises from the table and bids a cryptic, sad farewell: "Go on eating. Go on sitting there with your food and your wine. I saw you first that way, alone, so god-damned sure of yourself. This is right. I'll leave now. Do this last thing and stay as you are, here at the table with the wine in your hand."

This is all vintage Fisher: the juxtaposition of highly charged emotional moments with the need for gustatory fulfillment, the tension and ambiguity of human relations, the warm empathy and understanding, the melancholy resolve, and the recognition and honest acceptance of Fate. It doesn't matter whether champagne or beer is drunk or whether it's good or bad; and it's worth describing a fondue as "too thin, stringy, and gluey" only because her suitor's rejection of the dish says something important about his personality. Other food writers would wax endlessly and stodgily over why a certain wine or dish is palatable or atrocious; with Fisher, such secondary details are useless unless they contribute to the pathos of an event or sensation. She might discourse elegiacally on the pea, or the oyster, or a memorable meal in Dijon, or even a greasy fried-egg sandwich; but while doing so, she always manages to transform and transcend the subject so that the art of living takes supreme precedence over the more subordinate act of nourishing our bodies.

It was only a few years after my initial exposure to Fisher's work that I was approached by Patricia Brown, the editor in chief of *Bon Appétit*, told that the very private Mrs. Fisher had agreed for the first time to be interviewed for a national magazine, and asked if I'd like to take on the assignment and fly to California to have lunch with the author at her home in Sonoma Valley. Slightly apprehensive but excited over the opportunity to meet and get to know this legend, I accepted and proceeded to reread all seven hundred pages of *The Art of Eating* plus every out-of-print book of hers I could get my hands on. Then, to break the ice, I sent Fisher a cordial letter introducing myself, inquiring about driving directions from San Francisco, and expressing the hope that my visit would not be too dreadful an infringement on her privacy.

Our date set for a midwinter morning, I flew to San Francisco a day early for the express purpose of joining an old priest friend at a venerable seafood grill called Sam's to eat rare Olympia oysters, sand dabs, and petrale sole. The dinner was as exceptional as expected, the only problem being that I had a restless night back at the hotel and began feeling queasy by dawn. Knowing the importance of my meeting up in Sonoma, I still set out in the car as planned, popped a few Rolaids, and headed for the Golden Gate Bridge. Then, not fifteen minutes up Route 29, the nausea, now accompanied by horrific stomach cramps, only intensified, to such a degree that I was suddenly forced to pull over and begin heaving right there on the side of the highway. Remission was brief, however, and after stopping again at a gas station, I felt my clammy, feverish forehead and knew from tough past experience that without question this was a classic case of oyster poisoning—only worse. How I made it to the small, arched house on the Bouverie Ranch near Glen Ellen (fronted by a threatening sign that read Trespassers Will Be Violated) I don't know to this day.

"You look terrible," proclaimed the elderly but strangely beautiful lady with knowing blue eyes, impeccable skin, and silver hair drawn back sleekly over the ears adorned with dangling enameled fish. "Are you ill?" she asked, touching my candent forehead with the back of her soft, veined hand.

Of course I was taken aback and embarrassed, but realizing instantly that this was no woman to be duped, and that I could be retching again at any moment, I declared, "Yes, I'm sick as a dog—oysters I ate last night—and frankly, Mrs. Fisher, I'm mortified to say that I might have to use your bathroom and may not even make it through this interview."

Taking my arm gently and smiling, she led me into a large, nondescript, redwood-beamed room that served as sitting area, kitchen, dining room, library, and workroom and directed me to sit before a crackling fire on an antiquated sofa occupied by a cat named Charlie.

"Oysters," she mumbled almost wistfully. "Lovely creatures, but they do have ways of taking brutal revenge. Now, you just sit there with

---

EAUZE, FRANCE, OCTOBER 1981—

Witnessed for the first time the force-feeding (le gavage) of geese for foie gras on a small Gascon farm. When I asked the old lady cramming maize down gullets whether she ever felt sorry for the staggering creatures, she simply glared at me incredulously and said, "Mais Monsieur, it's what they're on this earth for, and they're never hungry—unlike myself and my family."

Charlie while I make you a cup of tea. And for God's sake, please don't call me Mrs. Fisher. I'm Mary Frances." If I had not known better, I would have sworn by her tone of voice and gestures that she was flirting.

In the profile that was eventually published, I wrote about sipping a gin and tonic while Mary Frances and I discussed her life and views on food; about eating delectable prawns in oyster sauce, sliced plum tomatoes and zucchini topped with mild chilies, and baked pears with fresh cream; and about drinking flinty chablis from a local winery—all that I knew the magazine editors and readers expected to read. Almost every word was untrue. She herself did nurse a cocktail, and that was indeed the beautiful, simple lunch that she prepared. What really happened was an awful, humiliating, extraordinary episode that remained Mary Frances's and my secret for years and enamored me to that remarkable lady more than all the other predictable, saccharine stories about her combined.

"I think I'm going to be sick again," I informed her sheepishly after taking a few sips of the tea and feeling my insides begin to churn.

"Good," said Mary Frances seated calmly and elegantly in her high-back chair and pointing toward the bathroom. "You need to purge your system completely of all the poison, and the caffeine in the tea helps. You might also try to smoke another cigarette—the nicotine stimulates the stomach in the same way."

I fought the urge a few more minutes, the wretched sensation getting worse by the second.

"Do you know how to vomit correctly?" she then asked bluntly.

Even though I'd read all about nostrums and elixirs and other folk remedies in her esoteric *A Cordiall Water*, the straightforward question stunned and almost distracted me.

"To be honest, I never gave it much thought," I moaned.

"Well, there's a right and wrong way to regurgitate, and it's important to do it correctly," she continued seriously, like some dedicated witch doctor. "You must not simply lean over the bowl, but get down on your knees. And in between heavings, be sure to raise your head all the way back to recirculate the blood and prevent dizziness and capillary damage to the face. It's all a matter of gravity. And try to keep it up till there's nothing but colorless bile."

Reeling from these graphic new instructions and unable to hold back any longer, I raced to the enormous, carpeted bathroom and emptied my raging gut just as she had directed. Then, recovering from the violent gastric ablution that left me dripping with perspiration and weak as water, I gazed foggily around at the huge tub in the middle of the room, an exotic array of multicolored bottles and jars, oil paintings that covered the walls, and books scattered everywhere. It was the most amazing bathroom I'd ever seen.

"Your color's returning," Mary Frances observed as I collapsed back on the sofa next to Charlie, "but now you should rest and stay warm, lie back, and let the stomach settle. I think we've tamed the wolf, but we must also respect him."

Worrying about how in hell I was going to do an interview and get my story (much less manage to taste any food she'd prepared), I had just taken the list of questions and tape recorder out of my bag when Mary Frances picked up Charlie, insisted that I stretch out on the sofa, and covered me with an Indian-style blanket that smelled faintly of eucalyptus. So weak I could feel my limbs tingling, I did doze off, but not so deeply that I couldn't hear her puttering around over in the kitchen area or didn't notice when she went to the front door to thank a young lady for delivering a large white paper cup. She next returned to the sofa and picked up my yellow sheets of questions and the recorder.

"Now, I tell you what: You're in no condition to conduct an intelligent interview, so you just keep resting, and if you'll show me how to work this contraption, I'll simply read the questions out loud to the recorder and give my answers. Then you'll have everything on the machine and can do with it what you want when you're back in perfect form. I think it's a brilliant idea and makes lots of sense."

With which she boldly moved over to the dining table and began very confidently and expertly interviewing herself as if I didn't exist.

For example:

JV: You have said that you don't write cookbooks, only books about food. How exactly do you make that distinction?

M.F.K.F.: For me there's always been so much more to food and cooking than just recipes or specific ways of preparing certain dishes. No doubt a good cookbook has its place in any kitchen, but I feel that if what I cook and eat doesn't relate somehow to my emotional and intellectual life, then something's wrong. When I compose a recipe, there's always some reason why, some personal inspiration that causes me to want to pass along a dish I enjoyed. If others care to try it, fine.

J.V.: How is your health?

M.F.K.F.: Pretty good, I suppose. Of course I have a horrible liver, but I really have no intention of doing anything about it.

I couldn't believe this was happening, but since, under the dire circumstances, it was surely happening and apparently working out well, I had little alternative but to adopt Mary Frances's philosophy and simply "lie back and enjoy it." For at least an hour, she studiously talked to herself and the recorder, and when she'd finished, she returned to the kitchen, made some strange-sounding racket, and announced that lunch would soon be ready but that, of course, I couldn't eat what she'd prepared for herself since we had "to respect the wolf."

"You'll have milk toast and Coca-Cola," she informed peremptorily. "Not just ordinary milk toast and Coke, mind you. This milk toast is made with our special sourdough bread and fresh Sonoma milk and butter, and to replace the bacterial flora in your tummy, a couple of spoonfuls of yogurt. And this is real Coke made with syrup that I called and asked my sweet neighbor to drive over and get at our old-fashioned drugstore. All I do is mix it with seltzer and crushed ice. There's no palliative like milk toast and Coke, and you'll have your strength back in no time."

Suffice it to say that nothing in memory ever tasted so good and comforting as that bland but miraculous concoction that Mary Frances

MILK TOAST FOR THE ILL, WEAK, OLD, VERY YOUNG, OR WEARY

SERVES 1 TO 2

1 pint milk, part cream if the person is not forbidden that

4 slices good bread, preferably homemade

Sweet butter, if butter is allowed

Salt and pepper, if not a child or very ill

In a saucepan, heat the milk gently to the simmering point.

Meanwhile, toast the bread slices and butter them generously. Heat a pretty bowl, deeper than it is wide. Break the hot buttered toast into the bowl, pour the simmering but not boiling milk over it, sprinkle a very little salt and pepper on the top, and serve at once. (To treat intestinal upsets, a spoonful or so of natural yogurt can also be added.)

(Adapted from *The Art of Eating* by M.F.K. Fisher)

put before me with the icy Coke, and that the combination so restored my stamina that I not only felt up to going over the tape with her later in the afternoon, but even ventured out to another restaurant that night when I returned to San Francisco.

Over the next few years, Mary Frances and I continued to see each other up in Sonoma, in San Francisco, and when she paid a rare visit to New York, and we never stopped laughing about the "sour stomach ordeal" and infamous self-interview. We carried on a lively correspondence, exchanged homemade preserves and confections, and gossiped wickedly about the food world on the phone. Much to my — and, no doubt, her — gratification, most of her old books were republished and a number of new ones brought out to great acclaim as her reputation soared and she was finally recognized by the American Academy of Arts and Letters as one of the twentieth century's most dynamic literary forces. Through it all, Mary Frances confronted the advancing years with the exact same curiosity, tenacity, courage, and stoicism that she had anticipated in her moving volume *Sister Age.* Even after Parkinson's disease had reduced her to an eighty-four-year-old invalid barely capable of seeing, writing, talking, and eating, she could still manage to receive visitors at her bedside, let me know caustically when I'd split an infinitive in one of my sentences, and . . . eat her beloved oysters from time to time with no ill effects.

When I had my last phone conversation with Mary Frances, I reminded her once again how she'd once mothered me through an awkward moment in my career, then lamely and stupidly asked how she was getting along. There was a long, difficult silence; then, in an almost inaudible whisper, the lady who had opened my eyes to so much wisdom slowly articulated her answer.

"Well, my friend, I'll tell you exactly what I'm doing. When I was a young lady, I learned how to cook and make love; when I reached the age of 50, I learned how to treasure friendship and grow old; now I'm learning how to die."

With New York Times restaurant critic Craig Claiborne, 1988.

Mother, Craig Claiborne and Daddy in the kitchen of my East Hampton home, Thanksgiving 1985.

Pierre Franey, Craig Claiborne, and I judging the San Francisco March of Dimes Gourmet Gala, 1983.

CHAPTER SEVEN

AN APPETITE FOR RISK

"Jim, it's Craig," croaked the weak voice on the phone early one morning. "I'm in jail."

"My God, what for?" I reacted with alarm.

"Whadda you think. Drunk driving again. I've been in the lockup all night, and the bastards won't let me drive home. Can you come get me?"

I couldn't remember whether this was Craig's second or third arrest for DWI, but I, not exactly innocent myself of driving after one too many and fully aware of the draconian crackdown by the East Hampton gestapo, knew that this time he was in serious trouble. It didn't matter that the woman who had slammed into his car while pulling out of her parking space was at fault—she would not even be indicted. It didn't matter that, as he often did, he'd been dining alone at a restaurant and, as usual, drank wine with his meal. And it certainly didn't matter to the cops that he was the celebrated author and food columnist of the *New York Times*. All that mattered was that he flunked the Breathalyzer test. No doubt, I figured, this time they would really throw the book at him (which they did), and no doubt, since he was Craig Claiborne, the otherwise routine news would make headlines everywhere as it had before.

Of course, it was no secret to anyone (himself included) that Craig had a longtime drinking problem, and while he had so far never killed anybody on the road or even had an accident, remnants of red taillight glass in my driveway and dents in my trees inflicted after one of the more uproarious dinners at my house were obvious signs that his luck was bound to run out eventually. Others were quick to cast moral judgments and condemn his wanton ways, but, naively or not, I always interpreted such traits in his personality and behavior as further indications of Craig's lifelong appetite for risk—whatever the consequences. Here was the man who had dared to cross swords in New York with the irascible restaurateur Henri Soulé of Le Pavillon fame by siding with the chef, Pierre Franey, when he resigned after a bitter dispute over staff wages; the journalist who had ventured into Vietnam at the height of the war just to sample the cuisine; the adventurer who had traveled a thousand miles in Brazil to taste a single dish and who had ingested poisonous globefish in Japan; the gourmand who enraged the Vatican itself by spending four thousand dollars on a single meal in Paris; the editor brave enough to quit his prestigious job at the *New York Times*; and the seasoned profligate with no qualms whatsoever about revealing in print his sexual preference for men when such an admission could still spell disaster. Another DWI violation was simply par for the course in the life of a maverick accustomed to danger.

All such personal drama aside, there is not and never has been any question in my mind that it was Craig Claiborne, not James Beard or Julia Child, who first introduced Americans to the glories of great cooking and fine dining. If this conviction strikes today's professional foodies as heretical, so be it, but despite Beard's saintly legacy and Julia's phenomenal celebrity—and despite my close friendship with both icons—the truth is that it was Claiborne who really pioneered this country's gastronomic sophistication back in the fifties when he invaded the "Women's Page" of the *New York Times* and not long after published his monumental first cookbook. Of course Craig never conducted cooking schools and developed an adoring flock like Jim Beard;

he never had Julia's glamorous television exposure; and perhaps most revealing of all, he never hobnobbed with or sought approval from his peers. A very complex and private man, Craig just preferred to be left alone in his work and personal life. Some perceived him to be a snob. But by maintaining a guarded sense of mission virtually unknown to others in the field, he almost singlehandedly established, articulated, popularized, and celebrated a new system of gastronomic standards that remains as valid today as forty years ago.

That I happened to meet Craig for the first time in the early seventies aboard the S.S. *France* was a coincidence that would affect my life in more ways than one. Although I'd crossed back and forth to Europe on a number of the great ocean liners during my years as a graduate student and college professor, my veritable passion for the *France* had remained steadfast ever since I boarded her as a Fulbright on the third voyage back in 1962. After my career at *Town & Country* and other magazines was launched, I was in the lucky position not only to travel first-class on the regal ship, but also to periodically undertake round-trips (with my beagle, Beauregard) for the sole purpose of consuming some of the finest classic French cuisine on earth and writing about the sybaritic experience. On those phenomenal crossings, I would meet—and sometimes dine with—such engaging passengers as Salvador Dalí, Hermione Gingold, Sir Stephen Spender, and a bevy of filthy rich, shady, fascinating older ladies from another age, who esteemed the attention and companionship of a young blade almost as much as they relished fresh beluga caviar and Taittinger Comtes de Champagne. The *France* was unique, the last floating palace of old-world charm and decadence, correct social manners and dress, inimitable cuisine, and lots of discreet hanky panky. By the time she succumbed pathetically to the encroaching vulgarity of 747s, glitzy cruise ships, health spas, and dietetic foods, I had already begun to acclimate to the only other liner that could approach the *France*'s distinction—namely, *Queen Elizabeth 2*.

Being a regular journalist on the *France* kept me in touch with certain top brass at the French Line office in Manhattan, and this, in turn, entitled me to engraved invitations to any number of exclusive press receptions held aboard the vessel when she was docked in New York harbor. It was at one of these decorous shindigs that I was introduced to Craig Claiborne, a cordial, shy, impeccably dressed gentleman who, not long before, had pronounced in the *Times* the ship's first-class Chambord dining room to be the greatest restaurant in the world. We tried to chat mainly about our Southern backgrounds and mutual acquaintances, but since, after all, Craig was already the most influential food writer and restaurant critic in the country, he was constantly besieged by photographers, journalists seeking a statement about the ship's cuisine, and fans eager to compliment him on a cookbook or article or restaurant review.

"Good God Almighty," he finally whispered to me in utter exasperation, "I just can't take any more of this. What say we clear out of here and go where we can talk and have a good martini and something like a club sandwich?"

Suffice it that we were soon perched at a quiet table in the Oak Bar at the Plaza Hotel, sipping ice-cold Beefeater martinis and discussing not only the *France* but the South, the way all displaced Rebels tend to do when alone together. Still a relatively unknown greenhorn in New York's vibrant food world, I was unquestionably dazzled being in the company of its most renowned and respected exponent—though Craig must have surmised immediately that it was just not in my nature to fawn over anybody. In a courteous but forthright manner, he asked if I were gay like himself, said how impressed he was with both *Town & Country* and *Esquire*, told me about lecturing and cooking with his collaborator, Pierre Franey, aboard the ship. He even insisted that I drive out sometime to visit him at his home in East Hampton.

We talked about lots of things, and even camped like two old queens who'd known each other for years, but what astounded me most was how little Craig alluded to his passion for food and fine dining. Here was the country's foremost authority on gastronomy, the man who had introduced Americans to everything from French *coulibiac* of salmon to Greek *garides* to Chinese sea slugs, the discerning critic with the power to make or break any restaurant in the nation with the stroke of a pen, the author whose insistence on recipe testing and precision had reshaped the entire cookbook industry. And he didn't care to talk shop, flaunt his culinary knowledge, impress me or anyone else. In the years to come, Craig would periodically express to me gastronomic wisdom that would greatly influence the tenor of my work, and frequently I'd turn to him for advice on any number of professional subjects. But to sit for hours and dwell on the components of a certain dish, or go on inordinately about such-and-such restaurant, or extol at great length the talents of some superstar chef the way most food journalists love to do was as pretentious and boring to

> BADEN-BADEN, GERMANY, SEPTEMBER 1982—
> *Here at Brenner's Park for sheep-cell therapy (prostate and lungs), stress reduction, and weight loss. Fifth day, 1,000 calories a day, no alcohol and minimum smoking, and I'm starving to death. Just called Jean-Pierre over at Auberge de l'Ill in Alsace and plan to sneak over tomorrow for some real food. Why do I torture myself like this?*

Craig as drinking wine at cocktail parties. Culinary erudition, enthusiasm, and conviction were to be communicated primarily in an author's writing, not in a social milieu more conducive to talk about recent travels and books read, music, politics, and, indeed, sex.

The house in East Hampton that has been my refuge from the chaos of Manhattan for the past twenty years, and where I've cooked countless meals and written almost a dozen books, would have never become a reality had Craig Claiborne not suddenly pushed me through the door of a real estate office one cold winter morning after we'd shopped at a meat market.

"Michael, this is a friend of mine," he announced abruptly to someone he knew at the agency, "and he wants to buy a house."

Never having so much as entertained the possibility of actually owning a home in the Hamptons, I was as stunned by Craig's proclamation as the agent was pleased. In those days, of course, East Hampton was still mostly the charming, pastoral, relatively quiet village it had been for centuries before uncouth developers and celebrities turned it into the glitzy summer resort it is today. I'd visited Craig fairly regularly in his sprawling, rather bizarre home, met and become equally good friends with Pierre Franey and his wife, Betty, and undoubtedly fallen in love with a place once pegged "the most beautiful town in America." To be enraptured by East Hampton was one thing; to buy an expensive house there, however, was another.

"Are you crazy, Craig?" I mumbled anxiously as the agent went to fetch his coat and we headed back out the door. "You know I can't afford a goddamn house."

"Of course you can," he dismissed in his dogmatic way. "You love it out here, and prices are just going to get higher and higher; so it's time you took the bull by the horns and made the plunge. All you need is another good book contract."

The second house the agent showed us—a new, modest, two-story saltbox in Craig's own neighborhood—captivated me from the minute I saw the kitchen with windows overlooking a wondrous forest of towering pines and scrub oak. It was certainly nothing on the scale of Craig's imposing waterfront spread perched dramatically high over Three-Mile Harbor, but as the shrewd agent pointed out, it was an ideal "starter house" in a prime area, the price was reasonable, and no doubt the value of the property would increase rapidly. Being as naive and downright dumb at the time as Craig when it came to practical matters (not long after, he would march into a car dealership and, with no haggling, pay sticker price for a new BMW), I fell blindly for the sales pitch, never so much as trying to bargain down the asking price. After Pierre Franey also had proffered his facile nod of approval the following day, I made a down payment on the "starter house," where I still live some twenty years later. The day I closed on the property, Craig, in his inimitable style, left a bottle of Dom Pérignon with a red bow at the front door.

I suppose that I came to know Craig as well as any friend was allowed. We dined periodically together in the city and country, cooked and entertained together, traveled and judged numerous March of Dimes "gourmet galas" together, plugged each other's books, got drunk and unruly together, and were always there to help and console one another when misfortune struck. Craig became close to my mother, Martha, and hounded her for recipes when she'd come to East Hampton to prepare Thanksgiving dinner and other feasts. I always had a standing invitation to his formal, high-profile New Year's Eve dinners graced by the likes of Jean Stafford, Joseph Heller, Lauren Bacall, Arthur Miller, and some of the world's most famous chefs. And rarely did he organize one of his rustic picnics or clambakes or I throw one of my rambunctious cookouts around the pool without including the other.

There were quiet evenings when he and I would simply eat fresh caviar and sip champagne at my house while discussing Southern matters, and there were much more festive occasions when, at his place, he and a brigade of helpers would produce on a buffet a staggering array of Chinese, Scandinavian, or Mexican dishes, or he would coax someone like Maida Heatter to make a dozen different cakes for a communal tasting. When Craig entertained at home for his celebrity friends, he pulled out all the social and culinary stops, and to be sure, these marathon events could make headlines. On the other hand, about once a year he'd call to say he wanted to do a small dinner for just a few close gay friends in the neighborhood, and I'd always know without asking that the main course would be the unusual, rather complex dish that he loved above all others, namely, his mother's chicken spaghetti.

Over the years, I spent many a morning in Craig's kitchen while he and Pierre Franey, to country music or Verdi blaring in the background, worked on recipes that would appear in the *New York Times* and their books. (Despite the lofty reputation of this team, no love was ever lost between Craig and Pierre, a phenomenon that always bothered me considerably given the full extent to which they had to depend on one

Chicken Spaghetti

One 3½ pound chicken with giblets

Salt to taste

3 cups canned coarsely chopped peeled Italian tomatoes

7 tablespoons butter

3 tablespoons all-purpose flour

½ cup heavy cream

⅛ teaspoon grated nutmeg

Freshly ground pepper to taste

½ pound fresh mushrooms, quartered

2 cups finely chopped onions

1½ cups finely chopped celery

1½ cups chopped seeded green bell pepper

1 tablespoon minced garlic

¼ pound ground beef

¼ pound ground pork

1 bay leaf

½ teaspoon hot red pepper flakes

1 pound dried spaghetti

½ pound sharp cheddar cheese, grated

Freshly grated Parmesan cheese

Place the chicken and giblets in a kettle with enough water to cover and add salt. Bring to a boil, reduce the heat to low, cover, and simmer till the chicken is tender, about 45 minutes. Remove the chicken and, when cool enough to handle, shred the meat and set aside. Return the skin and bones to the pot, cook the stock down over moderate heat about 30 minutes, or till reduced to 5 cups. Strain into a bowl and reserve. Discard the skin and bones.

Meanwhile, place the tomatoes and their juices in a saucepan, cook down over moderate heat to half the original volume, stirring often, and set aside.

Melt 3 tablespoons of the butter in a saucepan over moderate heat. Add the flour and stir with a whisk till well blended and smooth. Add 1 cup of the reserved stock plus the cream, whisking rapidly, and when smooth, add the nutmeg, salt, and pepper. Reduce the heat to low and continue to cook, stirring often, about 10 minutes. Set the white sauce aside.

In a large skillet, heat 4 more tablespoons of the butter, add the mushrooms, and stir over moderate heat till golden. Add the onions, celery, and green pepper and stir about 5 minutes till the vegetables are crisp-tender. Add the garlic, beef, and pork and cook, stirring and chopping down with a large, heavy spoon, till the meats lose their color. Add the bay leaf, hot pepper flakes, reduced tomatoes, and the white sauce and stir till the meat sauce is well blended.

In a large pot containing about 4 quarts of boiling salted water, cook the spaghetti till just tender, drain in a large colander, and rinse under cold running water.

Preheat the oven to 350° F.

Spoon enough of the meat sauce over the bottom of a 5- to 6-quart casserole to cover it lightly and add about one-third of the spaghetti. Add one-third of the shredded chicken, another layer of meat sauce, and a layer of grated cheddar cheese. Continue making layers, ending up with a layer of spaghetti topped with a thin layer of meat sauce and cheese. Pour in about 2 cups of the reserved chicken stock to almost cover the top layer of spaghetti, place the casserole on top of the stove, and bring it just to the boil. Cover with a lid or foil, place in the oven, and bake 15 minutes. Uncover and bake 15 minutes longer, or till lightly browned on top. Serve immediately with Parmesan cheese on the side.

another.) While I'm the first to credit Craig as being one of the most brilliant, exacting, and dedicated journalists I've ever known, it's also true that this legend who taught America so much about cooking was himself not a very accomplished cook and would never have attained such heights of success had Pierre (and other professional chefs) not been at the stove. Not that Craig couldn't turn out a perfect breakfast omelette or, so long as he followed a recipe to the letter and was given plenty of time, produce delicious *moules marinières*, a correct osso buco, and genuine chili con carne. What he lacked was Pierre's natural instincts for the mechanics of cooking, the ability to conceptualize a dish and bring about its execution deftly, comfortably, and with a sense of total control. From vast exposure to good food, Craig generally knew whether a dish was right or wrong—and he could explain in detail the reasons why—but when it came to actually reproducing a *brandade de morue*, chicken Pojarski, or even Brunswick stew, the amount of time he would spend analyzing the recipe, his nervous assemblage of components, and his awkward cooking gestures betrayed an insecurity in the kitchen that could have translated into serious problems without the help of the experts who usually surrounded him.

Nor was Craig's interpretation of certain dishes always as valid as implied in some of the recipes he published, as when he once decided to reproduce authentic North Carolina chopped pork barbecue after a trip to Goldsboro and stubbornly insisted on using two loins instead of fatty shoulders and on cooking the meat in the oven.

"But Craig, you can't use loin," I protested when he called to tell me his plans for a dish I was weaned on. "The flavor and texture will be all wrong, and the meat's got to be slowly roasted somewhere over hickory or oak coals and mopped with sauce—even if it's an ordinary kettle grill."

No amount of argument could convince him. Shoulder had too much fat for health-conscious readers, he insisted, and there'd be too much waste. He wasn't about to dig a pit outdoors, nobody wanted to go to all the trouble of searching for wood chips, and besides, he had figured out exactly how he could barbecue lean pork loins in the oven for five hours at 250 degrees, then simulate a smoky flavor by placing the roast for a while on a charcoal grill.

Suffice it that, in utter frustration and near anger, I finally capitulated and left him to pursue his fantasy. In late afternoon on the day of the big feast, scheduled at 8:00 P.M. and attended mainly by non-Southerners, he called to say that the barbecue looked and smelled "fantastic" and asked if I'd mind driving over with my hatchet so he could chop it properly. When I arrived at the back door, Craig, smiling proudly, offered a piece of meat he'd pulled off for me to taste.

"That's delicious roast pork, some of the best I've eaten," I declared truthfully, "but it's *not* Carolina barbecue."

"Oh, you're just a prejudiced Tarheel from the western part of the state," he mumbled, slightly wounded by my candid verdict. "My version is like the eastern-style barbecue they do in Goldsboro."

Since the damage has been done, I determined not to pursue the matter, nor to ask why traditional Brunswick stew and hush puppies were not on his menu along with what turned out to be a credible barbecue sauce, delectable cole slaw and potato salad, and exemplary pecan pie. Then came the ultimate shock after all the excited guests were seated. To wash down all this earthy Southern food was not standard iced tea, or beer, or even water, but . . . French champagne! I truly thought this man from Mississippi had lost his mind.

Still, I held my tongue as Craig and the others relished the food and bubbly with imperceptive glee, just as I bit the bullet of professional friendship when Craig ended the feature he soon published with a little more than poetic license: "It so happens that James Villas, food editor of *Town & Country*, is a good friend and neighbor, a native North Carolinian, and, if you will pardon the expression, a barbecue freak. I invited him over for a sample, and he pronounced my barbecue the best home-cooked version he had ever sampled. That is high praise."

To point out a few of Craig's salient limitations might seem scabby and disrespectful, the only justification being that his flawed example

My Authentic Carolina Chopped Pork Barbecue

SERVES AT LEAST 8

The Barbecue:

One small bag hickory chips (available at nurseries and hardware stores)

One 10-pound bag charcoal briquets

One 6- to 7-pound boneless pork shoulder (butt or picnic cut), securely tied with butcher's string

The Sauce:

1 quart cider vinegar

¼ cup Worcestershire sauce

1 cup catsup

2 tablespoons prepared mustard

3 tablespoons light brown sugar

2 tablespoons salt

Freshly ground pepper to taste

1 tablespoon hot red pepper flakes

Soak 6 handfuls of hickory chips in water for 30 minutes.

Open one bottom and one top vent on a kettle grill. Place a small drip pan in the bottom of the grill, stack charcoal briquets evenly around the pan, and ignite. When the coals are gray on one side (after about 30 minutes), turn them over and sprinkle 2 handfuls of soaked chips evenly over the hot coals.

Situate the pork shoulder skin-side up in the center of the grill about 6 inches directly over the drip pan (not over the hot coals), lower the lid, and cook slowly for 4 hours, replenishing the coals and soaked chips as they burn up but never allowing coals to get too hot. Turn the pork, lower the lid, and cook 2 hours longer.

Meanwhile, prepare the sauce by combining all the ingredients in a large, nonreactive saucepan. Stir well, bring to the simmer, and cook for 5 minutes. Remove from the heat and let stand for 2 hours.

Transfer the pork to a working surface, make deep gashes in the meat with a sharp knife, and baste liberally with the sauce. Replenish the coals and chips as needed (maintaining a low heat), replace the pork skin-side down on the grill, and cook for 3 hours longer, basting with the sauce from time to time.

Transfer the pork to a chopping board and remove the string. Remove and discard most (but not all) of the skin and excess fat and chop the meat coarsely with an impeccably clean hatchet, Chinese cleaver, or large, heavy chef's knife. Add just enough sauce to moisten the meat further, toss till well blended, and either serve the barbecue immediately with the remaining sauce on the side or refrigerate and reheat in the top of a double boiler over simmering water when ready to serve. (The barbecue freezes well up to 3 months.)

Serve the barbecue (plain or on a hamburger roll) with Brunswick stew, cole slaw, and hush puppies.

taught me that an eminent food journalist need no more necessarily be a master chef than an acclaimed connoisseur of Bach is expected to perform the composer's preludes and fugues with immaculate precision. Even after some formal training, I knew at an early stage in my career that I would never become—nor aspire to be—a gifted chef, a realization that might well have affected my ambitions and abilities as a food writer had I not witnessed how Craig Claiborne dealt so naturally and sensibly with the issue.

Equally important to me was the totally unpretentious way that Craig approached food and restaurants in general. Contrary to the image much of the public had of Craig as the authoritative bon vivant nourishing himself mostly on the world's most exotic foods, his tastes actually couldn't have been more elemental. He, indeed, relished an elegant caviar roulade as much as a Mongolian hot pot or intricate striped bass baked in phyllo pastry, but if you wanted to see his blue eyes light up, mention Southern fried chicken, or lowly French blood sausages, or pumpkin cream pie. Once, when my mother invited him to dinner in Charlotte after a television appearance and inquired what he'd really love for her to prepare, without a moment's hesitation he requested spaghetti and meatballs. Another time, while the two of us were getting soused on his beloved margaritas, I asked casually what he would say if forced to name the style of food he preferred over all others. "Well," he slurred after a moment of reflection, "actually, you know, I don't take this cuisine business all that seriously, since for me food is strictly a matter of pleasure, so I'd have to say . . . yes, I'd definitely say, any dish made with ground meat."

One further key lesson I learned from Craig in the early days came as a great surprise when, while still issuing his weighty New York restaurant reviews in the *Times*, he stated frankly one night at a lousy Italian place that he was bored with restaurant criticism and "wouldn't give a damn if most of the restaurants in Manhattan were shoved into the East River." The job had become frustrating, futile, and even demeaning, he had begun to realize; and one reason he was drinking so much was simply to endure another evening of dining out. At the time, I credited Craig's bilious outburst to either momentary disappointment or too many glasses of Barolo, but sure enough, not long after, he resigned from this duty at the paper. Many years later, having finally become fed up myself with the same fatuous task of tossing selective verbal bouquets at one capricious restaurant after another for magazines, I understood exactly what he had meant. "A restaurant is either good or bad—period," Craig would repeat in private over the years, "and for a critic to venture anything more than a brutally objective verdict and the essential details of an operation is both ludicrous and egotistical indulgence."

Despite finally meeting someone who helped to fill the void in his basically insecure and lonely personal life, and despite adopting certain measures to preserve his health and at least curb his heavy drinking, Craig's slow professional and physical decline began in the mid-eighties after the publication of his memoirs, which were dotted with a number of startling revelations about his childhood and career. Already his close working association with Pierre Franey had begun to crumble because of his inordinate demand that the French colleague sacrifice even weekends with his family to work on columns and books. While Craig continued to entertain lavishly and welcome the world's most distinguished chefs and food personalities into his phenomenal kitchen, the decades of relentless work, compulsive traveling, and reckless living were beginning to take their toll.

Still, it was nothing less than a shock to the food world and general public when, after thirty years of devoted service, Craig was suddenly "retired" by the *Times* at the age of sixty-seven, thus ending a glorious career that had virtually been his life's blood and, at least for a while, leaving a large gap in the newspaper. Into the nineties, however, we continued to socialize and throw parties at our respective houses, judge March of Dimes "gourmet galas" in various cities around the country, and drive out to Gosman's at the end of Long Island to eat clam chowder and fluke the way we always did. At a huge dinner given in his honor at Tavern on the Green in Manhattan, I delivered an address praising his accomplishments as a journalist and teacher; and when my fiftieth birthday was celebrated in great style at Le Cirque, Craig was the one who volunteered graciously to recap my life. Then, after publishing his nineteenth and final book (on dining etiquette), Craig was arrested still again for drunk driving, with shuddersome consequences, necessitating my having to pick him up periodically to shop, run errands, and catch the Hampton Jitney.

> EAST HAMPTON, MAY 1983—
>
> *Dropped by Craig's to deliver some beautiful N.C. country ham. Pierre at stove, Craig at typewriter, and when I began chatting about ham, C. bolted, "Please, Jim, can't you see we're working and trying to concentrate?" Rude but, alas, right.*

The final blow came in 1994 when doctors determined that Craig had to undergo bypass heart surgery, an operation from which he never really recovered. Alone at his East Hampton house most of the time and dependent on paid help, he became more and more reclusive and difficult, to the point where even I felt unwelcome when I'd go over to check on him. Next, there was a second serious operation, followed by what many interpreted as a series of small strokes. Eventually it was decided that Craig, now often in a wheelchair and increasingly confused mentally, would be better off living exclusively in his small Manhattan apartment with a full-time aid. There, the man who made cooking—indeed, the whole subject of food—a cultural and social phenomenon in this country straddled the edge of the abyss, and there, while a fickle, forgetful world went about its business, he existed in his own realm of fading memories till he died at the respectable age of seventy-nine.

In a gesture that was typical of his enormous generosity, Craig willed his famous East Hampton home and vast library to the Culinary Institute of America. Not long ago I drove over to the house for the first time in ages just to look around. The grounds were pretty unkempt and overgrown, but as I peered through the glass doors and windows, only a *New York Times* wall calendar in the kitchen that still read August 1996 gave an indication that Craig was not at home writing or cooking or preparing to entertain guests. Time had stood still, and in my ghostly imagination I saw him in his half-glasses at the IBM typewriter on the kitchen island, with Pierre sautéing a handful of vegetables at the gas range. In comes Paul Bocuse to bone and stuff squabs with foie gras and truffles, then Diana Kennedy to teach Craig and me the right way to make wheat tortillas, followed by Paul Prudhomme lugging a chest full of fresh crawfish. As the vision intensifies, I see Betty Friedan helping Craig set the long, pine refectory dining table, while farther back in the spacious, terra-cotta tiled living room overlooking the water, Sirio Maccioni refills Betty Comden's and Charles Addams's glasses with champagne. As Craig mixes himself another vodka and soda and moves into a small room next to the glass-fronted, refrigerated white wine cabinet to change the classical tape, Marcella Hazan and Jacques Pépin review the elaborate Scandinavian buffet that stretches almost the entire length of one wall. Once again, the old crowd is together, the party is in full swing, and Craig is happy.

Elaine Whitelaw in her element aboard Queen Elizabeth 2, 1989.

Elaine and I, 1987.

Elaine with Pat Brown and her husband John Brady at the Houston March of Dimes Gourmet Gala, 1988.

CHAPTER EIGHT

NEVER ENOUGH CAVIAR

EARLY ONE BALMY NORTH CAROLINA JUNE MORNING during World War II, I was getting out of bed and tumbled to the floor as my left leg gave way helplessly but painlessly. I think I was four years old, maybe five. My parents, terrified like all at the time, rushed me to the doctor, fearing the worst. It was indeed polio, he later confirmed, though a minor case restricted to the left knee and calf—at least so far. Of course there was no cure, but with plenty of rest and appropriate exercise, he speculated, there was a good chance that the condition would improve and that I'd be a lucky survivor of the dreaded disease that was crippling or killing hundreds of children every day in the U.S. Fortunately, his prognosis was correct.

Before being stricken and confined to our house and yard for the entire summer, I loved nothing more than going to the movies at the Carolina Theater in Charlotte and, while happy, dazzling tunes resounded from the enormous Wurlitzer organ at the side of the stage during intermission, dropping coins into a March of Dimes basket passed to help fund the battle against infantile paralysis. Charlotte was a major polio treatment center throughout the forties, and equally vivid is the memory of driving with my parents past acres of gigantic open circus tents virtually surrounding Memorial Hospital. Each was packed with victims enclosed in iron lungs, and even though I was too young and naive to grasp the full horror of the panorama (or appreciate my own good fortune), to this day I can still hear the protracted whoosh, whoosh, whoosh of those hideous machines struggling to prolong innocent lives—many of my school classmates included.

What I also had no way of knowing at the time was that roaming periodically through that very movie theater and those very tents was a dedicated, dynamic young lady from New York who, having been appointed by none other than President Roosevelt to head a network of volunteers for the March of Dimes, would not only eventually coordinate the nationwide field trials of the Salk polio vaccine, but, once the disease was finally checked, move on in the seventies to combat birth defects by creating a vast series of March of Dimes gourmet galas that would quickly become the country's premier charity. Given my position at *Town & Country* and my involvement in the food world, it was inevitable that our paths would cross. Little did I suspect, however, when Elaine Whitelaw first called me, that this vibrant woman would one day be recognized as a veritable legend in the eyes of hundreds of chefs, eminent journalists, entertainment personalities, scientists, glittery socialites, and politicians whom she gathered under her imperious wing. Nor could I imagine to what extent she'd become a dominant force in my own personal life.

"Is this Mr. Villas?" boomed the authoritative, husky, gravelly voice on the phone.

"Yes, sir, it is," I confirmed casually.

There was a long, silent pause, then a deep chuckle. "Well, my name is Elaine Whitelaw, and I'm with the March of Dimes."

"Oh, please excuse me, but . . ." I stammered with embarrassment.

"No worry, dear," she tittered. "Hotel operators and restaurants the world over have mistaken me for everyone from Tallulah Bankhead to Vincent Price."

She then went on to explain in precise, highly educated diction what the gourmet galas were all about, what her goals were, and why she was calling.

"I'm gradually establishing galas in every major American city. Local celebrities from each chapter participate in a formal cook-off, and I'd like to invite you to join one of our panels of culinary experts who judge the dishes, award prizes, and help us make lots of money to fight birth defects. In other words, I want your time, and you won't make a goddam penny, but it's lots of fun, and you'll be working with your peers for a good cause. What do you say?"

Accustomed to being cajoled into participating in any number of charity events, my immediate inclination was to beg off with one lame excuse or another. But the more this woman croaked frankly and inter-mittently about her involvement with Jonas Salk during the polio years, and her working relationships with Craig Claiborne and Beverly Sills and various city mayors, and her love of fresh caviar and opera and Flaubert, the more utterly compelling she became. No doubt I might have agreed to the offer solely on the grounds that I had a personal con-nection with the March of Dimes, but what really prompted me to accept was an anxious determination to meet this fascinating lady in the flesh.

And to be with Elaine Whitelaw was indeed to stand to attention, to heed her piercing dark eyes, shock of silver hair, and regal nose, to be bombarded with opinions and convictions and prejudices in language that modulated between Shakespearean prosody and dockworker pro-fanity. Dressed in one of her stylish but simple Dior or Adolfo outfits, Ferragamo shoes, and amazingly outdated chinchilla jacket, with a gloss of blood-red lipstick circling her broad mouth and her aristo-cratic ears adorned with dangling semiprecious jewels, she swept through a room with her Camel cigarette waving carelessly in the air like a cyclone of unrestrained glamour and energy.

Heads turned in ballrooms, maitre d's bowed in restaurants, chefs and politicians revealed secrets, and even taxi drivers did double takes when confronted with this oracular grande dame with flailing arms, whose otherwise rich vocabulary seemed to be dominated by the words *darling, glorious, vulgar,* and *appalling,* depending on the person or event or dish in question. No doubt Elaine was perceived as a blue-blooded eccentric, but she was also lionized from coast to coast as the woman responsible not only for raising hundreds of millions of dollars for this country's most successful charity, but also for pushing regional

American cooking to the forefront of the gastronomic revolution in ways that eluded even the most powerful chefs, restaurateurs, and journalists.

Of course, the concept of charity fund-raising was a virtue ingrained in Elaine Whitelaw from the days she volunteered as a young lady in the thirties to campaign for the Loyalists in the Spanish Civil War, and at the beginning of World War II, for the National War Fund. Never mind that she was raised in a wealthy yet fiercely liberal Democrat family on New York's Upper West Side, or that she attended Smith College during the Depression while other girls her age were destitute, or that her early grooming included dressing for dinner or the theater in Vionnet gowns, satin slippers, ten-millimeter pearl necklaces, and perfectly manicured nails.

"My father was lucky to be a diamond merchant when the Crash occurred, and it's for damn sure we suffered much less than most," she would inform anybody forthrightly. "But it's also true that I had a very strict social conscience drilled into me, the principle that what good fortune we inherit we must pay back. From the moment I left college, I knew I was going to work—but, mind you, not behind a perfume counter at a job somebody else needed more than I."

And for the next fifty years she remained engaged in a quixotic mission to balance the privileged and less fortunate in society, the entitlements of the rich with the responsibilities implicit in Roosevelt's New Deal, and the lofty, old-fashioned values in which she so strongly believed with an encroaching cultural shabbiness and vulgarity that she loathed. Elaine was a lady who dined regularly at New York's Le Cirque, but, even in her seventies, slogged through Grand Central Terminal each and every morning to catch a train to her office in White Plains. With sublime eloquence, she could quote at length from Henry James or *Henry V*, then barge into a flock of dainty socialites decorating tables for a gala with the reproach, "And where in hell are the goddam place cards my poor assistants spent all night filling out?"

She hobnobbed with Wolfgang Puck, Lidia Bastianich, Daniel Boulud, Jeremiah Tower, and most other superstar chefs; but let her hear about or sample the regional dishes of an obscure upstart in Cleveland or Memphis or Boston and, if impressed, she'd not only circulate the name among her many contacts in the food world, but call the rookie to serve as a gala judge. On the other hand, expose her to someone of prominence who didn't meet her professional, intellectual, or even sartorial standards, and she would be as "appalled" as she was when, as a young girl, she had occasion to watch Queen Marie of Romania step elegantly out of a limousine and noticed that she was . . . chewing gum! None other than Paula Wolfert, for example, once committed the unforgivable crime of appearing at an official food press reception in New York wearing jeans—designer jeans, but jeans nonetheless. And when Martha Stewart was scheduled to judge a gala in the Midwest and simply didn't show up, Elaine's reaction to the "shocking breach of manners" was simply never to invite her again.

> SAN ANTONIO, APRIL 1986—
> *Midnight snack in hotel coffee shop with Jacques Pépin after Gala. So refreshing to be with an educated chef who can talk about something besides food. We ate cheeseburgers and discussed mainly Baudelaire and Genet.*

Gradually, as my professional relationship with Elaine evolved into a very close and intimate friendship—based mainly on our mutual love of food and shared passion for great literature and music—I became privy to aspects of her former and current life that at once coincided with her public persona and revealed other complexities that only enhanced her mystique. Although she cleverly eluded all efforts to determine once and for all exactly how old she was and how many times she'd been married, it was clear that she had worshipped her last husband, a stockbroker who died just a few years before Elaine and I met. A very sensual woman who adored and cherished the company of men and had her fair share of beaus, escorts, and lovers over the years (I used to kid her wickedly about having an affair even with Franklin Roosevelt), she became quietly involved with a young man some thirty years her junior during the last years of her life, fully aware of the emotional—and financial—risks but determined to satisfy her strong female instincts the only way she knew how. The liaison worried me considerably, but I would no more have pried into the dangerous relationship or proffered advice than Elaine would have questioned my sexual preferences. Such circumstances simply existed for us both, never to be discussed in any depth and never to affect in the least our solid bond.

Elaine and I traveled together extensively, not only to the numerous gourmet galas we worked around the U.S., but, in more relaxed times, to London, Paris, Baden-Baden, and other glamorous venues for which we shared equal interest and where we loved to eat. Unbeknownst to the mostly gilded world in which she thrived and made her living, Elaine was as capable of sticking a finger in a peanut-butter jar, slipping into a pizza parlor, or devouring a greasy hamburger as the next rube. She was justifiably very proud of the authentic chicken soup (or "Jewish penicillin") that she taught me how to make, and she could, when pressed, turn out decent corned beef and cabbage with the help of her loyal housekeeper. But basically Elaine's idea of entertaining at home was limited to serving an exquisite side of smoked Scotch salmon with delicate brown bread supplied by an upscale delicacy shop, lobster in every guise imaginable, maybe a jellied fillet of beef or veal, and, to be sure, heroic sufficiencies of fresh caviar and champagne.

Elaine knew and appreciated good food, and she was fanatically adventurous in her eating habits at restaurants, but never have I known anybody in my entire life who loved, understood, and glorified caviar and champagne like this woman. Bubbly was her standard aperitif, cocktail, digestif, and all-purpose quaff, and she was one of the few who could detect in an instant the subtle differences between a beautifully made but nonvintage French brut and a truly noble Krug. Likewise, caviar was to her not an outrageously expensive delicacy spread sparingly on tiny toast points, but a prized commodity to be spooned and consumed lavishly (with no more than a few drops of lemon juice) on fresh blinis—washed down, naturally, with ample sufficiencies of Taittinger or Moët et Chandon. Given her fastidious nature, it didn't take much to shock Elaine, but never did I see her more stunned (and "appalled") than when the wealthy chairman of a Texas gala who was throwing a small reception for the judges and celebrity cooks asked her how many ounces of fresh beluga should be ordered for the appetizer table.

Jewish Penicillin

YIELD: ABOUT 3 QUARTS

One 5-pound stewing hen

4 quarts cold water

1 large onion, coarsely chopped

2 celery ribs, coarsely chopped

2 carrots, peeled and coarsely chopped

1 garlic clove, chopped

2 teaspoons chopped fresh dill

½ chicken bouillon cube

Salt and freshly ground pepper to taste

Combine the chicken and water in a large, heavy pot. Slowly bring to a gentle boil, reduce the heat to low, cover, and let simmer slowly for 2½ hours, skimming fat from the top from time to time.

Transfer the chicken to a plate and strain the broth into another large, heavy pot. Remove and discard the chicken skin and bones, chop the meat coarsely, and add it to the broth. Add all remaining ingredients and stir. Bring the soup to a gentle boil, reduce the heat, cover, and simmer slowly about 1½ hours longer. Taste for salt and pepper.

"Ounces?" Elaine stammered almost in disbelief, unfazed by the prohibitive cost of the precious eggs. "Darling, I do think you mean pounds, do you not? I'd say that one imperial pound tin sunk in crushed ice should suffice."

Always proclaiming that she'd never once had her fill of caviar, Elaine's eyes would glisten when the subject was so much as mentioned. Having heard me tell about devouring unlimited quantities of sweet beluga and sevruga (cured with Borax—outlawed in the U.S.) day and night at no extra cost during one of my many first-class transatlantic crossings aboard the QE2, she finally couldn't stand it any longer and insisted that we book a voyage with two equally hedonistic friends.

NEW YORK, FEBRUARY 1988—

My 50th birthday dinner at Le Cirque attended by 100 chefs and restaurateurs and friends from all over the country. Menu designed and prepared by P. Franey: foie gras frais, coulibiac de saumon, consommé double au fumet de truffe fraîche, pintade rôtie, poire tiède gratinée, mini crème brûlée. Wines: Gewürztraminer Trimbach '83, Chablis '86, Pommard '80, Malvasia. Memorable—and we ate like pigs.

The first three days at sea, Elaine was in her element, ordering soft-scrambled eggs with caviar and a split of champagne for breakfast in her stateroom; eating fresh oysters topped with caviar, mounds of caviar wrapped in smoked salmon, and jellied madrilene with red salmon caviar for lunch; and always dressed to the nines in her designer gowns and luxuriant chinchilla, tucking away double pots of beluga with buttered blini each night in the Queens Grill. And I wasn't far behind her. "It's almost embarrassing to admit, darling," she whispered at one point, a naughty expression of utter bliss on her seasoned face, "but do you realize we could almost pay for our tickets with the amount of caviar we've knocked off so far?"

This sinful routine proceeded accordingly till the fourth day, when the ship encountered a nine-force gale that sent half the passengers staggering down to the hospital for *mal de mer* injections. Elaine did feel a bit queasy by early evening, but she was ecstatic over our rather decadent table captain's suggestion that the chef prepare an extravagant caviar pie as a starter for dinner. Not even the raging sea could stop her from throwing the chinchilla around her shoulders, holding tightly onto my arm as she maneuvered about the convulsive ship, and showing up in the half-empty Grill for what she perceived would be the absolute ultimate in caviar indulgence.

And, indeed, the small, chilled pie, which was little more than about half a pound of pure fresh sevruga mixed with a little sour cream, snipped chives, and lemon juice, was a gustatory miracle, which along with a ceremonial bottle of Dom Pérignon, brought tears to all our eyes.

"I hope now, my dear, that you will have finally had your fill of caviar," I jested to Elaine next to me on the banquette.

Atypically, she didn't respond, placing the mother-of-pearl spoon very suddenly and delicately on her plate and looking straight ahead as if in a state of shock. The changeover occurred in a split second, and I noticed that she was now perspiring slightly at the hairline.

"Are you all right?" I asked worriedly, reaching for her wrinkled hand as our friends stopped eating and also appeared alarmed.

Slowly she shifted her eyes to me. "Goddamnit, darling, I think I'm getting seasick."

"Dizzy, or do you feel nauseated?" I asked.

"Not well," she muttered simply, opening her lapis cigarette case on the table, then closing it quickly.

"Do you think you can make it down to the hospital for a shot—or at least to your stateroom?"

She seemed to be contemplating the question as our table captain, Norman, ever aware of our every gesture, approached discreetly.

"God, I don't know," she rasped, her face visibly pallid even with all the powder and makeup.

"Let's try," I suggested, motioning to Norman that Madam was seasick and needed to leave.

QE2 Caviar Pie

SERVES 4

6 to 8 ounces fresh sevruga caviar
½ cup sour cream
1 tablespoon snipped fresh chives

1 tablespoon fresh lemon juice
Toast points

In a large glass mixing bowl, combine the caviar, sour cream, chives, and lemon juice and toss very gently till well blended. Mound the mixture neatly and evenly in a large, attractive glass or ceramic ramekin, taking care not to press the caviar grains. Cover with plastic wrap and chill at least 1 hour.

To serve, sink the ramekin in crushed ice in a large, deep, silver dish and use small spoons of either mother-of-pearl or bone to spread the caviar on toast points.

We began coaxing her up, but no sooner was she halfway off the banquette than she stopped suddenly, gasped "Oh, God," and sat back down.

Since the last thing anybody wanted was a terrible accident right there in the elegant restaurant, Norman hastened to the phone. Within minutes, a nurse appeared carrying a packet and, with no further ado, commenced to remove the cap from a syringe and insert the needle into a small vial. Then, taking my place on the banquette, she quite casually lifted one side of Elaine's silk gown well up her leg as the couple two tables away gawked in shock, wiped an area on the upper thigh with an alcohol pad, and after waiting for a break in the ship's sway, jabbed the needle directly through her hose into the old muscle. Elaine didn't flinch, but by the time the nurse had re-covered the leg, reassembled the packet, and told us that Madam should now go straight to bed, we could almost see a faint flush returning to her regal cheeks.

"Good Lord, what was in that incredible injection?" she soon exclaimed, now holding up a restorative cigarette for me to light.

"Miracle medicine, they all say," I informed. "But I certainly never knew they'd administer it right here in the dining room. I'm warning you, though, that it knocks most people out cold and that it might be a good idea for you to call it a night."

"Nonsense," she bolted, waving the cigarette in the air before snuffing it out and taking a quaff of champagne. "If you think I'm leaving all that divine caviar . . . ," with which she gleefully retrieved her delicate spoon and proceeded to carry on as if nothing whatsoever had happened.

Given the highly opinionated nature of both our temperaments, not to mention our mutual predisposition to combativeness when challenged to defend beliefs and principles, it's little wonder that Elaine and I were forever arguing, debating, and generally conducting ourselves in ways that could make others feel, well, . . . ill at ease. The subject could be politics (Elaine being a hardened liberal Democrat, I a philosophical anarchist who rarely even voted), the leitmotifs in Wagner's *Ring*, the decor of a hotel in Vienna, or how to deal best with the nation's health-insurance dilemma. No topic was beyond our scope of interest, but what really terrorized most of our skittish friends and colleagues was when we began sparring about the quality of a given restaurant, or which of two chefs was more talented, or how a certain dish should be prepared to be authentic, or why one food author was better than another.

Typically, the skirmish would begin innocuously in a restaurant with someone broaching a slightly sensitive subject (the correct components of a Cobb salad, Alice Waters's mode of dress, tipping in a Paris bistro). Elaine would advance an opinion, I would respectfully disagree, then she would reinforce her stand with increased stamina. This, of course, would flame my fire, which in turn would set her on a rampage with arms flying in the air. By now, others at the table would have stopped talking while we, lighting one smoke after another (usually to our cohorts' annoyance), engaged in full battle. To wit:

Friend: "Did I mention that last week we had a wonderful meal at Spago in Los Angeles?"

E.W.: "Oh, darling, of course you did. Wolfie's a genius in the kitchen."

J.V. (rolling my eyes at E.W.): "Isn't that a bit of an exaggeration?"

E.W.: "Why, I should say it's not. Wolfgang's food is extraordinary."

Friend (batting her eyes at E.W.): "And the service was impeccable."

J.V.: "Yeah, if you enjoy gazing at pubescents in baseball caps and jogging shoes and consider it a challenge to serve one of those silly designer pizzas."

E.W.: "Well, dear, I'll have to agree with you about the appalling outfits, but you're dead wrong about the phenomenal pizzas—not to mention the glorious pastas."

J.V. (swirling the cherry in my bourbon manhattan): "Raspberry and goat-cheese pizza. Nauseating. And you call that intelligent cooking? I think Puck's a real jerk who's making a mockery of American gastronomy."

E.W. (after taking a big sip of champagne): "Dear, you have no earthly idea what you're talking about. Wolfgang's a true original, and just in case you're getting ready to pontificate about traditional versus modern cuisine, let me remind you that he was trained at Baumanière. The boy knows how to cook, and the point is that his food is delicious—which is what matters."

J.V.: "Bull! He doesn't cook; he performs. And you're just prejudiced, since he or that harpie of a wife gives you a choice table on five-minute notice."

E.W. (starting to hyperventilate): "That's patently not true, goddammit, and you know it. I'd never—ever!—be so crude as to call *any* restaurant at the last minute for a table."

J.V.: (smiling wickedly): "Like Le Cirque?"

E.W. (rearing back imperiously in her chair): "Have you lost your mind, darling? You know I'm a regular there—three or four times a week—so it's perfectly correct and acceptable for me to call whenever I damn well choose. God, you're impossible!"

So it would continue for maybe ten minutes—standard banter for Elaine and me, which might be construed by some as spiteful dialogue, and which could—and once did—prompt an unconditioned sugar-plum to flee the table. And perhaps most unnerving of all was the way, once the two of us had vented our spleens, Elaine would playfully grab my hand and, fully stimulated, proclaim, "Now that, darling, was what I call a good fight." Anybody who happened not to appreciate the heated exchange was, in her opinion, "humdrum and not a very good sport."

Even when I would invite Elaine to visit me at my home in East Hampton, she took control in her assertive if highly civilized manner. Once, after frowning the entire weekend at the small, plain, dull pool towels stacked on the deck, she marched into Hermès back in Manhattan, spotted a few oversize, colorful, and ridiculously expensive ones stenciled with exotic wild animals, and had them shipped out to the house. Disapproving also of my practical, half-synthetic table napkins, which I found quite respectable, she wasted no time finding more proper all-cotton ones at Bergdorf-Goodman. And after she very politely made it obvious that my wire coathangers were "appalling," a huge box from Bloomingdale's arrived one day stuffed with enough smooth plastic ones in different shades to fill a dozen closet rods. Elaine had her paradoxical standards, and if she deemed it her mission to teach those friends whom she truly cared about how to attain her level of sophistication, I discovered it was useless to do battle.

As the gourmet galas assumed more and more importance and prestige throughout the eighties, Elaine not only knew and worked with virtually every major young American chef, but, as doyenne of the charity circuit, forever in search of volunteers who might contribute time, space, and money to her program, was closely involved with prominent restaurateurs all over the country, hoteliers, journalists, and a number of glittering stars of stage, screen, and television. She had no qualms, for instance, about picking up the phone and boldly cutting some deal with Sirio Maccioni at Le Cirque or Warner Leroy at Tavern on the Green for a big benefit party in New York, or with Tony Vallone at Tony's in Houston, or with Ella Brennan at Commander's Palace in New Orleans. She wouldn't hesitate to contact a city mayor, a state senator, or some bigwig like Donald Trump when it was felt that their presence at a major gala would double the attendance; and it didn't faze her to solicit the complimentary services of limo companies, photographers, and musicians. Judges for the annual San Francisco gala were nearly always guaranteed a deluxe room at her friend James Nassikas's Stanford Court. She could always count on Wolfgang Puck in Los Angeles, Jeremiah Tower in San Francisco, and Jasper White in Boston to come up with premium tables. And usually all she had to do to finalize gala participation of Beverly Sills (who has two children with birth defects), Craig Claiborne, Pierre Franey, Tim and Nina Zagat, Liz Smith, Jane Wyatt, and a roster of highfalutin fashion moguls was to ask.

Elaine had clout, and she certainly had plenty of chutzpah. While it's true that enormous amounts of March of Dimes funds were spent (some said wasted) flying her privileged bevy of judges first-class, putting us up in snazzy hotels, feting us in the finest restaurants, and generally spoiling and pampering us in the style to which she herself was so accustomed, it's equally true that her overweening business approach still managed to make millions for the charity every year. Exactly what qualified a person to be amongst the elect was a moot point that remained a mystery to all but Elaine. She had her reasons for favoring chef Paul Prudhomme, restaurant critic Bryan Miller, and Houston gossip columnist Maxime Messinger; and food-world figures like Craig Claiborne, Pierre Franey, and Daniel Boulud simply could do no wrong. She had little interest, on the other hand, in soliciting the services of James Beard, Julia Child, Charlie Trotter, and a few other big names that would no doubt have enhanced her gourmet galas tremendously. Perhaps she didn't approve of a chef's style of cuisine or social conduct.

Perhaps she frowned upon a given food author's fatuous pontifications or lack of writing sophistication (and even if Elaine Whitelaw had no other virtues, her literary sense was phenomenally keen). Or perhaps she simply wasn't convinced that some individuals, despite their towering celebrity, were sufficiently committed to a cause in which she believed with all her soul. She had her private standards and prejudices, and it's for sure that if Elaine decided not to include certain people in an enterprise that could always promise to elicit plenty of press exposure, advance reputations, and help book sales, no amount of coercion could sway her adjudication.

Assisted by former editor in chief of *Bon Appétit* and *Cuisine* Patricia Brown, Elaine was tough in the way she directed the galas for the same reason she was tough in the fight against polio: There was a definite goal to be accomplished and no room for hanky-panky. She cringed as she witnessed the perfunctory direction in which most other putative fund-raising charities were gradually heading, a trend that would result in today's almost farcical nationwide network of social extravaganzas masquerading as charity events intended to raise money for every medical research program, religious organization, school, museum, arts group, and animal shelter imaginable.

"What should matter is the immediacy of a charity—tangible projects that show tangible results," I heard her repeat over and over. "Worthwhile fund-raising cannot be abstract. It must be very specific, and it certainly must merit a great deal more than a crowd of rich socialites simply plopping down two hundred bucks a plate to have fun at a single dinner prepared by the latest hotshot chef. In another time, a project continued for years; now it lasts a week. We may have been forced to eat lots of rubber chicken, but at events in those days, dammit, we had serious wars to win, and we knew exactly how to win them."

Dining one evening in New York during the eighties with Elaine and Jonas Salk at Le Bernardin, I listened in horror as the renowned scientist predicted with apocalyptic insight that "AIDS has the potential to make polio seem like the common cold"—a prospect, he suggested, that the March of Dimes might be wise to address. While most of the world was still turning a blind eye to the terrible threat, Elaine not only heeded the warning, but made the bold attempt to convince the foundation that at least part of future fund-raising at the gourmet galas should be directed at combating what could be an emerging epidemic of immense proportions. Although she advanced the prescient and logical argument that eventually it could be the unborn children of AIDS victims who would present the greatest problem, her plea met ears as deaf as those in Washington.

After decades of serving the March of Dimes, developing the gourmet galas, and helping the foundation to evolve into one of the world's most respected charities, Elaine's contract was suddenly terminated in 1991, just as she was approaching her mid seventies. Although no explicit explanation was ever proffered, it was assumed that the official reason was her age (despite her continued robust energy and activity) and the immediate need to train a young successor to take her place. Some felt she was being accused of squandering too many funds; others guessed that she had become too tyrannical. I was convinced that her attempt to shift part of the emphasis from birth defects to AIDS was a major factor that just didn't sit well with the governing forces. Whatever the accounting, my instincts told me that without her March of Dimes responsibilities, a long-term goal to be achieved, and an overall grand purpose in life, Elaine wouldn't last more than another year. My instincts also told me that without Elaine's guidance, handpicked network of volunteers, and unique style, the gourmet galas would deteriorate almost to extinction. Basically, I was right on both counts.

Not that Elaine sat back and did nothing after her "retirement"; for actually, she spent much of her last year as none other than the volunteer director of a national organization devoted to tending the homeless, dealing with drug abuse and prostitution, and helping those with AIDS. Anybody else would have simply attended meetings and coordinated matters on the phone. Not Elaine Whitelaw, the champion of immediacy, who, still dressed in her finest Ferragamos and Guccis, literally spent night after night roaming the boroughs of New York City in a Planned Parenthood minivan, counseling victims of the streets. "The aim, of course, darling," she would explain knowingly, "is to get them in for treatment, and the only way you can do that is to feed them—not just cold cuts but nourishing hot meals." In no time, she had wheedled food donations from all over, procured cooking equipment, and assembled a group of volunteers to serve food from midnight till dawn. Not long after, the wheels were put in motion to apply the same strategy in other cities around the country. Others might have viewed the effort as an exercise in futility; Elaine Whitelaw was convinced it was as feasible and necessary as inoculating every child in the world against polio.

Because of the terminal disease that she was diagnosed with in 1992, Elaine didn't have much of a chance to pursue her new charity. Increasingly debilitated and refusing to see a doctor, she for a time secluded herself with the housekeeper in her handsome East Side apartment, and it was only after a few close friends asserted authority that she was finally forced to go to the hospital for tests. An ambulance was called, Elaine was helped to dress in an outfit that would have been more appropriate for one of her many Le Cirque lunches, and all went relatively well till a cocky attendant loading her into the back of the vehicle decided to comment on her hacking cough.

"Lady, do you smoke?" he pried.

Elaine's head snapped around. "First, young man, my name is Miss Whitelaw for your information," she growled in her gravelly voice, "and second, it's none of your goddamned business what I do."

I continued naively to hope that it was nothing worse than a bad virus, if not severe depression or exhaustion, and since Elaine had directed sternly that the hospital release no information and that there be no visitors, including myself, it was only after I learned that her daughter (whom nobody had ever met and whom Elaine saw exactly once a year) had been summoned from California that I suspected something much more serious.

"It's cancer, darling," Elaine finally announced calmly on the phone in her forthright way.

"Where?" I stumbled helplessly.

"Oh, everywhere, darling. You know I never do anything halfway. Why don't you come to the apartment and we'll talk about it."

Of course I was shattered, especially when she informed me that she had opted not to undergo any form of treatment and would have hospice. "I believe, dear, in simply letting nature take its course, as it always has." She was utterly dispassionate and stoical, as if relieved to be spared the inconvenience and indignities of old age. Many times we'd discussed death as a philosophical subject, as a literary and musical motif, and when dear friends passed on; but now that Elaine was actually confronting her own mortality and would be gone in a matter of weeks, it bothered me to realize that it was I, not she, who was selfishly frightened and angry. I certainly respected her brave decision to control her fate till the bitter end. What I could not accept was the prospect of a future devoid of a unique force that had contributed such depth and meaning and joy not only to my personal life, but to so many others.

Until the final days when Elaine had to be rehospitalized, she conducted her dying with the same authority, organization, and outright pleasure that had governed her existence in better times. She scheduled visitor appointments in a small diary, advised her charity volunteers on the phone, and even when she had difficulty eating, could always manage a few spoonfuls of the caviar I'd bring. Jonas Salk came, as did Beverly Sills, the ever-loyal Patricia Brown, chefs, food journalists, Elaine's paramour, and a contingent of friends and colleagues from out of town. Hardly a day passed that her favorite dishes from Le Cirque, Chin Chin, the Four Seasons, and other restaurants didn't somehow materialize at the apartment to be shared with visitors. She always wanted to know where I'd dined and what I'd ordered the night before, what I was reading and writing, and if I'd attended an opera, concert, or play, details of the performance. She even had her nails and hair done according to normal routine. It was all as if her condition were a mere temporary setback and she'd be back in her restaurants and theaters and airplanes and minivan in no time.

The last time I visited Elaine, I noticed on her bed table a recent biography of Harry Truman, a volume of Shakespeare's plays, and one of my own food books. She was very weak, but we laughed, first about the caviar incident aboard the *QE2*, then about a certain gala night when her flailing arms had caused a mortified waiter to dump a bowl of squash soup over her ridiculous but beloved chinchilla wrap. She took my hand, and for the first time, her dark, hooded eyes suddenly became solemn.

"Darling, I want to tell you good-bye today," she pronounced quietly, as I gazed at the freckles on her hand that I'd always found so beautiful. "No protest, no sentimental arguments, no more fights. Just do me one last favor." She pointed to the table. "Would you turn to the end of *Hamlet* and read to me the lines I've underlined. I'd like to hear those words read out loud—and slowly. Then, you'd be a real dear if you'd simply kiss me and leave."

I opened to the play, found the passage, and read:

"There is special providence in the fall of a sparrow. If it be now, 'tis not to come; if it be not to come, it will be now; if it be not now, yet it will come: the readiness is all."

A strange glow came over Elaine's face as she gazed into space. "Ah, yes . . . yes," she murmured to herself.

With James Beard, posing for a magazine shoot, 1982. Photo: Michel Tcherevkoff.

My first book party: Craig Claiborne, James Beard, JV, and Barbara Kafka.

CHAPTER NINE

MY
MASTER CLASS

MY FIRST BOOK, *AMERICAN TASTE,* PUBLISHED IN 1982, was a collection of essays that not only launched me formally as a champion of American cookery, but also certified me in the eyes of many as a highly opinionated troublemaker insofar as my irregular views on food, drinking, and dining out were concerned. I booed Texas barbecue, yogurt, cornflakes, and white wine as a cocktail. I glorified greasy hamburgers and fat french fries, unfashionable meat loaf and hefty stews, and chicken hash for breakfast. I challenged the U.S. government's draconian regulations on the production of genuine country hams, exposed the sneaky hidden charges on restaurant bills, and even, as an undercover table captain, revealed how customers in deluxe restaurants were ripped off by unprincipled staff members.

The volume did have some token recipes, but essentially it was a prose work in the tradition of A. J. Liebling, Elizabeth David, and M.F.K. Fisher. In other words, it was the sort of book that bottom-line cookbook publishers in the early eighties wouldn't touch with a ten-foot ladle, convinced, as they surely were, that all the cooking public wanted was recipes and that Americans were simply not sophisticated enough to appreciate an entire treatise on disparate and controversial aspects of American gastronomy. Years later, authors like John Thorne, Jeffrey Steingarten, Jay Jacobs, Betty Fussell, and John Mariani would have less trouble finding outlets for their literary endeavors (and *American Taste* itself would even be reprinted as a "classic"), but when my agent tried to sell this first book, one editor after the next responded with a respectful, polite rejection.

All, that is, except a tough, feisty, brave gent at Arbor House by the name of Arnold Ehrlich. He praised the book, saw its potential as a trailblazer, and agreed to publish it under one very demanding but important condition: that I convince none other than James Beard to write a foreword.

"But what if he doesn't like the book?" I reacted with real alarm.

"He will," Arnold assured me with typical steadfast confidence in his own judgment. "It's a damn good book with plenty of original and controversial stuff, but it needs Beard's endorsement to really take off. You know the guy, so turn on the charm and somehow get him to agree. Okay?"

And that was that. I had indeed known Jim Beard for a number of years, and I would have been totally satisfied with the same sort of complimentary blurb he'd sometimes dashed off for other books he felt had merit; but to ask the great lion to introduce my book with an entire essay not only frightened me, but seemed a potential abuse of our friendship. Yet we did talk (or rather gossip) on the phone frequently. We judged various food events together and dined out fairly regularly. And I was also one of the few queens with whom Jim felt at ease discussing his own difficult homosexuality. I therefore determined that, unlike so many vultures who took unfair advantage of Beard's enormous ego and generosity (especially in his vulnerable old age and increasing loneliness), I would simply invite him to dinner, level with him in the most honest, pragmatic way possible about the book, and respect his ruling.

"I won't bullshit you," I stated candidly after we'd perched across from one another at a New York steakhouse and ordered our respective Glenlivet on the rocks (for Jim) and bourbon manhattan (for me). "My book has been tentatively accepted, but they want you to write a pithy foreword. I hate to put you in an awkward predicament, but would you be willing to at least read the galleys and give it consideration?"

Taking a slug of scotch, he hesitated a moment, looked me straight in the eyes, and said, "Sure. When can you get the galleys to me? I won't make any promises, but I'd be happy to read what you've written. Now, let's talk opera."

Suffice it to say that Jim did read every word of the book, applauded it, and agreed to the request. I was thrilled and honored, to say the least, but what really gripped me and demonstrated Jim's inimitable support was the absolute hell he went through to deliver his commentary. As it happened, he was teaching cooking classes at the Stanford Court hotel in San Francisco when he realized that the deadline for the introduction was quickly approaching, no doubt an inconvenience but a responsibility to which he was committed. Holed up in a corner suite between classes with his cooking assistant and indispensable aide, Barbara Kafka, he spent a number of days carefully working on the text of the foreword, not only recapping in his scholarly way the literary history of American gastronomy, but discussing in zestful detail how my book was following in the tradition of Eliza Leslie, Theodore Child, and M.F.K. Fisher.

Having finally finished, much to everybody's relief, he sent the commentary on audiotape off to New York, only to have Barbara call me a few days later to report that, with the perversity of machines, the foreword had arrived mangled and unusable. Since, inexplicably, Jim had no copy made, my heart froze. For anyone else, of course, the disaster would have been met with profuse regrets and legitimate excuses for delaying publication. Beard, however, drawing on his phenomenal gift of recall and his sense of duty, simply sat back down with Barbara and, with great effort and love, redid the entire thing. The book, with Beard's name splashed under mine on the jacket, was a big success, and when everyone from Craig Claiborne to Liz Smith to famous New York restaurateurs to Jim himself showed up at a celebration sponsored by the Chaine des Rôtisseurs, I had no illusions over why they'd all really come.

13935 Sonoma Highway
Glen Ellen,
California 95442

April 23, 1982

Dear James:

Thank you for having the proofs of AMERICAN TASTE sent to me. I think it is a truly amusing and interesting and valuable look at our gastronomy (so-called, and quite often rightly!). Of course I don't agree with all of it, and some of your recipes are logistically impossible for me, but that's my problem and not yours! The overall picture is exciting and delightful. Jim Beard wrote perhaps the best introduction (sorry—*foreword*) of his life for your book, and I agree with everything in it. I wish I had said it myself . . . so just read him again, in quotes, and pretend it's me.

Thank you for giving me such pleasure, and accept my sincerest compliments and good wishes and all that. I know the book will be a success, of course, and I hope you have a lot of fun basking . . .

I trust you to let me know if there is ever another chance to see you up here. (You will understand after that bad oyster day in San Francisco, my special interest in the meal you were served once in Chicago when you felt fairly queasy about too much travel or something like that. You made a much quicker recovery there than here, thanks to the beautiful food, and finally faced something like a chocolate mousse with full courage . . .)

All best,

Mary Frances

M.F.K. Fisher

to
James Villas
C/O Arbor House
235 East 45th Street
New York, NY 10017

Since Jim's death in 1985, volumes have been written about his early years in Oregon, his love of picnics, his phenomenal teaching abilities, his working relationship with virtually every major food professional on the globe, even his temper tantrums and improper use of others to his benefit. For better or worse, these are aspects of his life I simply never witnessed. I knew Jim only the last decade of his life. We were occasionally thrown together at receptions and charity events, and I did feature a memorable photograph of him once in *Town & Country* to accompany a piece I did on chestnuts. But I never attended any of his cooking classes, we took no official trips together, I didn't mingle with his fans at various shindigs held at his house in Greenwich Village, and I was never exposed to any purported fits of rage.

> NEW YORK, NOVEMBER 1981—
>
> *Delightful dinner with Jim Beard at Post House. He practically devoured the entire menu, slugged Glenlivet, and sang a little Wagner after he became smashed. God, I pray he'll agree to write the foreword to my book.*

Our relationship was basically that of a casual but close friendship: placid, civilized, and respectful—due, perhaps, to the fact that, whether in New York or Paris or San Francisco, we usually met alone in the relaxed confines of a good restaurant. From time to time, when Jim was feeling lonely and depressed, I would go down to his house either to fix a real Southern breakfast or to share a simple, potluck lunch he'd whip up from leftovers. I never saw him happier than when we once sat around my pool in East Hampton sipping bloody bulls, eating *salade niçoise*, and "gissiping" about friends and foes. Although the subject of food was never far from Jim's mind, I think that part of his attraction to me was that I was one of the few (Barbara Kafka, San Francisco chef Jeremiah Tower, and magazine editor Patricia Brown were, I suspect, others) who made a concerted effort to spark his many other interests. Without question, he loved to talk about food and reminisce about all his dining experiences from the golden past. To hear Jim hold forth on the different varieties of apricots, the multiple ways to roast duck, the important historical links between a nation's food and culture, or the exact dishes he savored fifty years earlier at the Hôtel de la Côte d'Or in Saulieu was an enlightening, unforgettable experience, one which served me well as an investigative journalist. On the other hand, to tap such topics as ocean liners, British hotels, left-wing politics, grand opera, pretty boys, and other such disparate passions we shared was to expose altogether different and fascinating facets of the man's complex character that remained hidden from the public and most of the adoring colleagues who viewed him as little more than a cooking guru and walking gastronomic encyclopedia.

And if, partly by design, I didn't witness many aspects of Jim's life around which his lofty reputation revolved, there were, indeed, other aspects of his makeup to which only I was privy. I doubt, for example, that anybody else ever beheld Jim in a restaurant when, overstimulated by an operatic matter, he would suddenly and unabashedly lean back, clear his throat with Glenlivet, and sound forth a few measures of Verdi or Wagner in his best baritone. Even before doctors strictly limited his vinous intake, wine to Jim (as to Craig Claiborne and Jay Jacobs) was simply a commodity to be enjoyed with food and used in cooking. He had nothing but mild contempt for pretentious nerds who stood around at cocktail parties pronouncing a cabernet or chenin blanc to be "flowery," "weedy," "flinty," "woody," and all the other silly jargonistic terms. ("Who do they think they're trying to impress?" he once whispered to me about two pontificating food writers.) Jim loved fine wines as much as he respected great winemakers; but he neither wrote nor talked much about wine, and he always asked me to choose the appropriate bottles when we dined out. For Jim, a wine, like a dish, was either "very good," "so-so," or "bad"—no elaboration was necessary. And if this seems a surprising revelation to the pristine of mind and palate, no less piquant is how, after a prodigious meal, Jim would usually bum one of my cigarettes and puff away in postprandial ecstasy.

Much, in fact, was startling about Beard, but nothing so much as what and how he ate at home and in restaurants when he was relaxed and not expected to put on the dog. For lunch, he could be just as happy with a few cans of sardines, buttered fresh bread, and good ale as with the most elaborate composed salad and fancy wine, and his eyes would shine when, on his orders, I'd sometimes arrive at the house laden with multiple goodies from the neighborhood deli, which would be gone in no time. The only way he'd eat liver was if it was smothered with bacon and onions, he had no use for desserts in general, and who wouldn't have been a little shocked to learn that the dean of American cooking found roast holiday turkey to be a monumental bore? He liked any preparation of duck, he was rarely without some form of ham, he relished fresh corn on the cob by itself as an appetizer, and he waited impatiently each year for the first shad roe and rhubarb to appear in the markets. But the dish that Jim Beard loved above all others and considered to be consummately American by virtue of its being prepared with chicken stock instead of wine was simply braised sauerkraut.

Nothing gave me more pleasure (and no doubt inadvertently altered aspects of my own dining demeanor) than to watch Jim eat in restaurants. Although always the old-fashioned gentleman in his oversize jacket and tiny bow ties, he would first spread the entire napkin over his massive, elevated midsection, reminding me of one of the nineteenth-century gourmands depicted in Daumier engravings readying himself for assault on the table. Drink in hand, he would then study every single item on the menu, wonder, and make comments. Should there be the remotest doubt about a certain dish, he didn't hesitate to signal the waiter and ask questions. Finally, he'd make decisions, then maybe change his mind a couple of times, all the while visibly salivating as he tore off another piece of bread and again pronounced it good or bad. ("If the bread's no good, kiddo, you better watch out," he would warn time and again.)

Jim Beard was both a gourmet and a glutton (he loathed both terms), meaning that while his taste was keenly informed and fastidious, he was capable of devouring enormous quantities of any dish he liked. (Once, at

JAMES BEARD'S BRAISED SAUERKRAUT

SERVES 4 TO 6

2 packages (1 pound each) fresh sauerkraut

6 slices of bacon

Freshly ground black pepper

Bouquet garni (⅛ teaspoon each dried thyme and rosemary, 2 parsley sprigs, 1 bay leaf, and 5 whole cloves tied tightly in cheesecloth)

2 garlic cloves, peeled and halved

10 crushed juniper berries (or 2 tablespoons gin)

4 cups chicken stock

Place the sauerkraut in a large colander and rinse well under cold running water, tossing it with your hands. Line the bottom of a large pot with the bacon and layer sauerkraut on top, grinding pepper over each layer. Tuck the herb bouquet, garlic, and juniper berries among the layers (or sprinkle gin over the top), add the stock, and bring to a boil. Reduce the heat to low, cover, and simmer slowly 3 to 4 hours.

Remove and discard the herb bouquet and serve the sauerkraut hot with any pork dish.

La Grille in Paris, I sat in horror when, after classifying the copious platters of pot-au-feu and *pommes frites* we shared as the best he'd ever had,
he simply directed the waiter to repeat the entire order.) If Craig
Claiborne was an outright prissy eater no matter the circumstances, Beard
was a veritable trencherman when the food was to his liking. With
Rabelaisian gusto, he would consume without blinking an eye two or three
bowls of rich tripe soup at New York's Coach House, a brace of meaty
Dungeness crabs following a big bowl of cioppino at Tadich Grill in San
Francisco, and, at Savoy Grill in London, a half poached lobster before
proceeding on to a dozen or so flamed kidneys in a whisky mustard sauce.

Reared back comfortably and royally in his chair, Jim ate and drank
slowly but steadily—talking the entire time about some chef, the theater,
opera, his mother, wedding cakes, silly queens, phony journalism, anything. If he enjoyed the food (and was appropriately smashed), the
occasion was never less than a ravenous ritual; if he didn't care particularly about what he was eating, he'd simply grimace, nibble, and push
what he didn't like around the plate like a disgruntled child. Beard was
fully capable of sending truly bad food back to the kitchen, but never
once did I see him cause a scene or try to embarrass a waiter. Unlike so
many other self-styled experts out to impress, Jim didn't go to restaurants with a chip on his shoulder. He dined out because he was always
hungry for great food, because he loved people and good conversation,
because restaurants were his natural arena. And for me, every meal with
him was a master class in gustatory and social hedonism.

Myths about James Beard abound, but surely the most absurd is
one launched by a California colleague of his to the effect that Jim (by
his own putative admission) had never been able to truly love another
human being. This, I maintain strongly, is utter nonsense. I, of all
people, certainly never claimed to be an expert on affairs of the heart,
but if anyone ever gave of himself as much as he needed to be loved it
was the James Beard who confided in me not all but many of his long-
ings, frustrations, and romantic dreams. Never, for instance, did I

The Coach House's Tripe Soup

5 pounds honeycomb tripe

3 pigs' feet, split

3 pounds veal bones

1 beef tongue

3 onions, coarsely chopped

2 celery ribs (leaves included), coarsely chopped

2 carrots, scraped and coarsely chopped

3 leeks, rinsed well and sliced

6 garlic cloves, crushed

3 teaspoons dried thyme

1 large bay leaf

4 sprigs of parsley

Salt and freshly ground pepper to taste

½ cup cognac

10 large egg yolks

2 tablespoons potato starch

Juice of 2 lemons

Freshly chopped parsley

Rinse the tripe, pigs' feet, and veal bones under running water. Trim excess fat from the tripe, cut the tripe into chunks, and place in a large stockpot or heavy kettle. Add the pigs' feet, bones, and tongue with enough water to cover, bring to a boil, and skim off the scum. Add the onions, celery, carrots, leeks, garlic, thyme, bay leaf, parsley sprigs, and salt and pepper. Return to the simmer, cover, and simmer 3 hours, or till the meats are very tender, skimming from time to time. Transfer the meats to a working surface, skin the tongue, and cut the tripe and tongue into short, thin strips. Pick the meat from the pigs' feet and discard the bones.

Strain the broth into a large pot, let cool, then chill for 2 hours. Remove all fat from the top. Add the cognac to the broth, bring to a boil, and reduce by about one-third.

In a large bowl, beat the egg yolks. Combine the potato starch with 1 cup of cold water and add this mixture plus the lemon juice to the egg yolks. Gradually whisk in 1 cup of the hot broth, return the mixture to the pot, and mix well. Add the meats, taste for salt and pepper, and reheat—but do not boil—the soup till it thickens, stirring constantly. Serve sprinkled with parsley.

observe a more distraught, devastated individual than Jim when he learned that his beloved collaborator and associate José (pronounced *Josie*) Wilson had taken her own life. Rumors flew from every direction about Jim's difficult relationship with his longtime, clinging companion, Gino Cofacci; but the truth was that, despite Gino's increasing neglect and indifference, Jim always refused to abandon a liaison that had a highly emotional history. Carl Jerome—who besotted Beard in his seventies, assumed control of the house and cooking school, and alienated any number of old comrades—was a prime example of Jim's loving not wisely but too well; yet I had no doubt that the much older man's emotions over this flame were real and that his senses were virtually blinded by the proverbial love that dare not speak its name. Jim expressed deep affection for many people in many mysterious ways, and if love is not what he felt for M.F.K. Fisher, Marion Cunningham, Barbara Kafka, and, indeed, me, then at least in my book, the term needs to be redefined.

And to say the least, there was the more racy side of Beard that he concealed from all but his closest confidants—be it his subtle flair for camp or his inclination from time to time to indulge vicariously in bawdiness. Given his girth and unfortunate physique, I always just took it for granted that Jim had been sexually frustrated most of his life, but this certainly didn't prevent him, even in old age, from having a keen eye for handsome young men. I remember, for instance, telling him one evening over dinner about a notorious hustler bar in midtown Manhattan called Rounds where, shortly before AIDS began its lethal march, you might spot various titans of Wall Street and the publishing world, Tennessee Williams, and even several closeted sports heroes goggling the libidinal, cunning merchandise stalking the premises nightly. After we'd tucked away the last of a stunning almond soufflé washed down with a noble sauternes, he asked with a wicked glint in his eyes, "What would you say to dropping by that place you mentioned and looking at the pretty boys?"

Given Jim's difficulty getting about during his last years, I always hired a car when we dined out, and no doubt our driver raised an eyebrow when I directed him to wait outside the fleshpot on East Fifty-third Street while we caroused. Perched on a crowded banquette not far from the piano player banging out tunes of Carole King, Jim ordered his scotch, then immediately struck up a casual conversation with two lithe, stunning twits at the adjoining cocktail table, who seemed initially not to know whether to be repulsed or fascinated by this decrepit, 285-pound Buddha making their brand of small talk. Still naive myself about the general public's limited cognizance of even the most respected names in the insulated food world (Julia Child and Craig Claiborne included), I was shocked to realize that the curious boys who gradually huddled around our tiny table had no earthly idea who James Beard was. Vain as he usually was about his celebrity, Jim wasn't affected by this ignorance in the least and actually appeared to relish being prized by a bevy of beauties simply for the jolly and bewitching eccentric he could be.

The intrigue only intensified when, at one point, another well-known food writer and friend, Richard Sax, ambled over. Visibly astounded to see Beard cavorting in this den of disrepute, he couldn't decide at first how to greet the monarch, but when Jim held out a limp wrist in a very camp, regal fashion, Richard dropped to one knee, kissed his hand, and generated paroxysms of laughter from all around. I think Jim would have sat there all night ogling and babbling and chuckling had I not finally insisted that he get home. Back in the car, I told him not to forget that opportunism was the name of the game at a place like Rounds, a vulgarity he almost refused to acknowledge. "There's not one thing wrong with those delightful boys that a good meal wouldn't help," he quipped in typical fashion. "They just need to put some meat on those bones."

While I never saw Beard fly into one of the stormy rages others would tell about, I could always arouse his spirits by bringing up the topic of what was being touted as the New American Cuisine.

"First," he'd repeat over and over, "genuine American food is not 'cuisine,' it's 'cooking' or 'cookery'—in the old tradition of Fannie Farmer and Mrs. Randolph. Second, those who harp on developing a distinctive American style of cooking must know nothing of our culinary history. We don't need to initiate anything; the style is there and has been for three hundred years. It's in the regions. It's in succotash, and clam chowder, and cioppino, and club sandwiches. It's in the way Smithfield hams are cured, and the way a sourdough starter is made, and the way we compose fruitcakes. What the hotshots need to do is get out there to Kansas and New Orleans and California and learn to make the dishes those folks have been preparing for ages. They need to master the basics, learn how our ancestors used native ingredients and kneaded bread, absorb the various cultures, and taste, taste, taste. Then, and only then, do they have the right to mess around, and modify, and try to come up with some original ideas and contributions."

God only knows what Beard would have added had he lived long enough to witness the present-day abomination called fusion cuisine. And since I must have listened to him philosophize about the principles of American cookery dozens of times, it's little wonder that I developed the same antagonism toward cooks and journalists who believed they could usurp age-old traditions and reinvent the culinary wheel overnight.

The irony, of course, was that just about the time everybody was ready to write him off as a hopeless conservative steeped in the past, he suddenly and unexpectedly introduced in his final book, *The New James Beard,* a revised but sensible approach to food that was by no means a diet cookbook, but one that was to take both the public and the food community by storm. It was typical of Beard's never-ending passion for discovery and learning. "At my ripe age," he announced in a foreword, "I acknowledge with some pleasure that my lifelong liaison with good food has gradually been creating a new me."

My first inkling of this turnabout had occurred one Sunday evening in New York at Jim's beloved Coach House when he, now on a salt-free diet, began exclaiming about the nutty, delicate earthiness of a plain baked potato seasoned with nothing but a few grinds of black pepper. He then related how, with a fresh craving for robust aromas, he was coming up with all sorts of novel ways to prepare parsnips, turnips, salsify, celeriac, and other neglected root vegetables. He was investigating new varieties of wild mushrooms, different methods of preparing lentils, shad roe, and intensely flavored sherbets, and countless possibilities with secondary cuts of meat and fish. He would never abandon the classic, sound food combinations and solid cooking techniques that were the hallmark of authentic American cookery, he emphasized, but the time had come to address not only exciting recipe variations, the food processor, microwave ovens, and handy pasta machines, but ways to cut down on fats and starches. He had learned from his students that cooking was becoming a much more individual and challenging activity. Since every palate is different, cooks should begin developing a personal style that reflects keen knowledge and imagination—so long, that is, as the process didn't fall victim to the excesses and abuses of the French nouvelle cuisine.

Jim was almost like a religious convert as he recounted his new ideas and plans, and he convinced me that I, too, should be a bit more receptive to certain changes that were now inevitable and could benefit us all. I had to confess that I could never eat fresh tomatoes, pasta, or eggs without salt; that I had no intention of reducing the fat in my homemade country sausage; and that my doubts about the microwave were dead serious. But because of Jim's contagious enthusiasm and shrewd open-mindedness, I was prompted to rethink my approach to food in general and did manage to free myself of many prejudices. When *The New James Beard* appeared in 1981, Jim proved himself to be years ahead of his time, and with his revitalized energy, it seemed for awhile that he would indeed overcome his vascular and many other physical afflictions and live well into his eighties to continue spreading his amended gospel.

But any lifetime of wanton hedonism is doomed eventually to take its toll, and soon I realized that I was visiting Jim in hospitals more than picking him up, against doctors' orders, for still another of the heroic restaurant meals that he still loved and that I refused to deny him. When a stupendous dinner attended by friends, students, and colleagues from all over was given at the Stanford Court in San Francisco to celebrate Jim's eightieth birthday, Barbara Kafka and I literally had to transport him in an ambulance from the hospital to the event. Not long after, our few remaining rendezvous were in his room at New York Hospital, where, when he wasn't nibbling at luxurious food delivered regularly from the Four Seasons restaurant, he would relish his favorite thinly sliced onion sandwiches that I'd make and bring along. It was on a frigid January afternoon that Barbara called to say that Jim had died quietly of cardiac arrest.

Although Jim never liked to broach the subject of his or anybody else's inevitable death, I do recall clearly that when José Wilson died, he mentioned casually that when his time came, he wanted neither a funeral nor a memorial service. I found this strange coming from a ham who, consciously or unconsciously, often reveled in the limelight; but sure enough, at the end there were no ceremonies. Quixotic as he was, I have absolutely no idea how Jim would have felt about his beloved house in Greenwich Village being one day turned into a shrine venerated by chefs and foodies the world over, though I suspect he would have been very proud of the foundation established in his name and the way it has encouraged and helped young American cooks and authors. Over the years, I've often been invited to attend receptions and dinners, to lecture, and even to cook at the James Beard House, but since Jim's death, I've had my own private and perhaps illogical reasons for never once returning to the place that embodies so many wistful memories.

With Paula Wolfert in New York, 1988.

With Paula Wolfert in Cassis, France, 1989.

With Paula and Ruth Reichl in Provence, 1988.

CHAPTER TEN

ONE CHROMOSOME AWAY FROM HAPPINESS

T HE SUBJECT WAS ROASTED GOOSE HEARTS, and while the four other
food journalists sat predictably placid in the small hotel lounge
sipping harsh Madiran as if it were vintage Figeac, Paula Wolfert and I,
both cupping our first snifters of potent Armagnac, were at it again.

"I thought they were ghastly," I moaned loudly, referring to the strong,
rather tough goose hearts with grapes *en brochette* that we'd all been served
as part of our first dinner together at a country inn deep in Gascony.

"Oh, darling, that's all in your thick head," Paula countered, reaching toward the small cocktail table for one of my Gauloises and holding
it up for a light.

"Labouche, angel, if you're going to smoke, why in hell don't you buy
your own pack and stop bumming from me?" I scoffed as she puffed and
frowned, her eyes as glassy as mine from the evening's alcohol.

"Cheapskate," she shot back, as one of the other women fanned the
air with her hand. "Anyway, I thought the hearts were delicious—an
acquired taste, I admit, but delicious. What's happened to your curiosity and sense of adventure, Bozo?"

Sitting together on the small, tacky sofa, I patted her lovingly on a knee, then squeezed. "My curiosity's intact, *chérie*, but goose hearts will signal a limit to my sense of adventure from now on. I ate them, and that's that."

Our new acquaintances proffered no opinions but simply gawked while Paula, on whom I'd long ago bestowed the name Labouche because of her compulsive habit of pontificating at length on any food topic that interested her, began a passionate discourse on the virtues of roasted goose hearts.

"Well, dear," I continued, "I didn't travel all the way to Gascony to fill up on disgusting goose hearts. You might be an authority on this food and know all about *confit* and *alycot* and stratified sauces, but please, I beg you, just please spare me your goose hearts."

In a while the waiter appeared again, and when Paula ordered two more Armagnacs in her fluent but excruciatingly ungrammatical French, I casually corrected her.

Running a hand nervously through her unruly black mane of hair held somewhat in place by two cheap, multicolored clips, she turned and fixed her dark, glistening eyes on me.

"Jimmy, I do wish you'd stop taking out your homosexual hostility on me," she bolted.

The faces across from us froze.

"Well, Labouche, I'll make a deal with you. I'll stop taking out my homosexual hostility on you if you'll stop taking out your nymphomaniacal hostility on me."

Just as the others began to squirm, Paula let out a howl of laughter that filled the room, placing an arm around my shoulder and pulling me playfully close to her.

"Did I ever tell you, darling," she whispered out loud, "that you're just one chromosome—one tiny chromosome—away from true happiness?"

With that statement, I now roared gleefully, sinking my head momentarily onto her ample breast. "Ah, Labouche, then I might wander off the primrose path."

One of the other fidgety journalists, obviously dazed by our reckless behavior, announced meekly and politely that it had been a long night and he was exhausted. Without blinking, Paula held up the palm of one hand, then began rummaging frantically in her cloth purse.

"Wait!" she called, pulling out two thin glass vials of colorful liquid and holding them up. "What you need is this *fortifiant* called Léviture, which I discovered over in Bordeaux. They say the secret ingredient is fox urine. Personally, I take it for anxiety attacks, but it's also supposed to be great for exhaustion and hangovers. It's safe and cheap as dirt. Here, let me show you."

With that she emptied both vials into what little Armagnac remained in my first snifter, swirled all the liquids around like some witch mixing a special elixir, and directed the man to drink. Smiling guardedly, he declined as he rose from the chair, prompting me to take the glass and chug down the exotic potion with the comment that it might prevent my inevitable hangover.

Apparently that was the last straw, for when the first man got up, so did the other three, all looking a bit aghast and apologizing and explaining that we had an early start in the morning to visit a duck farm near Auch and then a wine tasting at Luppé-Violles.

"Well, how was that for clearing a room," Paula quipped, murmuring a sigh of relief. "God, we were terrible."

"Not as terrible as those dull creatures. Can you believe they had no comments to make, no opinions whatsoever, on the goose hearts—or anything else we ate tonight? Gastronomic zombies. And to think we have four more days and nights with them."

"Oh, we'll survive it, sweetheart," she assured me, taking my hand. "We've survived a lot worse just to find great food, and by now you should know what to expect on these damn press trips."

I did indeed know what to expect from dull journalists on such jaunts, but I'd also learned what to expect from one of America's most revered and respected cookbook authors, who happened to be one of my dearest friends. Being almost the exact same age, Paula and I first met shortly after I'd begun my association with *Esquire* and *Town & Country* and she had published her first landmark book on Moroccan cooking. It was platonic love at first sight, not because we necessarily had many common interests other than the quest for good food, but because our restive personalities were virtually identical. Actually, our professional affinities couldn't have been more different: Paula focused basically on Mediterranean food and cultures, while I was already championing nothing more than the legacy of American cookery. It's true that from the beginning we both held French cuisine and all its traditions sacred, but beyond that, our careers couldn't have been aimed in more disparate directions. Where our souls merged, and where there evolved a unique rapport that exists to this day, was in our rebellious determination to debunk as much phoniness in the food world as possible in the name of authenticity, and to overcome certain bosky forces in our individual natures that few others could even begin to comprehend.

Anyone who has ever used Paula's cookbooks has been at least partly familiarized with the landscapes of Sicily, Morocco, Syria, Crete, Algeria, and Estonia; and anyone who has tried to prepare her exotic, in-depth recipes learned from firsthand sources has known the frustration of having to find preserved lemons, squid ink, fenugreek, Aleppo pepper, and pomegranate molasses if the dishes are to be right. That, mainly out of ignorance, I personally have never cared much for either the types of food she celebrates or all the weird ingredients is no more egregious than her lukewarm reaction to the Brunswick stew, hobotee, and Hangtown fry I write about.

What matters in both cases is our mutual appreciation of the spirit behind the enterprise. Paula, for example, could be writing about how natives of the Sahara prepare an unusual dish of cat food, and my imagination would be sparked, such is her unadulterated passion for any topic she attacks and the sense that the approach is real, the flavors genuine. Who really cared that night in Gascony that I loathed the goose hearts? What was important—and what Paula has taught me over and over—was the serious, infatuated involvement in a dish that, for whatever reason, deserves exploitation. As we see it, the only cardinal sin committed in the search for memorable food is total indifference, and those who don't share our strong convictions in this respect learn quickly they'd best keep their distance.

Although Paula and I are not exactly unaware that, by nature, we're two of the most frenzied mavericks on earth, the decades we've spent together traveling, eating, cooking, commiserating, and confiding in one another have convinced me that Labouche's neurasthenia has a definite edge on mine.

"I live in a dark, fearful world," she first told me years ago. "I have a photo of myself when I was only five days old that I've studied carefully, and that look is already there in my eyes—that look of apprehension. Sure, I venture into the wilds of Dagostan, and cross deserts, and risk the backroads of Syria as a Jew, but no matter where I go or what I do, I'm frightened—of exactly what I never know."

> SAN FRANCISCO, APRIL 1985—
>
> *Joyce Goldstein's Brazilian churrasco last nite at Square One a sensation. Am more and more convinced that the best young chefs in this country are women and am determined to pursue subject for long feature. Zarela Martinez in NYC, Leslee Reis in Chicago, Lydia Shire in Boston, Elizabeth Terry in Savannah, Pamela Grosscup in Cleveland—lots of them and all top notch with that . . . female touch.*

This personality trait (rarely evident in her books) no doubt accounts for much of Paula's chronic hypochondria and dependence on clairvoyants, acupuncture, and all sorts of Chinese herbals. But never was it more manifest than one evening back in the early eighties when we joined friends in Paris at a small, offbeat restaurant named Gérard to sample what Paula had read somewhere was the best, most authentic pot-au-feu in France. Arriving before the others, the first thing I couldn't help but notice was the swarm of dachshunds that filled the place: dogs scampering about, dogs sprawled at the exposed kitchen door, dogs sleeping in the recessed windows, dogs cuddled in the arms of customers—not to mention the statues and photos and paintings of dachshunds that decorated every counter and wall.

"*Est-ce que Monsieur voudrait bien tenir Mimi?*" asked the waiter quite genuinely after I'd ordered a Ricard, holding an adorable female in his arms and offering her to me.

Noticing that practically every other table had a canine either in someone's lap or reclining close by on a banquette waiting patiently to be fed tidbits, I, loving dogs the way I do, took Mimi without hesitation, began stroking her soft head, gave her a piece of bread, and said to myself, "*Vive la France!*"

Shortly, in walked Paula and our two other friends. At first they all simply stared in disbelief, then asked me what in hell was going on. I, of course, professed total ignorance of the bizarre scenario, but when I signaled them to simply take a seat, Paula didn't budge. An expression of horror crept over her smooth face.

"I'm terrified of dogs," she stammered, glaring at the docile pooch on my lap and grabbing my cigarette pack on the table.

"Oh, Labouche, that's ridiculous," I began to argue. "This little mutt wouldn't hurt a flea—and, glory be, this is France!"

Carefully she maneuvered around the table to the banquette, looking about to observe all the other dogs nibbling away.

"This is the most incredible thing I've ever seen," she exclaimed, visibly fascinated but threatened. "Who's dogs are they?"

"Who knows?" I said, feeding Mimi another bit of crust. "Obviously, these people just have a thing for dachshunds."

Soon Andy and Pat were breaking off pieces of pâté for Mimi, which prompted me at one point to get up and carefully transfer the dog to the banquette on Andy's far side from Paula. Warily she kept eyeing the beast as we drank delicious beaujolais and waited for the pot-au-feu ordered for four.

"Oh my God, look at that!" Paula cried excitedly when the waiter positioned the enormous, deep platter in the center of the table. Distracted momentarily by all the food, she poked at the ingredients with a fork, pronouncing the meat to be the right cut, the bones full of rich marrow, the leeks large and properly intact, the carrots "soft and plump like perfect female breasts," and the broth thin and sufficiently fatty. Yes, she finally decided, this was indeed a glorious pot-au-feu, perhaps the best she'd tasted, and weren't we all glad and thankful she'd discovered this remote place deep in the then unchic third arrondissement? Stick with me, gang, she assured us, and you'll find good stuff.

Labouche was rolling along in typical loquacious fashion, till, that is, she grabbed a bone with her fingers to scoop out a little marrow and Mimi sat up alertly and nuzzled across Andy's lap in her direction. Screaming as if she were being attacked by a savage brute in the jungle, she went all to pieces, dropping the bone on her plate, knocking over her glass of wine (a common occurrence with Paula no matter where), and struggling so hard to escape the perceived onslaught that she almost ended up in the lap of the man at the next table.

"Labouche, the dog's just looking and begging, so would you please calm down," I scolded, reaching over to grab her arm while Andy placated Mimi with a nugget of meat and the waiter rushed over to cover the wine spill.

"Did you see that? Did you all see that?" she shrieked in horror, still pulling away. "He was going to bite me!"

By this time, of course, Mimi was quietly seated back at her place on the banquette, savoring her snack.

"First, darling, Mimi is a she, not a he, and don't be so absurd, the dog's just being a dog and she's hungry—just like you. Now please stop the hysterics. You've overcome this sort of anxiety a hundred times before." I spooned a small amount of marrow from the bone she'd dropped onto a piece of bread. "Here, sweetheart, just feed this to the dog the way everybody else in the restaurant is doing, and you'll see how gentle she is. It's part of the scene."

Regaining her control, Paula hesitated, her eyes still blazing and her hands shaking. Then, either because I'd challenged her sense of adventure or because she was simply determined once again to fight her hidden demons, she took the morsel, very guardedly extended it across

Andy, and watched as Mimi took it gently and gobbled it down. More reassured, she repeated the gesture, then offered the dog a piece of meat.

"God, this is so . . . primal," she declared, at last caught up in the madness of the spectacle. "I mean, sharing the earthiest, most primitive of dishes with an animal right at the same table."

Before long, Mimi was nestled between Andy and Paula, the two ladies became the best of friends, and everything returned to normal.

I've always suspected that the true origins of Paula's tension and paranoia can somehow be traced back to her youthful, formative years as a countercultural expatriot in Morocco, where she encountered such renegades as Paul and Jane Bowles and Tennessee Williams, immersed herself in numerous mystical traditions, and only after becoming convinced that the drinking water was being poisoned, fled back to America. The experience certainly inspired one of the most original, classic cookbooks of our era (*Couscous and Other Good Food from Morocco*), but I have no doubt that it also had tremendous psychological influence not only on the diligent and highly suspicious ways that Paula would always approach the subject of food, but also on her apprehensive outlook on life in general.

Fed up with her unwillingness to get behind the wheel of a car, for instance, I once tried to teach her to drive on a remote country road near my home in East Hampton, only to watch her agonize over the virtually nonexistent possibility that another vehicle was just waiting to slam into her. Having spent an entire morning during a trip to Finland scouring the food markets of Savo for the Scandinavian anchovies necessary to faithfully reproduce a potato and onion dish called Jansson's Temptation, Paula, an extremely sensual woman, decided that nothing would be more relaxing and erotic—or cleanse our systems faster of all the vodka—than for the two of us to take an authentic sauna together at our lakeside lodge. She tolerated the intense heat, she even tolerated my swatting her back and thighs with birch branches to enhance blood circulation, but when time came to jump into the frigid lake in fine Finnish tradition, she took one look at the still, ominous water and said in utter panic, "If I do, Jimmy, I'll drown. I know I'll have a massive heart attack and drown."

I've watched Paula turn white in restaurants when she had some sudden, illogical reason to suspect that canned tuna fish or red peppers might be infected with botulism. And she was never again comfortable eating vintage sardines after I once told her that I'd heard the tins should be turned every four years to prevent spoilage. A pimple on her nose could spread infection to the brain and cause meningitis. A toothache might lead to blindness. A long-winded recipe for *confit de canard* constructed to prevent people from killing themselves. A barely perceptible ring inside a pot would be certain to contaminate food. A platter of stewed pig offal in Spain containing what looked like a penis . . . I've seen and heard about every facet of Paula's distressing, occult, inner torments, most of which even she admits are utter mental fabrications that can't be explained.

"I'm not just some nut," she proclaims quite soberly. "I'm well aware of my fears, and all I can do is try to control them."

While nobody except my mother has taught me as much about cooking as Paula, preparing a meal with her when she's in one of her manic states has always been a test of nerves, the most riveting memory being the time we decided to make bouillabaisse at my house in East Hampton for six pretty savvy guests. Although even Paula—who's been labeled "Queen of the Mediterranean" in the food press—admitted that there's no authentic, definitive way to make this famous French soupstew, sitting down with her to determine how we'd go about it was nevertheless a knock-down drag-out. Yes, we had to use real fennel sticks and not bulb fennel, she insisted. No, I didn't have any ridiculous seaweed in which to marinate the fish initially, I puffed, and it was senseless to waste expensive extra-virgin olive oil. She demanded that the tomatoes be seeded, and I absolutely refused to include crabs and mussels. The heated banter continued for maybe an hour, but finally we agreed upon a formula that should produce a respectable if not sensational dish.

Trash Bouillabaisse

Serves 8

The Soup-Stew

*4 pounds fish heads, bones, and
   trimmings (scrod, tilefish, porgy,
   rockfish, grouper, or other
   combination of white-fleshed
   fish), gills removed, rinsed, and
   hacked up*

*1 cup good-quality French or Italian
   olive oil*

4 dried fennel sticks

*Salt and freshly ground pepper to
   taste*

3 quarts water

1 cup dry white wine

*3 medium-size ripe tomatoes,
   coarsely chopped*

*2 medium-size onions, coarsely
   chopped*

*1 medium-size leek (including part
   of the green leaves), split, rinsed
   well, and coarsely chopped*

4 garlic cloves, peeled and crushed

1 celery rib, coarsely chopped

1 bay leaf

1 tablespoon tomato paste

Pinch of cayenne pepper

*¼ teaspoon saffron threads,
   chopped*

6 medium-size boiling potatoes

*5 pounds various white-fleshed fish
   (sea bass, halibut, grouper, red
   snapper, monkfish, rockfish,
   etc.), gills removed, scaled,
   skinned, rinsed, and cut into 1-
   inch chunks*

The Bread and the Rouille

2 French baguettes

5 large garlic cloves

Salt to taste

2 egg yolks, at room temperature

*1 cup good-quality French or Italian
   olive oil*

Cayenne pepper to taste

In a large, heavy kettle or stockpot, combine the fish heads, bones, and
trimmings with ½ cup of the olive oil, 2 of the fennel sticks, and salt and
pepper. Add the water and wine, bring slowly to a boil, reduce the heat to
moderate, and let cook about 35 minutes, skimming scum off the top.
Strain the stock through a large colander lined with a double layer of
cheesecloth into a large bowl, discard the solids, and rinse out the pot.

Heat the remaining ½ cup olive oil in the pot over moderate heat, add the tomatoes, onions, leek, garlic, celery, bay leaf, and remaining fennel sticks, and stir for 10 minutes. Add the fish stock, tomato paste, cayenne, and saffron, bring to a boil, reduce the heat to moderate, and cook 30 minutes. Strain the soup into a large bowl and discard the solids.

While the soup is cooking, prepare the bread and *rouille:* Cut the bread into thin rounds, toast the rounds, and set aside. To make the *rouille,* peel and cut the garlic cloves in half, place in a mortar, mash very well with a pestle, and transfer the puree to a bowl. Add the egg yolks and stir to blend thoroughly. Drop by drop, begin adding the olive oil to the yolks, beating constantly, and continue adding oil and beating till the mayonnaise is thick and smooth. Add the cayenne and mix till well blended.

About 20 minutes before serving, peel and slice the potatoes, return the soup to the pot, and bring to a rolling boil. Add the potatoes and cook 5 minutes. Add the firm-fleshed fish first to the boiling water, then the more fragile varieties, and cook till they are cooked through but still firm for a total of not more than 10 minutes. Transfer the fish and potatoes to a large heated platter and keep warm. Season the soup with more salt and pepper and pour into a tureen.

To serve at the table, arrange portions of fish and potatoes in wide soup plates. Ladle the soup over the top and serve with the toast and a bowl of the *rouille* to be stirred in discreet amounts into the soup (or let guests smear *rouille* on toast and drop into the soup).

To get the very freshest and most varied fish possible, I called Roberta Gosman in Montauk to ask what time the boats would be unloading their catch the next morning at her fish market. At the crack of dawn, Paula and I were there to watch the sorting process and choose our groupers, bass, snappers, and whatever other specimens looked perfect.

"Any spots?" Paula asked one worker. When he shook his head, she then asked, "What about some heads and bones and trash fish? Do you have any trash fish that you can't sell?"

With a surprised expression, he pointed to a huge tub out back and told us to feel free to help ourselves. Truly excited, Paula began studying a pile of the most hideous, disgusting-looking creatures imaginable—small, bony, strangely colored critters that I could tell she feared touching.

"Get that one . . . and that one," she directed me imperiously.

"Labouche, is this really necessary?"

She glared up at me. "It is if you want a really great stock like they make in southern France. Richard Olney taught me all about trash fish when I visited him in Toulon. *Rascasse*, of course, would be ideal, but since we don't have any rock fish like that, these'll have to do. God, aren't they hideous?"

Typically, she was spooked by the weird fish, but just as her curiosity had forced her to surmount the terror of sharing pot-au-feu with a dog, such was her enthusiasm over finding some trash fish that she gradually brought herself to pick up a few and toss them quickly into the bucket.

With our stash of dressed fish and heads and bones and revolting trash fish, we returned to the house, took out all the cooking equipment, hacked up ingredients with a Chinese cleaver, and soon had everything simmering to make the stock for our soup. The pungent aromas that filled the kitchen were intoxicating. We didn't argue any more than usual about details, and all went well till Paula took it upon herself with great authority and elation to begin pounding garlic cloves for the *rouille* sauce in my alabaster mortar like a mad woman. I warned her to take it easy, but sure enough, before I could restrain her vigor, she managed to crack the vessel in half with a single hard blow of the pestle.

"Oh my God!" she screamed hysterically, truly shocked at what had happened. "Oh my God, I can't believe I did that. Oh Jimmy, darling, I'm so sorry. Please, can you ever forgive me? How could I have done that? I'll replace it, sweetheart, I promise I'll buy you another mortar and send it to you. Oh God, this is terrible . . . terrible! Everything's ruined."

I put my arm around her cuddly waist and pulled her close. "Don't be silly, Labouche, it's only an ordinary mortar," I said, trying to console her. "What's the big deal? Nothing's ruined."

Now wiping her moist eyes, she continued to stare down at the mess. "You don't understand," she murmured fearfully. "It's like in Morocco when somebody puts a *djinn* in a place."

"A what?"

"A *djinn*—a spirit—and when there's a *djinn*, the place is cursed. I've been using mortars for years, and never, never once has something like this happened. I guess I'm being punished."

"That's absurd, Labouche, utterly absurd," I laughed. "It was just an honest accident with a cheap mortar. And besides, I have another one somewhere down in the cabinet, so would you please just relax so we can get on with the soup?"

As always, the trauma did pass, though I had the definite impression Paula was convinced that the entire meal was now doomed and that nothing we did could make it perfect. We followed every procedure to the letter, the single exception being when, while I was seasoning the stock and vegetables and she was still busy with the *rouille* and cutting up the fish, I suddenly realized that I didn't have a smidgen of tomato paste in the house. I was on the verge of telling her so when, fearing she might again hit the panic button and demand that I get back into the car and go get a can, I decided just to keep quiet. I mean, what big difference could a mere tablespoon of tomato paste make in all that liquid, after all?

In the end, I thought our trash bouillabaisse was glorious. Our friends raved and raved, and there wasn't a leftover to be seen. If the house had, indeed, been visited by one of Paula's *djinns*, her animated behavior and nonstop blabbering about what constitutes a great bouillabaisse belied any anxiety she might still have been harboring. Only when the last guest had closed the front door did she make it quite clear that all had not been perfect in our culinary production.

"How could you have pulled that rotten stunt," she almost sobbed, wrapping remnants of the cheese we'd also served. "Did you think I wouldn't notice? I knew I should have tasted that soup more carefully."

"What in hell are you talking about, Labouche?" I asked, having already forgotten about my little deception.

"You know exactly what I'm talking about. The tomato paste. You left out the tomato paste when my back was turned, didn't you? Admit it."

I don't know whether I was more stunned or impressed. One measly tablespoon of tomato paste, and even with all the chopped tomatoes and various other thickening agents, Paula had detected instinctively my minor sin—which in her view was not minor at all. My explanation and apology didn't help much, nor did my assurance that surely nobody else had noticed.

She shook her head dolefully. "I'm sure they did notice and were just being polite. Of course I knew the soup was doomed when I broke that mortar, but I never thought you'd be the one to punish me."

"That's outlandish, Labouche," I rebounded, kissing her on the cheek. "The soup was delicious, and everybody loved it. I wish you'd stop acting so goddamned . . . defeated. Nobody could tell the difference, and you know it."

"I could," she snapped. "A dish is either right or wrong, and the bouillabaisse wasn't right—believe me."

As the years passed, Paula's influence on me and my career would only intensify as I learned to understand and accept the more phobic nature of her complex personality and depended on her friendship and exceptional prowess to guide me through my own murky waters. It hasn't really mattered that I've remained "one chromosome away from true happiness," or that her husband and I have absolutely no use for one another, or that her cookbooks win all the awards and sell twice as fast as mine do. We both perceive all that as superficial and basically irrelevant in the overcast, private world we share, never once forgetting that she's only "a lost little Jewish girl from Brooklyn," whose special bond with a "rootless Carolina redneck" has remained steadfast for over two tumultuous decades of mutual respect, profound devotion, and outrageous frolic.

Cooking with 3-star Michelin Chef Paul Bocuse in a private kitchen in Manhattan: (left to right) JV, Chef Paul Bocuse, and photographer Arnold Newman.

A thank-you note from Bocuse.

PAUL BOCUSE

Un très grand mercis, Mon Cher James, pour ce merveilleux reportage illustré de superbes photos parue dans "TOWN AND COUNTRY" et très bientôt à Collonges, j'espère et encore mille mercis.
avec toute mon amitié.
Paul Bocuse
5. 06. 91

69660 Collonges-au-Mont d'Or France Téléphone : 78.22.01.40 Télex Bocuse 375.382 Fax 72.27.85.87

Menu from a Bocuse dinner at the Four Seasons restaurant in New York.

PAUL BOCUSE DINNER, THE FOUR SEASONS, JAN. 18, 1973

WINES	RECEPTION
Paul Bocuse Aperatif	SAUCISSON DE LYON
	VARIETY OF OYSTERS
	SAUTEED CHIPOLATAS ON FRIED PARSLEY
	DINNER
Meursault-Perrieres 1969	SOUP A L'ECREVISSE, FERNAND POINT
Meursault-Perrieres 1969	PAUL BOCUSE FRESH FOIE GRAS, COLD and SALAD OF FRESH TRUFFLES
Musigny 1969 and 1966	STRIPED BASS EN CROUTE, PAUL BOCUSE
Chateau Palmer 1955 and Chateaux Margaux 1955	POULARDE MERE BRAZIER HARICOTS VERT
	SORBET DE POIRE AU KUMMEL
Le Musigny 1961	BECASSE ROTI
Mouton 1955 and Cheval Blanc 1934	CHEESE COURSE: - CHÈVRE
Chateau D'Yquem 1949 and Trockenbeerenauslese 1959	OEUFS A LA NEIGE
	MIGNARDISES
Brandy and Port	DEMI - TASSE

CHAPTER ELEVEN

BOCUSE AND ME

— "A grand restaurant kitchen is no place for today's woman."

— "Nouvelle cuisine is much more a story of ambitious chefs, gullible journalists, and shrewd businessmen than of particular dishes."

— "France must preserve a certain identity with its cuisine as it does with the rest of its culture, and we're sick of these dishes with an ethnic mixture of a little of this, a little of that, and a little of something else."

— "Just as a composer cannot create a symphony or opera every day, a chef cannot invent an original dish every day."

PAUL BOCUSE IS NO MORE MODEST in expressing his opinions about gastronomy than he is in promoting his face and name in the life-size portraits and on every napkin ring and plate and ashtray that adorn the Michelin three-star restaurant outside Lyon to which serious epicures have flocked for the past four decades. As a result, it's always been considered clever, even hip to certain practitioners in the food world to disparage and castigate the chef as a mere dilettante, a pompous ass, even a fraud. Many feminists, of course, view him and his blasphemous convictions about women in the kitchen (all except, that is, the rugged "*mère*" chefs of Lyon) as nothing less than monstrous. Flippant journalists (many of whom have never even set foot in his restaurant) love to condemn the way he travels and is often absent from his kitchen, and most young, new-wave chefs caught up in the latest cutting-edge culinary innovations simply perceive him as old hat.

As for myself, I consider Paul Bocuse to be the most dynamic force in the evolution of world gastronomy over the past three decades. Other celebrity chefs have come and gone, eating and dining habits have been subjected to every upheaval and insurrection imaginable; but through it all Bocuse, now in his early seventies, has remained the uncontested emperor, the legitimate successor to Escoffier and Dumaine and Point, the outspoken, combative, and brilliant champion of an unimpeachable style of cooking that continues to awe serious chefs and eaters all around the globe. Fickle, self-styled experts may tout the glories of a Ducasse or Robuchon, fatuous restaurant critics might suffer under the misguided illusion that provender produced in America and Britain now equals anything that France has to offer, but forever looming above the fantasies and brouhaha is the implacable, tyrannical, and immortal figure of Paul Bocuse.

When Alexandre Dumaine first introduced me to Bocuse one evening in the early sixties at the Hôtel de la Côte d'Or in Saulieu, the much younger chef still had only one Michelin star at his simple family restaurant in the Lyon suburb of Collange-au-Mont-d'Or. Even then, though, I found him to be a captivating, high-strung individualist who respected every sacred principle of classic French cooking but already had his own unorthodox ideas of what a chef's role should be in a profession that was beginning to demand radical changes. I had sat and listened to him and Dumaine argue heatedly, watched as he raved wildly with his thick hands, heard him describe dishes that seemed to baffle the old master across from him, and, to be sure, noticed the way he virtually undressed with his dark, intense eyes a young waitress as she moved about the room.

By the time I first visited his restaurant with my Grenoble friends Pam and Philippe later in the year, he had just received his second Michelin star and seemed to be more tense and full of himself than ever. Recognizing me when he came out of the kitchen in his extra-tall white toque, he began prancing around the still modest dining room and wasted no time dictating our menu the same way he'd do in the years that followed. It was obvious that he couldn't keep his eyes off Pam.

"You will all have sea bass," he announced bluntly, "then chicken and pigeon," after which he patted Pam playfully on the head and strutted back to the kitchen.

What he meant by sea bass was a large fish stuffed with a mousse of lobster, truffles, and pistachios and baked in pastry. The chicken for two was a fat Bresse bird bursting with foie gras, sweetbreads, and root vegetables. And the "pigeon" was actually a meaty, gamy, roasted Bresse squab served wrapped in robes of cabbage and golden puff pastry. I remember eating also the creamiest and most extraordinary potato gratin my untrained palate had ever tasted, as well as an ethereal individual orange soufflé baked inside an orange. If this was two-star dining, I told my companions, then I still didn't understand what three stars was all about — including the phenomenal cuisine of Monsieur Dumaine. Three years later, in 1965, Bocuse received his third star, an accolade he's never had to forfeit to this day.

I rarely went to France (even when I was in academic life) without returning to Bocuse's restaurant for what I knew would be a momentous experience. Eventually, after I had the rare opportunity of actually cooking with him (okay, standing by and helping while *he* cooked) at a private townhouse in New York for the purpose of writing one of my first stories for *Town & Country*, we gradually became good friends. In Lyon, I'd often go to the city market with him and his cronies in the early morning, drinking cup after cup of strong *café filtre* and eating *sabodet* sausage on toasted brioche at a local dive called Café des Fédérations. Then we'd move on to negotiate beaujolais orders at his favorite wine dealer, and more than once I'd be invited back to the restaurant to share a simple lunch of some rugged stew or roasted meat with members of his family and staff before all the glamorous activity began in the dining room. Why the privileged treatment? I'd like to think it was because Paul actually enjoyed my company and conversation, but it was more likely because I spoke French (and I never heard Paul utter a single word to anybody in any language but French) and was a journalist who had the right press and social connections in America to help an insatiable egotist in his zealous campaign to spread his gospel and conquer the universe.

Since those early days, there's almost no aspect of Bocuse's meteoric rise to fame and often outrageous career to which I haven't been a witness: his introduction of nouvelle cuisine to the world; then a vehement rejection of the movement after all the abuses in favor of traditional French cooking; his controversial involvement with Walt Disney World's Epcot Center in Florida and endorsement of various commercial products; his creation of the first global cooking competition, immodestly called the Bocuse d'Or; his opening of restaurants in the Far East and Australia that bear his name, not to mention three eclectic brasseries in Lyon. I was one of the first to sample the celebrated black truffle soup he created when accorded the Legion of Honor by the president of France in 1975, and I was seated with him the day in 1989 when he learned that the Gault-Millau dining guide had proclaimed him "chef of the century." I've watched Paul blow up to the size of a mini-whale, and then, when his health and amorous shenanigans were threatened, suffer the agonies of the damned to reduce his weight.

What drives others really crazy about Bocuse are the very traits I've always most admired about the man: his staunch respect for culinary tradition and contradictory willingness to redefine dishes as he sees fit; his utter disregard for cooking trends and foreign influences; his rejection of dietetic meals and so-called health foods ("I'm a chef, not a doctor"). I respect his unabashed predilection for leadership and grand gesture and self-promotion ("I travel to publicize French cuisine and defend my way of cooking"), and since I've never trusted a thin chef, his considerable bulk impresses and reassures me. The man who created such amazing "nouvelle" dishes as truffle soup, red mullet with crisp potato scales, turbot soufflé with champagne sauce, chicken roasted in salt, and casserole of sweetbreads and crayfish is also the

Chicken Roasted in Salt

SERVES 4

*One 3½-pound roasting chicken,
    trussed*
Freshly ground black pepper to taste
8½ pounds coarse sea salt

Preheat the oven to 450° F. Pepper the chicken inside and out.

Line the bottom and sides of a heavy roasting pan with heavy aluminum foil, allowing enough extra foil to cover the chicken later on. Spread a thick layer of salt over the bottom, place the chicken breast-side down in the center of the pan, and cover the chicken thickly and completely with the remaining salt, packing it down with your hands. Fold over the extra foil to enclose the chicken completely, secure it tightly with hands, and place in the oven for 1¼ hours.

To serve, place the chicken on a large platter, remove and discard the foil, and break the block of salt with a small hammer, discarding the pieces. (The chicken should be golden brown and moistly succulent.) Carve the chicken in serving pieces and serve immediately.

man who fights to preserve the sanctity of a perfectly spit-roasted duck, a correct pot-au-feu and *blanquette de veau*, and an authentic crème brûlée. "What people don't understand is that there's nothing really new in cooking and that even Apicius spoke of nouvelle cuisine in the first century A.D.," he once declared during a frenzied tirade, echoing the same sentiment as Alexandre Dumaine but adding a typical Bocuse analogy. "Cuisine is like sex: there's nothing sensible left to invent, so the trick is to modify and perfect the familiar."

SPRINGS, LONG ISLAND, JULY 1990—

Mother, Aunt Dee, and I at Pierre Franey's waterfront place for dinner. Couldn't believe how he whipped up an elaborate three-course meal in no more than thirty minutes—scallops, veal, & fruit compote with Cointreau—all impeccable. The man's a genius—best chef in America. Just wish he and Craig got along better.

Ah, sex, and women, and scandalous flirting, and sensual pleasure. To understand the real Paul Bocuse and his passion for life is to acknowledge his overt obsession with the ladies, his veritable worship of virtually any human creature who doesn't have an Adam's apple. French men have always had the reputation of being clever rakes, but I'm convinced that none manifests the foxy spirit quite like Bocuse. Make no mistake: The great chef is the consummate family man, happily married to and dependent on the same wonderful woman these many years, and utterly devoted to what she and their children represent. At the same time, at least privately, he still holds firm by his conviction that today's woman has neither the stamina nor temperament to function in a three-star kitchen.

If Bocuse is the ultimate macho, vulgar bourgeois who pays no heed whatever to the sexual revolution of the past decades, he's also a benign lecher who has the cunning and charm and wit to woo the very females who under most circumstances would have his inflated head on a platter. Over the years, I've had good reason to question the sexual makeup of all sorts of men, but when it comes to Paul Bocuse, I can truthfully say he's the most confirmed, inalterable, irrepressible heterosexual I've ever known — and one of the few secure and bold enough to have quipped jovially and approvingly when he first noticed my eye following a handsome chap in a Lyon restaurant, *"Je remarque, cher ami, que vous avez un petit penchant pour les garçons."*

I've watched Paul ogling half-naked damsels around a swimming pool while other chefs waited angrily for him to join them in a hotel kitchen. I've seen him chat up alluring felines at bars and snuggle indiscreetly with other men's wives at charity food galas just for the dangerous tingle. And since age, disposition, size, and nationality are apparently no criteria for his lusty but innocent pursuits, I've sat at tables totally and rudely ignored for hours while he worked his magic on hefty, feisty women of all backgrounds whose vigor just boosted his adoration. While others would probably classify Bocuse as just another dirty old man not unlike stereotypical, woolly, red-blooded, cigar-chomping, alpha American males, I say that's too facile an interpretation of this highly charged but sensitive chef whose multiple passions are so intermingled that no single one can be said to explain his primal instincts. Yes, there's as much crudeness in the way he esteems the opposite sex as in the manner he wolfs down food, decorates his restaurant, and preens on TV, but to criticize him solely for these foibles is to ignore totally a strange aesthetic that governs his brilliance and creativity in the kitchen. I've observed the phenomenon for years, and perhaps no incidence has been more revealing than one that transpired some time ago when Paul was visiting New York and called one morning out of the blue.

"Bocuse ici," his voice boomed over the phone. "Where can we eat tonight?"

"But Paul, I already have an important dinner date," I stammered truthfully, exasperated as usual that he hadn't called earlier.

"Cancel it," he ordered in expected fashion. "I'm here for only one night, and we have things to talk about. Now, where should we eat that's good? I'm hungry."

My curiosity piqued (unwarrantedly, as it turned out), I did indeed change my plans and began the ordeal of deciding where we should go. Faithful to the paradox that he is, Paul made it clear that he was in no mood for French cuisine — and especially the contrived French cooking emerging all over the city. I remembered from the past that what he'd always really loved was a fat American steak or lamb chops at the venerable Coach House, but that beloved institution had since closed following its owner's serious illness. It dawned on me that he might not only enjoy the no-nonsense, delectable Italian food at Felidia, but relish meeting the restaurant's affable, buxom, and curiously voluptuous chef-owner, Lidia Bastianich, who bore a resemblance to the sturdy Lyonnaise *"mères"* and who spoke French. A table was booked, and I told Paul I'd meet him at the bar at the old Le Cirque since he was staying upstairs at the Mayfair Regent Hotel.

When I arrived, there he was perched like a behemoth at the far end of the bar, already lapping up the adulation proffered by fans who recognized him instantly.

"What's that?" he asked excitedly about the Negroni placed in front of me.

After tasting the potent gin and Campari cocktail, he ordered one for himself, studied it carefully, and proceeded to toss it back in two gulps.

In a few minutes, we were again interrupted by a short, well-dressed, cordial man, who commenced to inform Paul that the highlight of his trip to France every year was the meal he and his wife always had at Collanges and that, in their opinion, Bocuse had no equals. Of course Paul didn't understand a word the gentleman was saying, and as he sat there smiling and politely uttering only *"Merci . . . merci,"* I couldn't help but notice that he kept staring over the man's right shoulder.

"Did you catch what he was trying to tell you?" I asked when the admirer finally moved on.

"No, and I don't care," he almost panted, his flaming black eyes still fixed on something in the restaurant. "That woman, just look at that ravishing woman with long blond hair on the banquette. The hair, the eyes, the pale skin, the way she slowly lifts food to her fleshy lips — everything is perfect, *formidable*. Just look. *Formidable!*"

Walking across town and discussing the differences between French and American cheeses, we stopped momentarily on Park Avenue so Paul, like a tourist in town for the first time, could gaze in wonder at all the soaring skyscrapers lighted in the distance. At the sophisticated but unpretentious Italian restaurant, Lidia, dressed alluringly in one of her tight sweater outfits that gave Paul immediate pause, was in awe of the famous Frenchman as she led us to a choice table in the main ground-floor dining room and began reeling off a litany of enticing specials before returning to the kitchen. Suddenly the otherwise merry area became almost silent as savvy customers recognized Bocuse's distinctive face and came over to pay homage. I found such intrusive, audacious behavior appalling; Paul ate it all up with the same gusto he displayed in attacking the rough country bread and wine, nodding his head up and down proudly as if he understood every compliment and repeating *"Merci"* over and over when I wasn't being inopportuned to translate a question.

Once all the social hoopla subsided, Paul resumed discoursing about food, about Michelin and the ignorance of most restaurant critics, about the fantastic collection of fairground steam organs he was having reconditioned back at Collanges, about the American chefs he admired and how he planned to send his own son to the Culinary Institute of America, and about the enjoyment, *le plaisir*, that must be derived from every mouthful of food, every sip of wine, every trip, and, to be sure, every human encounter.

"All that matters to me is living life to the full," he proclaimed at one point. "I cook only dishes that I know will make me and my family and my customers happy. I travel to preach but also to learn. I read intelligent books and listen to good music. I associate with people who share my own interests but have something special to offer. And if kissing a few girls and pinching a few bottoms gives me a thrill, it also makes me feel younger and more alert. What's wrong with that?"

If there is one activity that actually stops Bocuse talking, it is eating. You only have to watch him mount an assault on a good bowl of soup, or plate of charcuterie, or big hunk of meat to realize that his love of food is entirely natural and unaffected and without restrictions. Since I had foolishly told Lidia to prepare whatever specialties suited her, the array of dishes that appeared on the table was staggering: an earthy ragout of wild mushrooms with fresh asparagus and white truffles; homemade fusilli with a sublime duck sauce; aromatic Istrian fish stew chock full of a half dozen varieties of seafood; massive veal chops stuffed with broccoli and pine nuts; and heaven knows what all vegetables and cheeses and desserts. Obviously, Bocuse was impressed by this woman's talent and respect for traditional food.

Being the culinary master he is, Paul would instinctively study and smell and often quickly manipulate each dish with a finger before tasting, his keen senses no doubt curious about components and balance and freshness and certainly flavor. Then, taking one or two more bites, he would casually air to me one of three pat verdicts that I'd heard so often in the past and learned to interpret: "*Ça va,*" which meant he didn't think much of a dish; "*C'est bon,*" quite acceptable; and "*Formidable,*" exceptional. And once a dish was judged *formidable* (as most were this particular evening), he would pounce like a real Lyon trencherman, devouring every morsel with great zest and slugging wine as if it were water. Of course, when Lidia would pop out of the kitchen to solicit our reactions to a certain dish, Paul, also the consummate gentleman under someone else's roof or around strangers, would automatically bellow "*formidable,*" his head turning and nodding and swiveling in some putative gustatory trance.

Or so I believed at first till it became clear to me that much of his attention was directed at the staircase not far away that led up to a small second-floor dining room. Thank God Lidia didn't notice, but the truth is that at least some of those *formidable*s were being uttered to rave not so much about the delicious food as about the flock of delicious females parading up and down the stairs with their legs exposed to full measure. There Paul sat, savoring delicious cuisine and drinking lavishly, indulging in ardent conversation with at least one frisky woman who knew how to cook well, and letting his libidinous eyes roam freely. He was a happy man.

Despite Bocuse's shortcomings, his generosity is such that not only are friends dining in his own restaurant often presented a bill that reads only *"Les amis sont toujours bienvenus,"* but when a young couple he has never met before turn up and are obviously enthusiastic about food, he is just as capable of giving them their dinner gratis. When, on the other hand, I asked for the check at Felidia and was told that the meal was with Lidia's compliments, Paul, signaling me to put away my credit card and taking out his, almost threw a fit.

"Ma belle," we're not in this business for charity," he admonished her playfully, reaching around her waist and pulling her close, "and this type of true pleasure should not come free." As always, Bocuse proved to be an utter paradox and enigma.

Just as we were preparing to cross back over Park Avenue after dinner and had to wait at an intersection while a passenger got out of a cab, I noticed the wistful way Paul again seemed to be taking in all the imposing buildings and lights and zooming traffic — almost like an astonished child.

"Formidable," he exclaimed quietly, still glancing up the street with a fixed expression on his face.

"Yes, it is a remarkable town, isn't it?"

"Don't be absurd," he growled indignantly, his stare even more intense. "I'm talking about that incredible woman walking up the street, the one who was in the cab. Just look at that figure — the legs, the shoulders, the bottom . . ."

Formidable!

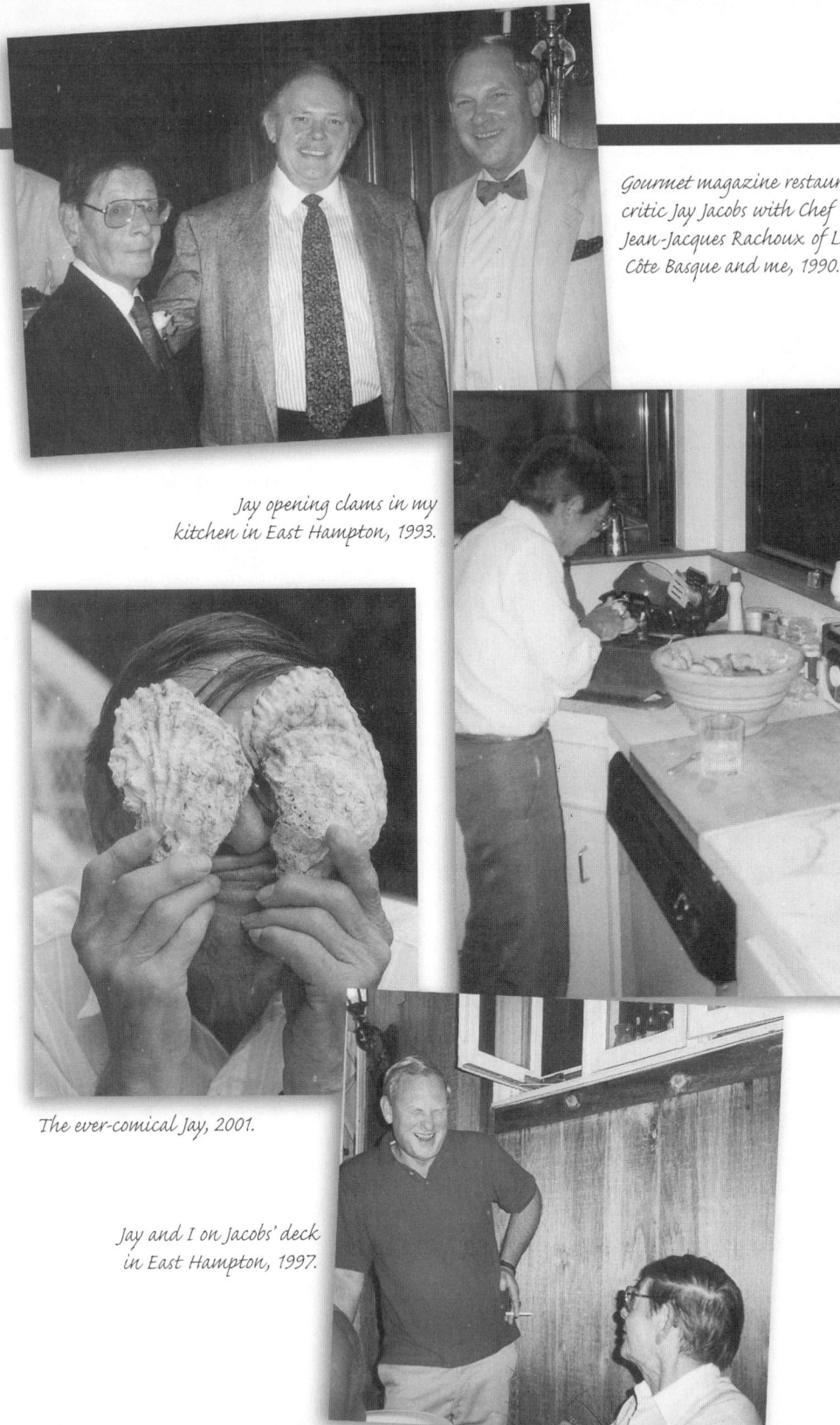

Gourmet magazine restaurant critic Jay Jacobs with Chef Jean-Jacques Rachoux of La Côte Basque and me, 1990.

Jay opening clams in my kitchen in East Hampton, 1993.

The ever-comical Jay, 2001.

Jay and I on Jacobs' deck in East Hampton, 1997.

CHAPTER TWELVE

DUBIOUS LESSONS FROM A HIRED BELLY

M UCH TO MY WONDER and utter consternation, the single aspect of my career that has elicited the greatest public response and fascination is not my food essays and cookbooks but my role as a restaurant critic. I can shed gallons of ink on the origins of crème brûlée, expound on the latest artisanal cheeses in the U.S. or Britain, or describe a half dozen different ways that Brunswick stew is made in the American South; yet none of these (for me, at least) engaging topics attracts the same attention as a piece on the finest restaurants of Chicago or the new bistros of Paris.

Ever since dining out became an obsession and virtual spectator sport for Americans back in the early eighties, my magazine coverage of restaurants from Vancouver to Saint Barts to the wilds of the Dordogne has, by necessity, been extensive. This professional duty has certainly had its rewards, but it's also been responsible not only for a wretched digestive track, a pathetic liver, and numerous bouts of food poisoning, but for that ubiquitous, loathsome question that plagues any recognized critic: "Oh, where do you recommend we eat?"—in

Munich, or on Mozambique, or in Kansas, or on Mars. Forget the assumption that I've traveled to every city, hamlet, island, and planet in the universe. What is truly irritating is that, on the spot, I'm supposed to surmise by ESP what style of food the plotters are seeking, the setting, the price category, the mode of dress, any dietetic restrictions, everything but the color scheme they prefer in restaurant bathrooms.

EAST HAMPTON, JULY 1988—

A phenomenal Portuguese feast chez moi prepared by Jean Anderson for me, Craig C., Pierre F., Pamela F., et. al. Caldo Verde, Cataplana (18 lbs. of mussels!), a huge vegetable salad, beer bread, an orange torte, and bottles of dry porto. Everybody impressed.

When I was starting out in the late sixties as a greenhorn in this racket, scouting and reporting on restaurants for Silas Spitzer at *Holiday* was an exciting, challenging hobby involving serious enterprises operated by serious professionals serving truly serious food. But with the advent of the nouvelle craze (not to mention the public's phobic obsession with health) and its subsequent influence on the budding abomination to be called New American Cuisine, dining out increasingly became more a frolic in food playpens than the sane, civilized culinary and social experience it had been for over a century. By the late 1970s, the only major American restaurant critic who still championed the dignified old guard was Craig Claiborne, who would eventually bow out to a contingent of self-styled experts around the country eager to wave their flags in the new-wave revolution and add their respective kiwi fruits to the countercultural *salade folle.*

A disciple of Claiborne (and, to a lesser extent, Baron Roy Andries de Groot at *Esquire*), I was decidedly in the minority when it came to my conservative approach to the global restaurant scene and the way I reviewed restaurants for *Town & Country* and other magazines. While colleagues like Gael Greene at *New York* magazine, Phyllis Richmond at the *Washington Post*, Raymond Sokolov at the *New York Times*, and Lois Dwan at the *Los Angeles Times* swooned orgasmically over Michel

Guérard and Roger Vergé in France, Alice Waters and Wolfgang Puck in California, Anton Mosimann in London, and Barry Wine in New York, I generally rejected the trendy wizards in favor of established practitioners of classic cuisine, traditional cookery, and above all, those regional dishes that should be the bedrock of any culture.

This, of course, didn't make me very popular with either the new culinary masters of the universe or my professional cronies, who surely perceived me as out of touch with future reality. In turn, I had little respect for any critic who somehow found revelation and salvation in tough, bleeding, fanned duck breasts floating in puddles of berry coulis; miniature packets of undercooked, pristine baby veggies; cutesy goat-cheese and sun-dried tomato pizzas; rosemary sorbet; pretentious, oversize, designer dinner plates; and pubescent, untrained chefs preening about dining rooms like peacocks.

I knew that most of the silly dishes and rites would soon lose their novelty, but I also feared that a careless, dangerous journalistic precedent might be set that could eventually not only bastardize all great cooking, but pervert the very nature of sophisticated dining (as, indeed, proved tragically to be the case). To me, such a threat was very real in the seventies, since restaurant critics were being granted more and more power in newspapers and magazines all over the nation, and quite frankly, the only one I esteemed a true professional was a man whom I'd never laid eyes on, much less dined with, who covered the restaurant beat regularly for *Gourmet* magazine: Jay Jacobs.

Throughout the seventies, I followed Jacobs's reviews of restaurants in New York and other cities as steadfastly as other fans of the magazine, admiring his keen knowledge of food and cooking in general, his erudite command of the language, his candor, and a worldly sophistication and subtle sense of humor that connoted a tall, handsome, debonair figure not unlike that of Cary Grant. He was never without a female companion, whose alluring attributes he didn't hesitate to note, he assessed gin martinis with the same vigilance he applied to a restaurant's decor, service, food, and wine list, and he indulged in none of the inane psychodrama that characterized the scribblings of more arrogant commentators.

Jacobs, like myself, also had absolutely no use for the wackier new styles of French and American cooking that were making a mockery of gastronomy. While he was one of the first to recognize dining out as theater, his interpretation of the concept, unlike that of his less perceptive peers, involved an insistence on appropriate dress, the need for intelligent, wide-ranging table conversation, and a vital attempt to immerse the reader in the action so that he or she could vicariously share the enjoyment to the fullest.

I liked the way he wrote in the first person singular, and I admired the obvious fact that he didn't waste time, ink, and money rendering worthless, self-serving negative reviews. But what impressed me most was the prospect that, working from his informative, precise critiques, any reasonably adept home cook could produce respectable approximations of any number of the dishes described (I finally perfected my Italian minestrone, for example, only after studying the details of Jacobs's review of the dish at New York's Aperitivo). His role always seemed to be that of a highly enlightened, cordial host, ready to elucidate matters instructively to his tablemates without being pedantic and to make sure that all were having a good time. There was, in short, no nonsense about Jacobs, and I found myself striving to emulate his method.

Some years passed before I finally met and got to know the mysterious, elusive Jay Jacobs, in an indirect encounter that didn't exactly get us off to a rousing start. As it happened, shortly after I published my first food book in the early eighties, some obtuse interviewer asked for my opinion on certain other journalists, Jay Jacobs at *Gourmet* included. "I think Jacobs is the most brilliant food writer and restaurant critic around," I answered ingenuously. "Of course, I've never met the man, so as far as I know, he can't boil an egg." When the piece appeared, my modified statement read simply and viciously—you guessed it: "Jay Jacobs can't boil an egg." And through a mutual friend, I learned that Jacobs had seen the swipe.

Subsequently, Jacobs, too, was asked to proffer his opinions of current food writers in a lengthy article for *Gastronome* magazine, in which he justifiably infused his arrows with plenty of poison, took careful aim, and, excoriating every facet of my professional demeanor, savaged me as a "pretentious, narcissistic twit." Given the opportunity by the magazine's editor to cross swords in print, I instead retorted by trying to explain the unfortunate gaffe and reiterated my conviction that Jacobs was in a class by himself.

The childish misunderstanding festered till the two of us, unbeknownst to each other, were invited to a dinner party in Brooklyn. Jay was pointed out to me shortly after I arrived. I was stunned by what I saw, to say the least. There he sat alone, all 110 pounds of him, a martini in one hand and cigarette in the other—hardly a threatening adversary, and certainly not the Clark Gable of the food world I had expected. Boldly, I made my move.

"Hello, Jay," I stuttered, introducing myself. "I just want you to know that I do think you can boil an egg."

Very politely and graciously, he rose from his seat, put the cocktail on a table, and extended his tiny hand.

"Oh, screw it all," he uttered casually. "I doubt you're really a twit, either, but we guys have to make a buck any way we can, and we shouldn't take anything personally. Where's your goddamn drink?"

And from that moment on, Jay and I remained close chums and fellow rebels, standing our ground against an often phony profession that was taking itself far too seriously. As it turned out, we also became neighbors in East Hampton. That we had little in common except a passion for great food and cooking (he loved baseball, championed anything Italian, and was a womanizer; I relished opera, traveled extensively in France, and was gay) gave me pause at the start. But what really staggered me was the realization that this putatively suave, elitist man-about-town was actually, despite his phenomenal intelligence, one of the most outwardly modest, generous, and profligate creatures I'd ever met.

When we dined together in Manhattan (usually, by mutual choice, at a humble bistro and always in the company of a feline from his amorphous harem), I roared with laughter at the way he would refer to himself mockingly as a "hired belly" and "mercenary eater," then proceed to dismiss all food journalists (ourselves included) as self-styled pundits "whose work, alone among all human vocations, culminates in ignoble defecation." Convinced that white wine as a preprandial quaff was not unlike "kissing one's sister," this perceived highbrow was usually smashed on "juniper consommé" by the time the first courses were served. Yet he could communicate brilliantly with a head waiter or chef without a trace of intoxication, analyze and judge a dish with the dexterity of a teetotaler, and remember with arrant clarity every item that was tasted.

More self-righteous, less secure writers (not to mention his fawning readers) accustomed to Jay's astute, elegant reviews would no doubt have been utterly mortified by his reckless boozing, racy conversation, and indeed smoking. I, however, not only began to identify with his unorthodox behavior, but viewed his ability to carry out a job while indulging his senses amply to be a sign of the seasoned professional. As Jay would later write in one of his food books, "Gastronomy is the least hermetic and most associative of the arts. Its fullest appreciation and deepest understanding depend on an adequate knowledge of food history, lore, nomenclature, and customs that few who practice the craft possess, as well as a whole body of personal and collective associations and extravagant pleasures."

If Jay's many distant admirers might have been a bit disconcerted by his wanton hedonism in restaurants, I shiver to imagine what they would have thought of certain facets of his personal life in East Hampton, habits that I soon came to consider normal, much as I became accustomed to drinking a rare '69 Bâtard-Montrachet with one of his clam pies.

Witness, for instance, this typical scene with my low-life friend, who never even finished high school. Jay and Big Leroy squat on small wrought-iron chairs at a wobbly wooden table cluttered with manuscripts and magazines, a couple of time-worn art books, a portable typewriter, a wicker basket of freshly picked ripe tomatoes, a screwdriver, a huge ashtray with a Vesuvius of cigarette butts, and an open, half-empty bottle of gin bearing an unrecognizable label. The overall space—which purportedly serves as dining room, kitchen, and sitting area—resembles not so much a littered Goodwill depository as the blowsy interior of a camping trailer. Should a visitor venture out the back door without looking down carefully, the probability of a leg plunging through a rotted board on the puny deck would be extremely high. Suspended from one wall is a net of garlic bulbs; hanging over a platform sofa with threadbare cushions in another corner is an unframed oil landscape of dubious provenance; and dangling from a ceiling fixture near the ancient refrigerator is Jay's prized collection of perhaps eight different-sized, black, encrusted cast-iron skillets.

His right ankle swollen to the size of a medium grapefruit, Jay is once again in excruciating pain. It's gout, of course, but this time the certain cause is not some organ meat or spicy Mexican stew or champagne. This time the cause is lobster, or rather a brace of two-pound lobsters, or even more precisely, a brace of forbidden lobsters sluiced with acidic still white wine consumed rashly the night before. He's taken a pill, but so far it hasn't helped much. Jay knows that he deserves his torment. He knows also that his sins will be repeated not long after he survives this attack.

Since Jay is approximately the size of a bantam jockey, he's virtually invisible next to Big Leroy, who might conceivably be mistaken for a 350-pound sumo wrestler instead of the retired cop he is. Jay wears a faded denim jacket, Leroy a short-sleeved knit shirt that might well fit the Incredible Hulk. The two are very close buddies, both smoke like chimneys, and although it is still midmorning and Jay is suffering, each nurses a wine glass half-full of straight, cut-rate gin on the rocks as they carry on an intense discussion of which bays and harbors and canals in and around East Hampton yield the finest fresh littleneck clams, mussels, crabs, and bluepoint oysters.

"Oh, come on," Jay urges as I take a seat and light up. "How about just one nip?"

He reaches for the gin bottle and is about to get up to fetch another glass when I beg off again, explaining that I'm actually fighting a hangover, have a dinner to prepare for guests, and just dropped by to plead for a few exotic greens from his vast garden out back.

As usual, Jay's eyes are wet and glassy from too much booze and too little sleep, and as usual, Big Leroy's eyes simply bulge like those of a hyperthyroid primate. Once conclusions have been reached about where the two should head that afternoon to harvest plenty of fat clams if Jay's foot improves, he begins talking about pig, then the tapas he had recently on a trip to Spain, and eventually such disparate topics as the work of some Renaissance painter from Verona he's been studying, his pal Rusty Staub's batting record, the cathedrals of southern England, and the most compelling firehouses in Manhattan. It doesn't matter that, for different reasons, Leroy and I have trouble following half of Jay's monologue, but then, anyone who's spent lots of time around Jay, whether he's pickled or stone sober, is accustomed to being intimidated by his multifaceted interests, daunting intellect, and despotic control of the English language.

Jay's outbursts of erudition have hardly been limited to mere restaurant reviews. In his many books and articles, he has written with authority on everything from oriental sea dates to Carolina pork barbecue to shark steaks; but in a less restrictive realm, it is also his offbeat essays on saloon singers, rookie ballplayers, and Europe's finest small museums that have inspired me to modify and expand the scope of my own subject matter. On his desultory beat over the years as author and illustrator, biographer and book reviewer, poet manqué and even puppeteer, Jay has known success and dismal failure, but never once has he not painted his own Indians.

As a result, there's rarely been a time when this small but virile maverick hasn't suffered professionally, socially, and financially for his sins against conformity. Forever at odds over personal principles with his longtime editor in chief at *Gourmet*, he was at one point axed as the magazine's restaurant arbiter, only to be reinstated as a contributing writer when the head honcho herself was summarily "retired." While token foodies in New York routinely get invited to snappy press luncheons, book parties, chefs' dinners, and wine tastings, Jay's name is on very few guest lists, and just the idea of his attending journalism award ceremonies or other such formal events and mingling with his peers seems ludicrous.

"When my primary beat was reviewing restaurants, I was considered a journalistic hit man," he recalls with typical irony. "Now I'm more closely akin to the anteater, the sapsucker, or the flycatcher."

Even when he was covering restaurants on a lavish expense account and traveling professionally on the cuff, Jay's resources have never been exactly what I'd call flush. I've known the man when he couldn't buy heating oil for his small co-op in East Hampton, the same man, incidentally, who, after an early divorce from his first wife, somehow managed by himself to raise and support four very respectable and successful sons. I've driven with him in a series of cars that looked as if they left the assembly line shortly after World War II and would cause even the foreman of a junkyard to wince. Although Jay is as neat physically as he is courteous socially, sartorial poise in private means little to him. Since he refuses to write anything so potentially lucrative but mundane as a cookbook, preferring instead to manifest his gustatory obsessions not only in *Gourmet* but in such astute and often hilarious books as *A History of Gastronomy*, *Winning the Restaurant Game*, and *The Eaten Word*, his cash advances are usually no larger than what some glossy authors get for a couple of magazine articles. Yet in all these years, I've never once heard him bellyache about

VENICE, OCTOBER 1990—

Dinner at Da Fiori with Natale and Connie and Marcella and Victor Hazan. Memorable risotto colle seppie, and Marcella taught me correct way to eat risotto: never hot and always spread on plate with fork—literally till you can count the grains. Amazing.

his deplorable and relentless pecuniary dilemma. In his own way, Jay, like A. J. Liebling, M.F.K. Fisher, and Waverley Root before him, is a martyr for some noble cause that only he can fully interpret.

To dine out with Jay, travel and shop with him, or be privy to one of the exorbitant buffets he prepares periodically at his East Hampton shanty for a gang of indigent locals (Bonackers), artists, and loyal friends is to gain some hint of what this unorthodox, complex man is all about and how he's influenced my special approach to gastronomy. Although he has perched on the plushest restaurant banquettes of the world and consumed his fill of foie gras and caviar with the snootiest of moguls, never have I seen Jay more content and satisfied than when he's face to face with a bowl of tender tripe, an overflowing platter of fresh shellfish, or a heroic pork shank in some raffish bistro. Bliss to him is searching the Chinatown markets of cities for genuine sea slugs, geoducks, quail eggs, exotic mushrooms and noodles, shrimp roe, and various organ meats. Turn him loose on the back streets of Málaga, a village in Provence, or a bay in Montauk and you can bet he'll end up with a tub of squid, a bag of briny black olives, or a mess of blue crabs.

"To this day," he confesses, "my first order of business in an unfamiliar town is to dog down its more obscure streets and alleys, following my nose along whatever digressive paths an intriguing odor may lead it, mingling with the street people, haunting the street markets, eating street food." And, whenever possible, I'm right along with him.

Despite being prone to debilitating attacks of not only gout but pancreatitis, Jay forges bravely ahead in his search for any comestible that might pass safely down the human gullet, and almost no food seems foreign to him. Of course he was relishing Aztec *nopales*, Trevisan radicchio, and chanterelle mushrooms ages before America's juvenile maestros trumpeted such ingredients. While Scottish haggis, Puerto Rican *cuchifritos*, Chinese shark's fin soup, French *andouillettes*, and Rocky Mountain oysters (testicles) are high on his list of gustatory superlatives, he also has a strong penchant for razor clams, any preparation of eel, boiled calf's head, and hog snout. I've heard him say that he'd love to sample the sex glands of lampreys once favored by English royalty, but he did draw the line in Hong Kong one evening when a waiter suggested braised stag's penis, soliciting Jay's mannerly reply, "Not tonight, thank you. I have a bad headache."

One of our more memorable (if controversial) trips together was a few years ago with epicurean peers eager to introduce us to the gastronomic glories of Istria and the northeastern region of Italy known as Friuli-Venezia Giulia. Accustomed to such jaunts, which somehow always end up involving the participation of local brass determined to showcase every historical monument, church, cemetery, museum, and flophouse at their disposal, Jay and I were initially on our best behavior as we schlepped dutifully through one predictable winery after the next, slogged pointlessly about sodden mushroom fields, incinerated our craws with half a dozen grappas, and indulged in torturous three-hour lunches that never failed to feature some bizarre risotto variation, overwrought scampi or lobster creation, maybe a distorted beef or lamb dish, deluges of acidic pinot grigio, *Tocai friulano*, *ribolla*, and any other wines to be promoted, and, assuredly, endless discourses delivered by mayors and cheese producers and winemakers and distillers.

"Where in hell is all the regional chow we were dragged over here to sample?" Jay finally exploded to me in private as we guardedly smoked in the back of the van like leprous teenagers on our way to another staggering lunch hosted by officials in a small Friulian town.

"Don't ask me," I snorted, "but ten bucks says we're about to encounter another weird risotto."

"Well, goddamnit, I need an honest drink," he pronounced decisively, eyeing a café across the street from where the van was parked. "Are you game?"

Suffice it to say that we told our cohorts we needed to buy cigarettes, and we might have an espresso, and we'd catch up with them shortly at the snazzy restaurant up the street. All glared disapprovingly at us, but in a matter of minutes we were standing desperately at the seedy bar pointing to bottles of Gordon's gin and dry Cinzano and directing the hefty, suspicious barmaid how to at least approximate two lukewarm but restorative martinis.

"*Digami*," Jay asked the buxom maiden in halting Italian that was still more proficient than my own, "where in this town can we find some really good food—the type you yourself prepare at home?"

Suddenly her chubby, rosy face lit up as she uttered some name, pointed out the door and to the right, and mentioned such dishes as *frico*, braised octopus, fried zucchini blossoms, polenta with snails, and stuffed squid.

Slugging down his gin and reaching into a pocket for some lira, Jay turned to me with that familiar glow of excitement in his slightly bloodshot eyes and directed, "Let's go—fast!"

"If we do, we'll be skinned alive," I protested half-heartedly, thinking of the others no doubt now obligingly sipping spumante before another fancy feeding marathon.

"To hell with it," Jay mumbled. "This could be our only chance to have some genuine regional food. How much money do you have?"

Not fifty feet around the corner, we spotted the tiny place, peeped in at the people eating and drinking and laughing, sniffed the lusty aromas, and proceeded to take one of the two free tables. A rather gaunt but smiling elderly man approached us with a basket of focaccia in his hand, placed it on the table, and, since apparently there was no printed menu, began simply reeling off the names of dishes available, half of which we didn't understand. Shifting my eyes to where I heard lots of racket, I glanced through an open door in the back. Two stout women were busy in the kitchen, one stirring an old pot, the other chopping with a big knife as she bawled about something or another. It was a good sign, and I nudged Jay to look.

After we asked the man lots of questions the best we could, within minutes I was raving about a gusty porcini mushroom soup of almost miraculous flavor, while Jay tucked into a small, crispy cheese cake, called a *frico*, filled with sausage and radicchio. Next were fresh, billowy

SAUSAGE AND RADICCHIO FRICOS

YIELD: **4 *FRICOS***

½ *pound hot bulk Italian sausage*

2 garlic cloves, minced

2 cups coarsely chopped radicchio, washed and dried

Salt and freshly ground pepper to taste

1 pound medium-aged Montasio or Asiago cheese, rind removed

Break up the sausage into a medium skillet, add the garlic, and cook over moderate heat, stirring to break up the sausage completely, till the meat is browned, about 10 minutes. Add the radicchio and salt and pepper, stir well, reduce the heat to low, cover, and cook about 5 minutes, or till the radicchio is wilted. Pour off any excess fat and transfer the filling to a bowl.

To cook the *fricos*, scatter about ½ cup of the cheese in a 5-inch nonstick skillet over moderately low heat and let it soften. Spoon about one-quarter of the sausage-radicchio filling evenly over the cheese, sprinkle another half-cup of cheese evenly over the filling, and cook about 6 minutes, or till the bottom is golden brown when lifted with a metal spatula. Slide the cake onto a small plate, invert it back into the skillet, and cook till the other side is golden brown.

Transfer the *frico* to a large platter and keep warm in the oven while repeating the procedure to make the remaining 3 *fricos*. Serve the *fricos* whole or cut in half.

gnocchi with a coarse venison sauce, and I thought I'd have to fight Jay for a bite of his garlicky squid simmered in stock and olive oil and served with creamy polenta. We drank a bottle of zesty, red *uvaggio* wine that we were told was made with blended grape varietals, and instead of dessert, we settled for a few pieces of some semifirm, pungent local cheese and purple plums. It was, without question, one of the most remarkable meals either of us had ever had. The bill for two—I'll never forget—was about eighteen dollars, and the only negative was that we'd been forced to rush.

"What's going to be our excuse?" I asked as we lumbered back up the street toward the other restaurant, aware that we'd been gone over an hour and prepared to be skewered.

"I'd say that we stopped in the local whorehouse," Jay snickered wickedly, "but they might question your credibility. God, have you ever tasted anything like that *frico*? I've got to find a recipe and learn to make that."

As anticipated, when we finally ambled into the rather flashy dining room the piercing stares from our mates were like daggers. I proffered ingeniously if disingenuously that we'd been delayed by a fascinating lady who offered to show us around a town bakery we'd noticed near the café. And as anticipated, the group was just being served a main course of prosaic beef filet in a strange-looking sauce, which was about as Friulian as spaghetti and meatballs. With absolutely no appetite left after our repast back at the dive, I pushed my meat around the plate, noticing in the process a telltale, embarrassing smudge of venison sauce on the front of my shirt. It was unsettling, but not nearly as disconcerting as Jay, who didn't so much as take a second glance at the silly beef and who, when eventually one of the officials rose to pontificate on pecolit, a Friulian dessert wine, promptly fell sound asleep at the table.

I suppose our behavior was less than genteel, if not downright rude. But thanks to Jay, we'd taken the bull by the horns for once and fulfilled a worthwhile gastronomic mission that we talk about to this day. Needless to say, the organizer never invited either of us on another such ramble.

Not only did I learn years ago that Jay can indeed boil a very nice egg; I also realized after attending the first of his extravagant buffets in East Hampton that he's one of the few dedicated journalists capable of reproducing virtually any dish he judges in a restaurant or features in an article. Of course these ultra-casual, laid-back bashes are hardly the type of entertaining that would make the pages of even the most stolid women's magazines, much less *Gourmet* or *Town & Country.* Jay's contingent of disparate characters is a far cry from the chichi Hamptons set, little effort is made to introduce strangers to one another, and basically guests simply mill about the cabin's one big room or tiny outside yard while Jay works happily, nonstop in the kitchen. Lining a shelf are half-gallon bottles of cheap booze, mixers, and generic wines to which people help themselves. Beer is kept in an old cooler in the middle of the floor, and the glasses are plastic. When the place is packed, it's not unlike being in a holding pen with hungry cattle.

Most of Jay's cooking equipment (or, as he calls it, his "battered *batterie de cuisine*") was found at yard sales, flea markets, and the town dump, but it fulfills his every need. (Such is his culinary ingenuity that when he bakes his delectable small pizzas in five-inch cast-iron skillets, common ceramic ashtrays are pressed onto the tops to produce a thin interior and puffy, crisp edges.) At any one of his bacchanalian shindigs, I've never seen fewer than twenty separate dishes displayed on tables, counters, and shelves, and since Jay suffers also from chronic insomnia and rarely sleeps more than three hours at night, he typically begins cooking all the victuals and baking two or three types of bread in the wee hours, consumes sufficiencies of gin in the process, and continues into the morning till stricken with narcolepsy. Why his heavy drinking has no effect on his ability to function is a phenomenon that baffles everybody except me, but the results of his intoxicated labor (which might well spread over two or three nights) are usually a big pot of Carolina pork barbecue, a baked country ham or side of beef, Scandinavian gravlax, a French *pâté en croûte*, Provençal mussels stuffed with pureed artichokes and smoked oysters, an Italian seafood salad, Spanish *gambas a la plancha*, Asian quail eggs wrapped in anchovies, Mexican seviche, Texas chili, Portuguese squid stuffed with chopped spinach and ham, and . . . well, you get the idea. Jay's cuisine has no territorial boundaries, and most of the guests have absolutely no idea what they're eating half the time, but the food is always extraordinary, everybody has loads of fun filling their bellies, and Jay once again proves himself to be the ultimate gourmand. That nobody has ever contracted food poisoning from mussels, squid, or shellfish left out for hours on a sweltering summer evening is a truth best not pursued.

Interestingly enough considering his self-professed resemblance to Kermit the Frog, Jay has always been a real ladies' man, a trait that has led to any number of rewarding flings but also to less felicitous encounters with his many female admirers. Witness, for example, a blind date at a French restaurant with a certain "waddling Venus du Jour" described in graphic and irreverent detail in his book *A Glutton for Punishment:*

> I suppose she wouldn't have been considered unattractive by a similarly cross-eyed hippopotamus of the opposite sex. She grunted a perfunctory greeting and fell on her *salade de foie gras Pompadour* with the purposefulness of a ravening hyena. She polished off a roast pigeon as though it were a hummingbird, wore out a team of busmen, who rushed breadstuffs to her in relays, and, unable to decide which dessert looked most tempting, ordered a portion of everything from the trolley. Then it turned out that she did indeed have a mind, but there was only one thing on it: sustained postprandial sex, either at her hotel or my apartment, or, if need be, in the form of manual stimulation right there at the table.

For years I watched Jay cover the turf, but as he approached his seventieth birthday, the escapades became more fruitless and monotonous, his basic loneliness led to depression and even more wanton drinking, and the night he had to be rushed to the hospital with acute pancreatitis, I knew his days were numbered, barring a minor miracle.

And the miracle materialized not long ago in the form of a lady friend and artist twenty years younger over whom Jay (unbeknownst to me and other friends) had been pining in his romantic way and whom he finally drummed up the nerve to call. For months I heard nothing from him—no calls, no messages, no invitations to come over for "pot luck." Then, once the silence was broken, it was announced that a companion and I were to be introduced to the mysterious Pam one evening at Ben Benson's Steak House in Manhattan. There at the bar sat Jay, cuddling not only an ample dry martini (despite strict orders from his doctor), but also the most attractive, charming, equally undersize gal imaginable. The two were like giddy teenagers on a first date, and Jay wasted no time breaking the news bluntly that 1) they were newly smitten with one another, 2) they shared the same interests, and 3) they were getting married during an upcoming trip to England. To this day, nobody (Jay and Pam included) has yet to come up with a sensible explanation of exactly why the marriage took place in England, but suffice it to say that since the momentous occasion, the lovebirds are virtually inseparable.

> LONDON, SEPTEMBER 1994—
>
> *Dinner at Ivy with Saint Delia Smith and hubby Michael. Everybody gawking at her, but she couldn't have cared less. Two million books sold! Hilarious when I forced her to eat her hamburger with her hands, à l'américaine, and watched it drip all over her. Must have shocked everybody in the place, but she's a good sport—and still so cute. An icon in the U.K., but unknown in U.S. Strange.*

But has Pam reformed Jay's slipshod ways, changed his social habits, or influenced his gastronomic activities? Not on your life. Together they share the same cramped digs in East Hampton when not at Pam's loft in Manhattan; together they tend a vegetable and flower garden that's larger than the house itself; together they throw the same outlandish feeds for the same ravenous vultures or come to my home for similar blowouts; and together they gluttonize foreign venues at every possible opportunity. Disgusted with the mounting prices, chaos, and pretentiousness in the Hamptons, they think seriously about pulling up stakes and migrating to the wilds of Pennsylvania, and they could easily make the move overnight, leaving me to grow my own arugula, go clamming alone, and fend for myself against the vulgarians. They're a reckless team cut from the same rough fabric, a couple of survivors who ask very little of destiny and yet somehow derive more satisfaction and joy from life than those with far greater social and financial advantages.

Meanwhile, Jay, Big Leroy, I, and any number of other Neanderthals continue to gather periodically around a gin bottle at the rickety table to talk food and solve the planet's problems, and over the years, I'd say I've learned more about the sources, nature, and preparation of the provender that sustains us from these guys than from any food magazine, cookbook, or cooking school. Jay's gout just gets worse as he religiously succumbs to his passion for crustaceans, organ meats, and spicy stews. And to gratify his irrepressible literary appetite and keep the wolf at bay, he still unfurls his erudite, waggish screeds in various magazines, in his eclectic books, and any place elsewhere his feisty pluck might be appreciated.

If the public has mistakenly perceived Jay Jacobs as (in his own words) "some sort of James Bond in the body of James Beard," at least to me he has always been bigger than life itself—and, to be sure, of a creative stature considerably more elevated than that of many heavyweight foodies secure in their phoniness and self-importance. Since I am a confessed elitist who subscribes vehemently to the notion that it's not the yahoos of this world who add anything to our lives, I thank my lucky stars to have been exposed to a few of the disfranchised but superior food writers like Jay who've had the courage and determination to buck the shallow system, confront an intractably fatuous, unfair, and often lethal world, and transform it in their work into a bright universe of intense color, mood, intelligence, and scrupulous honesty. M.F.K. Fisher took on the dangerous challenge, as did Richard Olney and Elizabeth David, and they would no doubt have joined me in endorsing Jay's elementary but cogent philosophy that "behind the soigné facade of any connoisseur of caviar, truffles, or pedigreed wines huddles a naked infant blindly groping for the breast, a toddler smearing its face with mashed potato, a sick child consoling itself with warm milk."

With Mother and restaurateur extraordinaire Sirio Maccione of Le Cirque on the Greek island of Santorini, 1998.

Robert Tréboux, proprietor of my home away from home, Le Veau d'Or restaurant in Manhattan.

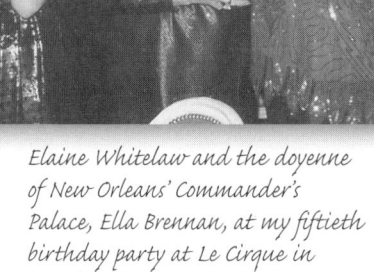

Elaine Whitelaw and the doyenne of New Orleans' Commander's Palace, Ella Brennan, at my fiftieth birthday party at Le Cirque in Manhattan, 1988.

Chef Jeremiah Tower at his restaurant, Stars, in San Francisco, 1990.

CHAPTER THIRTEEN

FEASTING WITH GIANTS

O N A BRISK FALL EVENING sometime in the late fifties, my mother, sister, and I, all dressed to the nines, followed my worldly father through the revolving door of Le Pavillon restaurant in New York and stood solemnly while he shook hands and exchanged a few pleasant words with the short, rotund, balding man standing archly at a small lectern in a double-breasted tuxedo. With a great swoop of the arm, the man escorted us to a nearby table, whisked the large, starched white napkins off the table and laid them in our laps, directed a waiter to pour flutes of Champagne by simply wiggling a finger in the air, and bowed slightly as he backed away.

A short while later, the same imperious man with round, tortoise-shell glasses returned. He carefully answered my father's questions about certain dishes in his distinctive French accent, nodded and shook his head in approval and disapproval, and finally, without so much as jotting down a single item on a pad, discreetly reeled off from memory our entire order to a hovering captain. Throughout the meal, he roamed the quiet, opulent room incessantly when not greeting guests at the door. He would dramatically scoop copious mounds of fresh beluga caviar from an ice-encased tin and supervise, closely inspect, and often stop to help a captain prepare tableside dishes. He would pour wine, replace ashtrays, and even remove dirty plates when things got too busy. What he would never do was peck arriving ladies on the cheek or pat gentlemen on the back, sit down at a table or linger standing to chitchat, or fail to ask if something was wrong with a half-eaten dish. Nothing escaped his concentrated attention, no detail was too small to be addressed personally, and while my inchoate knowledge of fine dining still had me at a disadvantage, I remember having the impression that no nonsense from his staff, the kitchen, or indeed the gold-plated customers was ever tolerated. The man's name was Henri Soulé, this was his exclusive domain, and, quite frankly, that first night he frightened me to death.

Throughout the fifties and into the sixties, Le Pavillon was considered not only one of the world's finest restaurants, but a magnet for the social elite, the international set, and captains of industry. Later, I did have a few more memorable meals there, chatted briefly and formally with Soulé, and watched the restaurateur in action. Since I was still busy becoming the great academic scholar, however, and Soulé died in 1966, much of my knowledge of the legendary man was derived from his many disciples who moved on to open their own prestigious French restaurants in Manhattan or become renowned chefs (Robert Meyzen at La Caravelle, Charles Masson at La Grenouille, Georges Briguet at le Périgord, Robert Tréboux at Le Manoir, Pierre Franey, Jacques Pépin, and many more). No matter the source of my inspiration, Soulé always stood out in my mind as the quintessential restaurateur, the example to be emulated in any distinguished restaurant, the monarch who set and maintained the highest standards imaginable and who could not be bullied by anybody. Soulé often said, *"Le Pavillon, c'est moi."* The restaurant was truly a Valhalla he rarely left, and indeed, after he died and less capable zealots tried to make a go of the place, Le Pavillon's days were numbered.

"Soulé really had no life outside his restaurant," Pierre Franey once told me. "His family was his staff, he didn't travel or socialize, and I don't think I ever saw the man relax. He himself admitted that his only hobby was paying the bills promptly."

No doubt Soulé was a benevolent autocrat, a perfectionist who cajoled, snarled, raged, and refused to make compromises on any level. In other words, he was an aristocrat, and his influence on the way luxury restaurants would be perceived and operated in the U.S. for years to come was monumental.

Mainly because of Soulé, I came to respect and revere nobody in my profession more than a legitimate restaurateur, and the fact that so few are left today to carry on the proud tradition he established remains a major frustration. The problem originated, of course, when, back in the early eighties, most restaurant management began to be assumed by newly liberated, upstart star chefs eager to operate their own restaurants and make big names for themselves all by themselves. The gastronomic revolution was in full swing, and while the movement would produce dozens of young, talented, creative chefs with startling new ideas, what diminished was the number of experienced, devoted, truly professional martinets necessary to coordinate day-to-day staff activities, oversee wine cellars, tend personally to the clientele, and generally transform otherwise ordinary restaurants into world-class institutions.

Fortunately, I was lucky enough to know and work with some of the most renowned restaurateurs in America and abroad, all standard-bearers of a proud legacy and some still blessedly as active today as they were twenty-five years ago. Just in New York City, to have witnessed Tom Margittai and Paul Kovi at the Four Seasons, Leon Lianides at the Coach House, Michael Tong at Shun Lee Palace, Faith Stewart-Gordon at the Russian Tea Room, Robert Meyzen at La Caravelle, and Sirio Maccioni at the original Le Cirque was to understand fully the canon that any superior restaurant is no more than the reflection of its owner's personal involvement and high principles. So intimately connected was Jovan Trboyevic with Le Perroquet in Chicago, Maude Chasen with Chasen's in Los Angeles, Lester Gruber with London Chop House in Detroit, and the Gotti brothers with Ernie's in San Francisco that when these giants died or retired, I knew instinctively that their unique creations couldn't last for long. These individuals could hardly chop onions, but each had a singular vision, and each demonstrated in no uncertain terms that, no matter how talented the chef, efficient the staff, and delectable the cuisine, a great restaurant, like a brilliant orchestra, must have a mighty conductor—a full-time conductor in residence.

LONDON, APRIL 1997—

Jennifer Patterson arrived at Dorchester for tea on motor scooter wearing sequined helmet, proceded to order a gin and tonic, and consumed almost a whole plate of sandwiches and pastries. We smoked, discussed clotted cream, and cursed health fanatics in America. I do adore this "fat lady"—and, damn, she knows about food.

Never one to worry or care about anonymity the way most of my fellow food writers do, I've always made it a point to get to know and associate as closely as possible with any restaurateur whom I admire. This certainly doesn't mean that I've compromised my ethics or professional responsibilities, pandered to superegos desperate for good reviews or coverage in feature food articles, or allowed my objectivity to be overruled by personal concerns. My philosophy has been simple: If I've held a restaurateur in high esteem, I've gone out of my way to establish a solid relationship; if not, I've kept my distance. No doubt some peers would scream foul and say that instinctively I've played favorites, exploited confidences, and, even on a hefty expense account, accepted the occasional free meal; and to some extent, perhaps they're right. What these same colleagues may not know, however, is that some of my most scathing restaurant reviews have been of disappointing meals proffered by eminent restaurateurs whom I respect and consider to be friends. After once tracking down the original crème brûlée in England, for example, I criticized in print the famous version at Le Cirque in New York as being utterly inauthentic and contrived—even though Sirio Maccioni had on several occasions placed the dish gratis on my table. Our heated argument continues to this day, but in the meantime, Sirio has taught me all about white truffles, risotto, *vin santo*, and numerous other foods and wines; we've shared bowls of gumbo in New Orleans and eaten barbecue together in Houston; and aboard the *Sea Goddess* in the Aegean, I've shown him how to prepare and eat an American hot dog correctly. We understand one another.

One of the most profound influences on my early career was Pearl Byrd Foster, owner of the tiny and exclusive Mr. & Mrs. Foster's Place in New York, who is still remembered for the way she insisted that customers order their complete dinners in advance over the phone and expected them to knock on the restaurant's front door upon arrival. Pearl was a tough lady, but once she'd taken me into her confidence, we not only dined together in Paris, London, and aboard the S.S. *France* when her restaurant was closed in August, but spent many a night in New York discussing what was right and wrong with American restaurants and cookery. Equally demanding was Jovan Trboyevic at Le Perroquet in Chicago, the man I once tagged as Soulé's legitimate successor and the despot who allowed me to work undercover in his famous restaurant in order to write about the experience and subjected me not only to his brilliant version of French nouvelle cuisine, but to an iron-handed discipline I'd never forget. Eventually bored with serving a fickle public, the melancholy Serb sold Le Perroquet (which soon closed forever), opened a more intimate, private bistro called Les Nomades strictly for his discerning friends, charged an annual membership fee of one dollar, and barred all journalists except me from the premises. After he retired completely, Jovan and I became drinking buddies in the more louche fleshpots of Chicago, New York, and San Francisco, gorged on foie gras and pigs' feet at Girardet in Switzerland and Chez Henri in Paris, and today still meet regularly hither and yonder to nourish our swollen livers and criticize the restaurant business.

Over the years, I've watched the late, oligarchic Joe Baum train brigades of captains, waiters, and busboys with military precision at Windows on the World and the Rainbow Room in New York, then slipped away with him to a bar to drink manhattans, chain smoke, and rap about restaurant management. At Gosman's Dock in Montauk on Long Island, I've studied the amazing ways that Roberta Gosman deals with unruly children (and often their parents), charts tables as if the restaurant served 75 instead of 750 customers on a busy night, checks every steamed-to-order lobster and broiled fluke that comes out of the kitchen to ensure quality, and, alas, cleverly changes the subject whenever I, like Craig Claiborne before me, beg for the cole slaw recipe.

At Tony's in Houston, I've not only seen the driven, obsessed, fastidious Tony Vallone storm back to the kitchen and almost throw a plate of overcooked pasta in the chef's face, but viewed the restaurateur's stupendous collection of different-sized tuxedos necessary to accommodate his ever-fluctuating weight and assure that his sartorial appearance is always impeccable. And I've had Ella Brennan pick me up in her vintage Rolls Royce at the New Orleans airport, drive me directly to Commander's Palace to sample Emeril Lagasse's latest creole dishes, and later, after bidding farewell to her last dinner customers, regale me and other pals at her house next-door with magnums of Taittinger and outlandish stories about Truman Capote and Paul Prudhomme's "pot cooking" and how she and her brother created Bananas Foster at Brennan's back in the forties.

Because of my unvarnished relationship with Ella, I didn't hesitate a second in the early seventies to call one night after tasting a certain sensational jambalaya on a hotel buffet and suggest she contact an unknown Cajun chef by the name of Paul Prudhomme. And had I not bonded with this most venerable of female restaurateurs, I would never have had the rare opportunity to watch her at Commander's Palace confront both Prudhomme and Legasse about new culinary ideas with such stern questions and observations as, "Does the dish really make sense?" "Are the ingredients indigenous to our area?" "The presentation is just too cute and pretentious for my customers," and "I think the roux stinks."

THE FAMILY OF RESTAURANTS
ELLA, DOTTIE, TI, LALLY, AND BRAD BRENNAN

June 1998

Dear Jim—

In response to your questions about how Bananas Foster was created—Around 1950, my brother, Owen, was appointed Vice Chairman of the Vice Commission by Mayor Chep Morrison—the Chairman was Richard Foster—and Owen loved to tease Dick that the Vice Chairman of Vice was a much more desirable position than Chairman.

One night they were to have dinner and Owen asked me to create a dessert to be named after Dick Foster. I was tossing around ideas and we came up with Bananas. New Orleans is a big banana-importing town and bananas were available all year round. So, we plodded along and began with sauté bananas (which was a dish my mother served with scrambled eggs and we all loved it). So, on we went. We added banana liqueur and rum and this dessert was getting good. Then, we added a base of vanilla ice cream. Then, we decided to sauté the bananas tableside using brown sugar and cinnamon. Then we used the cinnamon to flicker in the flame and the world loved it. It became the most popular dessert to this day.

We enjoyed your recent visit and look forward to seeing you in New York. We'll enjoy more of the city's fabulous restaurants.

Regards from *all* the family!

Fondly,

Ella

Ella Brennan

THE ORIGINAL BANANAS FOSTER

SERVES 2

¼ cup (½ stick) unsalted butter

¼ cup dark brown sugar

*2 ripe bananas, peeled and sliced
   lengthwise*

¼ teaspoon ground cinnamon

2 tablespoons banana liqueur

3 ounces light or dark rum

1½ cups French vanilla ice cream

In a flat chafing dish or skillet, melt the butter over medium-low heat. Add the brown sugar and stir till sugar has melted. Add the bananas and sauté till tender, about 3 minutes on each side.

Sprinkle the cinnamon over the bananas. Pour the banana liqueur and rum over the bananas, shake the pan to distribute the liquid, ignite the liquid, and baste the bananas with the flaming sauce till the flames die out.

Immediately serve the bananas and sauce over the ice cream.

I've fought rousing battles with Giselle Masson over outrageous wine prices at La Grenouille in New York, and had Vincent Bommarito at Tony's in Saint Louis cut me down to size when I arrogantly and stupidly tried to lecture him about gnocchi. Not long after first meeting Alice Waters and puffing a cigar at Restaurant Georges Blanc in Vonnas, France, I horrified her salubrious customers back at Chez Panisse in Berkeley, California, by lighting up after dinner. My relationship with Jean-Claude Vrinat at three-star Taillevent in Paris has been such that, convinced that Michelin is as obsessed with clean bathrooms as flawless cuisine and service, he once literally demonstrated for me the correct way to swab a toilet. And how else could I have convinced the otherwise discreet, arch, unflappable Jean-Pierre Chevallier at the Connaught in London to reveal exactly which sartorial sins disqualify one for a choice table in the luxurious restaurant if I hadn't made inordinate efforts to establish a close rapport?

Perhaps no restaurateur in the U.S. was more universally misunderstood and often loathed (except, of course, by his favored, loyal, upscale customers) than Glenn Bernbaum at Mortimer's in New York, for the way he snubbed the ordinary public; but I had utmost respect for the man and his controversial viewpoint, admired the ways he'd try to move mountains to learn about various foods and acquire the finest ingredients on earth for the simple dishes on his menu, and even met him once in the Périgord region of France to survey fresh goose livers used for foie gras. The problem was that Glenn refused to play games—with his staff and suppliers, with clientele, and indeed with fawning journalists frantic to report on the international celebrities who made Mortimer's their canteen and whom he was determined to protect. As with Soulé, his restaurant was his castle, guests were expected to observe a certain code of conduct suggestive of more gracious and enlightened times, and anybody who disagreed with his keen sense of propriety or disapproved of his strictly traditional cuisine were simply encouraged to stay away.

Since I lived around the corner from Mortimer's, I'd often stop by to talk food with Glenn at the same small table where, glued to a phone and glass of wine, he'd rant and rave with wholesalers, chat with the likes of Bill Blass, Nancy Reagan, and a contingent of royals, and carefully chart dinner tables for his small, exclusive flock of regulars. On one occasion, Glenn's new obsession happened to be classic American chicken hash—like that he'd had as a child. What was the best chicken hash I'd ever tasted? Did I have a really sophisticated recipe? The version he'd had his chef testing repeatedly just wasn't right—not the taste, not the texture, not the . . . pedigree. And damnit, if somebody could come up with a perfect chicken hash, he'd recognize it after a single bite.

For weeks he called about chicken hash. I provided recipe after recipe, tasted one example after the next, communed with chef Steve Attoe, and even enticed Paula Wolfert to help solve the great mystery. Still, nothing satisfied Glenn. Finally, fed up, one day I marched across the street to the coffee shop on the corner, asked the Greek cook to describe exactly how he made the hash I'd always found very respectable, gave the recipe to the chef at Mortimer's, and told him to keep the prank our secret.

"That's it! That's it! That's the hash I've been dreaming about!" Glenn roared ecstatically after we sat down to taste. And never till the day he died did he ever suspect that the wildly popular chicken hash he proudly added to his menu was the same as that served at a fraction of the price next door at the greasy spoon. Had he known, he would probably never have forgiven me.

My introduction to Jeremiah Tower took the form of a bold, sassy, but highly intelligent letter he wrote in the early eighties claiming that, contrary to what I'd stated in an article on San Francisco restaurants, it was he, not Alice Waters, who had created the new "California cuisine" while working at Chez Panisse. Despite my revulsion over this phony movement, it didn't take long for me to realize that Jeremiah himself was one of the most gifted, complex, and indeed eccentric men in the

Jeremiah's Garlic Soup with Ham and Sage Butter

Serves 6 to 8

15 garlic cloves, unpeeled

3 cups chicken stock

¼ cup diced cured country ham or prosciutto

5 fresh sage leaves

3 tablespoons butter, softened

Salt and freshly ground black pepper to taste

½ cup heavy cream

3 large egg yolks

In a large, heavy saucepan, combine the garlic cloves and stock and simmer over low heat till the cloves are soft, about 30 minutes. Let the mixture cool slightly, then puree it, using the fine-mesh disk of a food mill or a food processor. Press the mixture through a sieve back into the saucepan and set aside.

While the garlic is cooking, chop together very finely the ham and sage and place in a bowl. Add the butter and salt and pepper, mix till well blended, and set aside.

In a bowl, whisk together the cream and eggs and set aside.

Bring the garlic soup to a boil, remove from the heat, and gradually whisk in the cream and egg mixture till the soup is thickened slightly. (If soup does not thicken, return it to the heat for 1 minute while whisking but do not let it boil.) Ladle the soup into warm soup plates and spoon equal amounts of the ham-sage butter onto the center of each serving.

business. When Barbara Kafka and I donned hard hats in 1984 at the site where Stars was being constructed in San Francisco and listened to Jeremiah outline his plans for the American brasserie, I had no doubts whatever that the spectacular restaurant would transform the dining experience in America. Over the next fifteen years, I carefully followed the fashionable venue's evolution as Jeremiah produced some of the most innovative food the country had ever tasted, trained chefs and staff by literally taking and exposing them to some of the world's great restaurants in their spare time, exposed California premium wines like nobody else, and demonstrated how the perfect dining experience must involve an intimate partnership between the customer and the restaurant.

NEW YORK, MARCH 1984—

Mortimer's—Held official blind sardine tasting for article with Glenn B., Paula W., Bill Blass, Pat Brown, and Claudette Colbert. Expensive Rödels, Gravier Aínes, plus a few fancy Scandinavian and Portuguese and Greek. Winner: Port Clyde from Maine, 89 cents a can. Shocked!

Jeremiah could be as brutal and unforgiving as Henri Soulé when it came to enforcing his vision, and even I'd shiver when he'd notice a burnt-out lightbulb, or a napkin on the floor, or a waiter carrying glasses without a tray. But I also got to know his other, more waggish and patrician side, as when he once swaggered into a snazzy hotel lounge wearing a full-length white alpaca coat; or when, spotting the fins of a chrome-glistening '59 Lincoln Continental convertible sticking out the service door of a car dealership in San Francisco, he marched in and bought the vintage beauty; or when, after stoking ourselves with ample sufficiencies of beluga caviar and iced Stoli at a March of Dimes gourmet gala reception in Houston, we sneaked out in black tie to a notorious gay cowboy bar and danced the Texas two-step together as a throng of butch queens gawked in awe.

Then, a couple of years ago, poor business decisions, overwrought ambition, a refusal to compromise standards, and plain rotten luck finally turned Jeremiah's dream into a nightmare as Stars slipped out of his hands as tragically as when Soulé was once forced to temporarily close Le Pavillon for many of the same reasons. This, however, by no means diminishes the model that Jeremiah set not only for dozens of youngsters who worked under him and have moved on to emulate his example, but for professionals like myself eager to understand what makes and breaks a great restaurant.

"I learned first that nothing is more difficult to cope with in a successful restaurant than one rave review after the next, since the challenge to top one's self becomes more and more impossible," Tower opines today. "I learned also that arrogance and an exaggerated stance of authority can only bring about loss of staff respect and loyalty. And after trying to expand my operation, I learned, above all, that no world-class restaurant can maintain its edge for long unless the owner is there at all times—for the staff and for the customers."

This sort of honest and painful self-appraisal is rare indeed amongst egotistical restaurateurs. While I have absolutely no idea whether Jeremiah will eventually attempt somewhere to equal or surpass his success at Stars, if he does, my guess is that the place's fame will derive as much from the restaurateur's new awareness of sound management as from culinary brilliance.

In any evaluation of how fine restaurants are developed and supervised in today's turbulent world, a clear distinction must be made between restaurateurs and entrepreneurs—a distinction that, in my opinion, not only separates the grandees from the vulgarians, but governs the very future of the dining experience. I suppose it's all well and good to have the Drew Nieporents, Alan Stillmans, Rich Melmans, and slew of hot shots in Las Vegas forging monticolous empires from every direction. Greedy for money or fame or power or whatever, exigent luminaries like Daniel Boulud and Jean-Georges Vongerichten in New York, Marco-Pierre White and Gordon Ramsey in London, and Alain Ducasse in France are bound to make a fugitive impact on the ever-gullible public desperate for novelty as they expand their purviews and delegate responsibilities. And when even truly experienced and expert restaurateurs like Sirio Maccioni in New York, Piero Selvaggio in Los Angeles, and the younger Brennans of New Orleans and Houston can't resist the opportunity to plant new flags hither and yonder, I can only hope that these big-city, bold-type sentinels have learned more than I have over the past decades about what guarantees distinction and longevity.

In the meantime, I look for reassurance and inspiration in this country not in the cutting-edge, fashionable haunts operated by canny entrepreneurs and superstar chefs, but in the few remaining establishments run either by veteran impresarios or family members determined to safeguard a tradition. In New York, I certainly have tremendous interest in what relatively young professionals like Danny Meyer at Union Square Cafe and Gramercy Tavern, Terrence Brennan at Picholine and Artisinal, and Robert Caravaggi (son of the late Bruno of Quo Vadis fame) at Swifty's have already accomplished; and how can I not be impressed to see the offspring of Giselle Masson at La Grenouille, of Tony May at San Domenico, and of Lidia Bastianich at Felidia following in their parents' footsteps? The question is whether these eagerly ambitious individuals so readily susceptible to ever-changing popular tastes and overnight trends will one day attain the utter self-confidence and lofty stature of André and Rita Jammet at La Caravelle, Alex von Bidder at the Four Seasons, Georges Briguet at Le Périgord, and, certainly, the master of them all, Sirio Maccioni. Will they, in other words, build strong foundations and stick to one big vision, or will they succumb to all the fads and gimmicks that threaten to destroy the integrity of the whole business?

What's so ironic is that, contrary to what the snob food press and crazed restaurant guides would lead us to believe, some of the greatest restaurateurs left in the U.S. are not in the putatively sacred canyons of Manhattan or glitzy avenues of Hollywood, but are out where considerably more sanity still exists. Imagine, for example, what it feels like at the venerable Tony's in Saint Louis being greeted and attended to by the same savvy Vincent Bommarito who virtually introduced me to northern Italian cuisine over thirty years ago. Or to return after many years to Jasper's in Kansas City and find the familiar Josephine Mirabile and her son sustaining the standards introduced so long ago by Jasper, Sr. At the illustrious, decades-old La Maisonette in Cincinnati, Lee Comisar may have finally turned the reins over to son Michael, but neither the social hype, ubiquitous Adam Tihany designs, nor daft multicultural culinary trends that have infected more pretentious restaurants from coast to coast have fazed this place, with its tasteful setting, formal service, and impeccable classic cuisine.

It does my heart (and stomach) good to know that Chris and Alice Canlis are protecting the traditional Polynesian-American menu that has dazzled diners at Canlis in Seattle since the fifties, and why should I give a damn about Spago Beverly Hills, Campanile, Citrus, and Joachim Splichal's latest conceit in Los Angeles when, after a quarter century, Gerard and Virginie Ferry's dignified L'Orangerie still has the most splendid food, mind-boggling flowers, and polished, personalized service of any French restaurant in America.

In Chicago, Mary Beth Liccioni quietly but sternly carries on the legacy of Jovan Trboyevic at Les Nomades, while out in La Grange, Illinois, seasoned restaurateur Reinhard Barthel is not only totally content at Cafe 36 dealing with the reservation book, staff training, and wine list the way he's done for the past thirty-five years, but already prepping Reinhard, Jr. to step into his shoes when time comes to retire. I know I can rest assured that Tony Vallone (whose son Joey is already coming up in the ranks) will be kissing hands and ranting and perspiring nervously at his bespoke Tony's in Houston whenever I'm craving the rich seafood *linguine bucaniera* or inimitable roast duckling with fig sauce. And with not only Ella Brennan, but her younger sister Dottie and daughter Ti Adelaide holding down the front desk, testing the waiters on the most minute points of table service, and roaming the various dining rooms at Commander's Palace in New Orleans, I'm never in the least surprised when, once again, this Creole shrine operated by three dedicated women of different generations is proclaimed by various food and travel magazines to be one of the best restaurants in the U.S.

No matter when and where I've dined out over the past decades, the most important aspect of the experience has always been that elusive bliss, that bewitching rapture that the French call *le frisson*. It's a sensation that seizes me when I arrive at a restaurant and encounter not some postpubescent receptionist named Cindy or an aspiring thespian posing as a maitre d', but a recognizable director ready and willing to orchestrate the entire affair, proffer advice and maybe deliberate, and supervise every aspect of the meal as only a truly professional restaurateur with an invested interest can do. Until just a few years ago, these were always the commanders who lent integrity to the whole industry and made dining out the special adventure it should be, and today, as I follow the performances of developing candidates like Danny Meyer and Joseph Bastianich in New York, Michael Comisar in Cincinnati, and Ti Adelaide Martin in New Orleans, I have every reason to believe that there is evolving a newly enlightened generation of dedicated, hardworking, and even autocratic restaurateurs who might eventually provide that real sense of authority and know-how, that utter control, that intense involvement I find so essential to plenary customer satisfaction and enjoyment. No doubt these fresh stewards have already realized how competitive and downright deadly the restaurant business can be, but I hope they've also learned how critical it is to formulate and maintain a well-defined vision, to buck social crazes and fatuous trends, and to deal better than I could with those undiscerning clods responsible for transforming at least half the locales in this country into playpens and food laboratories. And who knows, some might even manage to create that *frisson* that can spell the difference between a mediocre fun house and a first-class, dignified institution.

Unfortunately, I can't resurrect Henri Soulé to serve as a model for those potential gastronomic skippers, but I can do the next best thing by steering them to an old-fashioned, neglected, glorious haven in

New York owned and operated by one of Soulé's few remaining active disciples, namely Robert Tréboux. It's no exaggeration to say that Le Veau d'Or has virtually been my second home for over forty years, even before I actually moved to the city and long before Tréboux bought the venerable restaurant in 1985. I first dined at Le Veau d'Or as a teenager with my parents. On the small red banquettes, I've negotiated a career change; fallen in and out of love; shared *les cuisses de grenouilles* and *la poularde en cocotte* with Craig Claiborne, Elaine Stritch, and Bobby Short; signed book contracts; watched Tennessee Williams pass out from too much chablis; and entertained a sundry contingent of students, colleagues, lovers, chefs, friends, and benign enemies. Nor is it an exaggeration to report that not one facet of the place—not the portrait of a sleeping calf and French photos on the walls, not the tiny mahogany bar, not the slightly eccentric clientele, and certainly not the classic French menu—has changed an iota since my first visit. Le Veau d'Or is in a time warp, a vestige of a gracious, unrepressed, utterly adult era in New York when three-hour lunches, Bombay martinis and flotillas of vintage Talbot, smoking, feathery *îles flottantes*, and perceptive conversation were hallmarks of the good life.

And directing all the outdated, almost decadent activity with an iron arm and beguiling smile is Monsieur Robert, assisted only by the former lordly maitre d' of the much lamented Laurent, Jimmy Rapacioli, and a Veau d'Or waiter of twenty-eight years, Thierry Leroy—both always decked out in neat tuxedos. It is true that Monsieur Robert is considerably more relaxed than Henri Soulé ever was, but while I've known the man since he ran Le Manoir back in the sixties and seventies, such is his breeding and training that it would be inconceivable for either of us to address the other by a simple first name. Never have I seen Monsieur Robert without a vested suit and handsome necktie, and despite the fact that the restaurant is never, ever full, I can't imagine going there without first calling to make a reservation since it's expected. In all these years, I've not once seen the kitchen or been introduced to the longtime chef, and as with most other regular customers accustomed to merely informing Monsieur Robert what they'd like to eat, I can't remember when I was last shown the never-changing menu.

To the best of my knowledge, Monsieur Robert, now in his mid seventies, has, in order of priority, exactly four passions: his restaurant, vintage Bordeaux wine, his grandchildren, and ravishingly beautiful women of any age. I don't think he knows or cares that other restaurants exist or that the world is in the throes of gastronomic revolution and change. Not only is he on the premises day and night, he also lives above the restaurant. When on the job, which is always, he greets customers at the door, checks coats, mixes drinks behind the bar, answers the phone, takes orders, discusses and pours wine when Jimmy and Thierry are busy, prepares dishes tableside in the old manner, and—*pace* Soulé—doesn't hesitate to flirt with the ladies or sit down momentarily with old friends or visiting chefs to discuss food and wine, relate bawdy tales, or vent his spleen about one topic or another.

If customer satisfaction (of friends and strangers alike) should be the first commandment in any serious restaurant, Monsieur Robert adheres to the doctrine in ways that would baffle if not shock most of his peers. Order a Pernod or Ricard at Le Veau d'Or, for instance, and in all likelihood the whole bottle of pastis, a small pitcher of water, and a glass of ice cubes will be placed on the table. Can't decide between the pâté and *céléri remoulade* as an appetizer? Portions of each are served on a single plate. Craving something not on the menu like *salade niçoise*, or steak tartare, or *poularde à la normande*, or just a soft omelette with *pommes frites*? Inform Monsieur Robert, and somehow the dish materializes. Complain that the air-conditioning is too chilly, and in minutes you're more comfortable. Mention that it's the birthday of someone in your party, or that there's a new baby, or that your beloved dog has just recovered from a serious illness, and chances are an iced bottle of champagne and special vase of fresh flowers will appear on the table. Express real enthusiasm over a certain claret you've ordered, and Monsieur Robert might not only ask excitedly to taste the wine but refuse to add it to the bill.

So should it be assumed at Le Veau d'Or that understanding, tolerance, and geniality are steadfast virtues extended automatically to all and that, according to the old adage, the customer is always right? Not on your life. Monsieur Robert is indeed the most courteous and accommodating restaurateur I know today, but disrupt the decorum of his refuge, question his inviolable standards, or insult him rudely and the same wrath that fired the potentate under whom he trained so many years ago can be unleashed. Once, when the restaurant was unusually busy, a woman and her husband, neither particularly well dressed, showed up for an early prix-fixe dinner and complained haughtily and loudly throughout the entire meal about the table location, food, service—everything. Demanding freshly brewed tea instead of the French coffee included on the special menu, the woman refused to listen as Monsieur Robert tried to explain that, with the pretheater rush, the small kitchen was simply not equipped at that time to brew a quick pot of tea. He apologized profusely and, against his better convictions, even offered her instant tea, but the incensed woman wouldn't let up, disturbing those around her and testing the owner's patience to the limit. Finally, Monsieur Robert drew back his head in Gallic outrage, informed the couple that there would be no bill, and told them bluntly never to return to his restaurant.

"Well, all I can say is it's no wonder this place is not full," the woman then huffed at the door.

"Madam," Monsieur Robert countered quietly with utter indignation that would have made Henri Soulé proud, "any fool can operate a full restaurant, but it takes a genius to successfully operate an empty one."

With Mother, preparing Thanksgiving dinner in East Hampton, 1985.

Martha Pearl Villas picking strawberries on the North Fork of Long Island, 1993.

With Mother, putting up her famous strawberry preserves, 1993.

CHAPTER FOURTEEN

IN THE END IS THE BEGINNING

ALTHOUGH THE JUNE SUN OVERHEAD is already hot enough to make the early morning air feel heavy, Mother sports a white long-sleeve shirt, a pair of loose khaki pants, and a spiffy straw hat as we leave the car and make our way deep into the remote, vast strawberry field on the north fork of eastern Long Island.

"Don't say I didn't warn you about wearing that skimpy golf shirt and those shorts," she nags, linking the handle of her large bucket over one arm while trying to position a small stool between two rows of bushes laden with fat, ripe strawberries. "Haven't you learned after all these years that chiggers will eat you alive?"

She leans down, plucks three luscious berries from the middle of one plant, and studies them carefully in the palm of her hand. "Lord, have you ever seen such beautiful berries? Pretty as our Southern ones, I do believe. And it looks like these bushes haven't even been touched. A dollar a quart. Can you imagine? Almost like the old days."

By the time I've begun picking not far away, Mother has already cleaned berries off the tops and centers of at least three plants and is maneuvering to sit on her stool in order to negotiate the full clusters down below.

"Ugh," she moans in exasperation, hesitant to lower her ample girth squarely on the stool till she's absolutely sure that it's firmly in place on the ground. "Honey, you better give me a hand over here," she directs. "I just can't pick the way I used to with these old joints. Makes me mad as a hornet."

Once she's settled, I watch momentarily as she resumes her labor with almost childlike enthusiasm, her short, chubby fingers rummaging about the clusters as she gathers the choicest berries and drops them carefully into the bucket. Already beads of perspiration have begun to drip from her silver hairline down her wrinkled face, and as she manipulates the fragile berries and globules of scarlet juice gradually stain the glabrous skin on the back of her hand, I notice how the surface blue veins and patches of brown spots only reinforce the fact that she's well into her eighth decade of life.

"Make sure you also pick the stems, so the berries don't bleed," she blurts as I return to my area. "And, for heaven's sake, son, do watch out for chiggers!"

Watch out for chiggers . . . Watch out for chiggers . . . The words ring in my memory, transporting me, for a moment, back some fifty-five or so years to a large strawberry field in Union County, North Carolina, about twenty miles from our home in Charlotte. It was another early warm June morning, and there, along with me, my younger sister, Mother, and Daddy, were my grandparents, Maw Maw and Paw Paw. At the edge of the field, an old farmer at his wooden stand passed out cardboard quart boxes, collected fifty cents a box, and told us that there were plenty of Cokes on ice in his red and white cooler.

"Remember y'all: the bushes are always fuller at the far end of the rows," Daddy reminded everybody as we followed him deep into the field.

From time to time, my sister and I would pop the largest, reddest, warm sweet berries into our mouths, only to hear Paw Paw warn, "You young'ins better watch out. Didn't I tell you that if you eat too many strawberries, they'll grow bushes in your stomachs?"

"Lord have mercy," Maw Maw exclaimed out loud, getting up from her stool after about thirty minutes, checking her boxes, and peering over at Mother. "You know, Martha Pearl, if we keep picking at this rate, we're gonna have enough strawberries for preserves, shortcake, *and* a big churn of ice cream."

Squatted in front of a large plant, Mother, her slender body clothed from head to toe and her long, radiant chestnut hair pulled back from her smooth face into a tight bun, was just standing up when I rushed over to proudly display my half-filled box of berries and continue picking next to her.

"Son, I see a little white on some of those strawberries," she reprimanded mildly, running her beautiful, still youthful fingers carefully through the lot, tossing the imperfect ones on the ground, and holding up a medium-size, bright red berry for me to observe. "Now look, if you're gonna help me put up preserves, you've gotta pick the right berries and stop eating every . . ." She suddenly noticed me scratching the inside of my thigh as we started picking together. "Unhuh. Chiggers!" she exclaimed sternly, reaching over to inspect my legs. "You wouldn't listen to me and your daddy when we told you about wearing shorts, and now . . . I'm telling you: You've got to watch out for chiggers!"

By ten o'clock, the Long Island sun is blazing. Our buckets overflowing with exquisite berries, Mother and I return to the rough country road to pay the farmer for our bounty, then drive to my home on the south fork so she can begin immediately to make the preserves that will last us through the year and help fill all her holiday gift packages. For years at home in North Carolina, Mother was never at a loss for relatives to participate in this annual summer ritual. But time passes, peo-

> EAST HAMPTON, MAY 1998—
>
> *If Julia Child can love Pepperidge Farm Gold Fish as much as Craig Claiborne loves Ruffles potato chips, why shouldn't I indulge my indiscriminate passion for peanut butter—crunchy? I eat some every day of my life. Ditto cocktail peanuts—Planter's only. Man does not live by truffles and foie gras alone, I say.*

ple disappear for one reason or another, and today there's only Mother and me left to carry on a tradition that is as sacred to her as making fruitcakes for Christmas. Of course every June when she comes to visit me on Long Island, she complains about her stiff knees and weak hands and threatens not to go strawberry picking. Then, after she rages about the poor quality and outrageous prices of market berries, prompting me to suggest that we just ride over and check the north-fork field, she inevitably forgets her ailments and off we go.

"I need a drink," she announces in the kitchen, reaching for the Bloody Mary mix while I begin rinsing some ten quarts of strawberries and placing them on paper towels spread out over every inch of counter space. "Now, sort them carefully, honey, and make sure the ones for preserves are firm and the same size," she instructs as if I hadn't been through the procedure a hundred times over the years. She then opens a new package of pectin, measures cups of sugar, and takes a big slug of her restorative libation.

Cooking strawberries for preserves is a very serious and private affair for Mother, and nobody, not even my neighbor Craig Claiborne when he was alive, would ever risk distracting her. Once the hulled berries are in a big kettle and the first measurement of sugar is added, I step away as she brings the mixture very slowly to a boil and begins stirring attentively with a large wooden spoon. More sugar, a little lemon juice, a slight heat adjustment, then further careful stirring as she quietly watches the berries gradually yield their juices, blend with the melted sugar, and almost magically turn a deep, glistening red. Her concentration is intense.

"Quick, help me move this pot off the heat," she suddenly directs, lifting one side of the large vessel up before I can grab the other side.

"I thought you said you had no strength left in your hands," I jest.

"Hush. I don't have time to think about that now," she huffs, stirring pectin into the mixture. "Have you got those bowls ready?"

Together we slowly pour the hot berries into two large mixing bowls, after which Mother begins the tedious but important task of skimming foam off the tops so that the preserves will not be cloudy.

"Here," she says, handing me the spoon, "stir them steadily till they cool slightly and begin to thicken. I'm dead." She wipes her hands on her apron and reaches for her drink.

Quite often, the cooled strawberries must stand overnight so that they will jell and plump enough to remain in suspension when preserved. After we've had lunch and taken well-deserved naps, however, Mother determines by early evening that the texture and consistency of the berries are already ideal, rousing her to begin sterilizing half-pint canning jars and lids in a steaming water bath while I melt paraffin in a saucepan. At one point, she drops a lid on the floor and asks me to pick it up, complaining about how she can't bend down that far.

"Sometime I'd like to drop a hundred dollar bill on the ground and watch you scramble for *that!*" I jeer.

"Smart aleck," she mumbles, popping me on the rear.

As I ladle luxurious preserves into the jars, Mother, with her experienced and expert touch, pours hot paraffin over the tops, slowly tilts each jar back and forth till the waxy substance begins to set and seal every edge, and caps each with a lid and ring band as a precaution against any improbable but always possible seepage. We then take each jar and apply a label that reads "From Martha's Kitchen."

"Pretty, aren't they?" Mother comments quietly, standing back with her tired hands on her hips and surveying the twenty-odd jars lined up across the counter. "But Lord, that's a lot of work and . . . well, honey, I really do think my strawberry-picking days are over."

Playfully I put my arm around her broad waist, tell her not to be so ridiculous, and suggest that she go change clothes so I can take her for a good dinner. Outside, the warm setting summer sun now filters gently through the towering oak trees, and as I gaze wistfully at this season's fresh, brilliantly red preserves that will bring such happiness to so many, I'm once again seized by all sorts of confused childhood, adolescent, and even recent nostalgia pertaining to the lady known to family as Martha Pearl, to friends simply as Martha, and to me as Mother, Missy, Big Mama, and, when she gets particularly overbearing, Brunhilde.

MOTHER'S STRAWBERRY PRESERVES

YIELD: 4 HALF-PINT JARS

1 quart fresh, ripe, firm strawberries, stemmed and washed

4 cups granulated sugar

2 teaspoons fresh lemon juice

2 tablespoons pectin (Certo)

If the strawberries are very large, cut them in half. In a large saucepan, combine the strawberries and 2 cups of the sugar. Bring slowly to a boil and cook rapidly 5 minutes, stirring all the while. Add the remaining sugar, return to a boil, and cook 10 minutes longer, stirring in the lemon juice about 2 minutes before removing pan from the heat. Add the pectin and stir well.

Pour the mixture into a large mixing bowl. Skim off as much foam as possible, cover with plastic wrap, and let stand till the berries are fully plump (at least 6 hours and possibly overnight), stirring occasionally.

Spoon the strawberries into hot, sterilized jars and seal with hot paraffin. When the paraffin is fully cooled, screw lids onto the jars. Store the preserves in a cool area and let age at least 2 months.

I can't remember everything exactly, but I know the war was still raging overseas and that, due to strict rationing, Mother was forced to use not only white margarine instead of butter, but also minimum sugar for the jelly treats I'd help her make. It's my first memory of cooking with her, a happy time when she'd show me how to roll small balls of dough between the palms of my hands, make indentions in the balls with a floured finger, then fill the holes with smidgeons of her homemade preserves. My next responsibility was to watch the cookies carefully as they baked. If I started fooling around while Mother was busy with other cooking and allowed them to overbrown, the tongue lashing could be severe—followed, of course, by a consoling hug and explanation of why I had to learn to pay more attention to serious matters like baking cookies and making biscuits and . . .

"Son, if I've told you once I've told you a hundred times not to handle that dough so much," she fumes when we're making buttermilk biscuits some years later. As usual, she has used only soft, Southern Red Band flour and Crisco shortening, measured none of the ingredients, and is watching like a hawk every move I make. Disregarding the timer as she peeps through the glass on the oven door, she commands, "Take 'em out, they're done." To my eye, the biscuits don't appear nearly brown enough, and I say so. "I'm telling you to take 'em out *this second* or they'll be hard as rocks," she insists as I continue to argue. "Lord, how stubborn can you be?" Out they come, and sure enough, despite the unmeasured ingredients, and reduced cooking time, and my wounded pride, the biscuits are as puffy and even and golden and perfect as every batch she's ever baked to accompany our beloved short ribs of beef . . .

"You've been playing around again, and you've absolutely ruined these ribs," she barks after a first bite of short ribs I've modified by adding green olives and a few fresh herbs. "You know, Buster, you still haven't got it through your thick head that the secret of great Southern food is its natural simplicity. Southern short ribs of beef are *not* French pot-au-feu (pronounced "potty foo").

French pot-au-feu. Just the name evokes still another random, distant image of Mother sitting on the edge of her and Daddy's bed in her frilly nightgown and dropping quarters into small paper cylinders. Times are still lean after the war, Daddy has a job selling trucks after having worked for the government supervising the local rationing of gasoline, but nothing will do but for Mother to save enough money so that we can splurge one night at a fancy French restaurant during a planned trip to New York City to visit relatives. That extra money might well go toward a down payment for a washing machine or spent on a new dress. She knows, however, that Daddy is eager to take her, my sister, and me to a deluxe restaurant he's heard about called Le Chambord, and as she sees it, what does another small personal sacrifice matter if she can help to make her family happy? So she collects her quarters and dollar bills month after month, she even finds a way to buy me a new blue suit for the anticipated occasion, and at the restaurant she and Daddy order a glorious pot-au-feu that she will insist for years to come is the greatest dish she's ever tasted.

No doubt food and cooking have always been the major catalyst in my long, complex, and often labored relationship with my mother. But to explain the most important force in my life merely in terms of gustatory affinities not only misrepresents this most sacred of unions, but reduces the close bond we've established over the past six decades to an almost casual substantiality. Thousands of sons have acknowledged either the beneficial or the malevolent influences of their mothers, usually from the perspective of an adult distanced by geography or marriage or both. As a single gay man, by contrast, I have always maintained the proverbial childhood link with my mother that psychiatrists love to analyze in such depth, an alliance that neither time nor space nor different lifestyles have ever altered in the least. Others come to refer to their mothers as a friend, a confidant, or a pal. My mother is none of these to me. She is simply my mother, the same mother who nursed and corrected and spanked me when I was a child, the one who taught me how to cook at her knee, and the irrepressible, feisty, remarkable lady who can do no wrong. She's on a pedestal—and this, as I see it, is the way it should be.

Southerners tend to be family-oriented in the extreme. I never was and still have little in common with relatives other than my mother. I loved and respected my father in the ancient Greek tradition that is in my veins, and his influence on my social and intellectual development was profound—especially in the area of dining sophistication. But even his impact on my life was modest compared with that of Mother's. She was the family bulwark while I was growing up, the one who saw to it that I was never in need of clothing or money or attention, the one who encouraged me to take piano lessons even though she had no interest at all in classical music, the one who supervised my schooling and spent grueling hours helping me with homework, and of course, the one who instilled in me a love of cooking. No doubt Mother perceived instinctively at an early date that I was cut from a different cloth than that of my classmates—a loner determined to map out and follow his own direction. And when the time came for me to seek new horizons while my friends remained safely in the nest, it was Mother who never once questioned my intentions and lent full material and emotional support. She understood me.

Those who have read the three books that Mother and I have coauthored on her Southern cooking were exposed not only to her amazing culinary abilities, but also to multiple facets of our unique partnership in and out of the kitchen. They got to know a gracious but stern lady who tolerates no nonsense when it comes to her vast legacy of Southern dishes, just as they became acquainted with a highly opinionated, often difficult, but respectful son. They followed us through peach orchards, oyster beds, blackberry patches, and remote mountain hamlets in search of luscious country hams. They learned how to cut up and fry chicken properly, make congealed salads and pimento cheese, and even produce Carolina pork barbecue. And they were privy to our heated debates over the most minute cooking problems, our constant fussing with one another, and the conflicts that erupt when two strong-minded individuals assert their sense of authority. All the arguments, cajoling, and hilarity were, of course, legitimate, and I think we did manage to convey the true spirit of Southern cooking. However, like most cookbooks, which by their very nature must project a superficial idealism that appeals to a mass middle-class audience, these hardly delved into the more intimate aspects of Mother's and my personalities or attempted to explain how we've managed to function so well together for so many years.

VENICE, OCTOBER 1998—

Here at Cipriani with Mother to teach a week of classes on Southern cooking. Julia Child arrived yesterday to follow us on Monday, and all she wanted was for Mother to teach her how to fry chicken and make buttermilk biscuits. Amazing woman.

And contrary to certain impressions one might get from the books, our lives actually couldn't be more antithetical, a fact known only to our closest friends and one that has engendered more than a little frustration and, at times, anguish for us both. Mother is a very outgoing, social lady who gets along with anybody; I'm basically a solitary. Having had little education, she shares none of my literary or musical passions, the highlight of her weekdays being a series of afternoon TV soap operas, which subject her apartment and my house to hours of romantic mush that drives me up the wall. A devoted fan of *Reader's Digest* and heart-throb novels, Mother can't imagine what I find engrossing about the London *Spectator*, *Opera News*, the *New Yorker*, and Kazuo Ishiguro, and she calls me a snob. When not discussing food or travel, her idea of engaging conversation revolves mostly around family and others' children, subjects I find repellent. She forever challenges my deep-rooted cynicism with her eternal optimism, and while I'm a self-centered, neurotic misanthrope, her compassion for others is as selfless as it is genuine. I envy her sunny disposition and wish I could imitate it.

For whatever reasons, much of our respective lives remains shrouded in or camouflaged by enigma and paradox. Why around

Mother, for instance, my Southern accent suddenly deepens and my overall vocabulary and mien become almost sloven I can't explain. Generally, I curse like a drunken sailor, but in front of my mother I can't bring myself to utter so much as an innocuous "damn"—much less a more characteristic "goddamn." While I do consult her on virtually every food topic I write about, a literary profile or a piece of fiction is work that I keep confidential. Nothing is more important to Mother than her religious beliefs and involvement in the church, but since I gave up on God decades ago, her fervor remains a very private and mysterious affair. As for my homosexuality, the subject has never once been broached and probably never will be. First, I respect fully that Southern ladies of my mother's generation have never been comfortable confronting openly such delicate matters. Second, even when I was young and active, I never felt the need to reveal and deliberate my sexuality with my parents, and to do so today with Mother would be an exercise that even she would find ludicrous and embarrassing. No doubt her wise motherly instincts informed her of my libidinous proclivities long before I myself came to terms with my sexual makeup, and while I know she wouldn't hesitate a moment to discuss this facet of my life if I so chose, I also know that our Southern breeding has always precluded sex on any level as an appropriate topic of conversation. And that's the way it should be.

I am one who fiercely believes that it's a son's or daughter's moral duty to repay parents who made tough and repeated sacrifices to assure a child's well-being. In most areas and with most people, I hardly consider myself very charitable, but when it comes to my mother, I profess that much of my adult life has been spent trying to show my appreciation and bring the same happiness to her that she's given to me and so many others. Not that I pretend to be noble, but I don't forget the deprivation of the war years, or the way she was forced for so long to care for not one but two aged grandmothers, or the utter hell she endured when my sister was stricken with a near-fatal brain aneurysm that rendered her an invalid and destroyed most of her personality. I remember the homemade cookies and toilet paper and extra money that Mother mailed three thousand miles away every month when I was a student in France. It made me proud that for more than twenty years she never once failed to send an enormous carton of baked Christmas goodies to the staff at *Town & Country*. And how could a son not be beholden to a mother who, on her own lone initiative and with typical authority, dealt with the deaths of two of my beloved dogs by combing the back roads of North Carolina till she found suitable replacements? No, indeed, the explanations of my filial devotion and love extend far beyond the narrow confines of a kitchen, and if it's no more in my neurasthenic nature to constantly hug and kiss and make a fuss over her the way others do so obligingly with a parent, I never doubt for a moment that she senses the emotions. And, I'm convinced, that's the way it should be.

In addition to giving Mother material goods as she did for me when I was young and needy, I also began years ago involving her in my professional food world—especially after my father died—in hopes that this would add new dimension to and perhaps prolong her very active and energetic life. Little did I know at the time how the casual collaboration would evolve, but the truth is that it not only produced three successful cookbooks but turned Mother into an octogenarian celebrity, the darling of chefs and the media alike. Craig Claiborne and Pierre Franey used to beg her for recipes, Paul Bocuse adores her, Paula Wolfert calls her for cooking advice, and when she was invited to conduct classes at the prestigious Cipriani Cooking School in Venice, none other than Julia Child (there also to teach) engaged her in intense discussion on the correct way to make Southern fried chicken and buttermilk biscuits. She's demonstrated her dishes on *Good Morning America*, the Food Network, and other national broadcast outlets, and when we were both interviewed recently aboard the *QE2*, the throngs who lined up afterward at a book signing were there to meet not me but my crazy mother. Of course, she pretends indifference to all the attention and rebels when I accuse her mockingly of being a ham, but I know that deep down she relishes it all. As for myself, I beam with pride and satisfaction.

SOUTHERN BUTTERMILK BISCUITS

YIELD: ABOUT 16 BISCUITS

2 cups all-purpose flour

4 teaspoons baking powder

½ teaspoon baking soda

½ teaspoon salt

¼ cup Crisco shortening

1 cup buttermilk

Preheat the oven to 450° F.

Sift together the flour, baking powder, baking soda, and salt into a large mixing bowl, add the shortening, and cut it in with a pastry cutter or two knives till the mixture is well blended and mealy. Add the buttermilk and mix with a large spoon till the dough is soft, adding a little more buttermilk if necessary.

Turn the dough out onto a lightly floured surface and, using a light touch, turn the edges of the dough toward the middle, pressing with your hands. (Do not overwork the dough.) Press the dough out to a ¼-inch thickness (do not roll with a rolling pin), cut straight down into even rounds with a biscuit cutter or small juice glass, and place the rounds ½ inch apart on a large baking sheet. Gather up the scraps of dough and repeat the procedure. Bake the biscuits just till lightly browned on top, about 12 minutes.

Perhaps the most amazing and revealing aspect of my long association with Mother is how I perceive her uncanny wisdom today to be as sharp as when she was ruling the roost at home some half a century ago. After years of challenging her cooking ideas and techniques and, as she says, "fooling around," I've come to the grudging realization that, dammit, with few exceptions, she's always right in the kitchen. Her instinctive ability to whip up perfect fresh mayonnaise and virtually any style sauce without glancing even at her sacred but impossibly jumbled black "receipt" book, to turn out homemade bread and pastry with the same ease as she does intricate needlepoint, to butcher anything from a chicken to a thirty-pound pig, and to transform the most rudimentary of ingredients into sumptuous feasts with no more than her time-tested old battered pots and pans—these are talents and practices and habits that defy interference and make a mockery of most novelties in today's fickle culinary world. "You'll learn someday, son," Mother has ribbed more often than I care to remember when I've done something stupid, "but just like when you were a child, you'll have to learn the hard way." Indeed.

Equally intimidating has been the way my tastes in food, after years of putatively sophisticated transformation, have devolved almost inscrutably to those of my mother's. No longer, for example, do I like any fish or steak gussied up with a sauce. I'd rather have it simply broiled or grilled with minimum seasoning—and preferably at a fine seafood emporium or steakhouse. Beans and peas taste utterly bland unless they're fully cooked with a small piece of pork fat; a great shrimp and corn chowder is eminently more satisfying than a rich lobster bisque; and having for years rejected with contempt all congealed salads and meat casseroles, I now prepare and serve them as proudly and regularly as Mother does. Because of her, I've learned how delectable a full summer meal of nothing but fresh vegetables can be. She's taught me not only the virtues of using only soft winter flour for baked goods, only white cornmeal, and only Crisco shortening, but also convinced me that Greek feta cheese is far superior to Bulgarian, that no onion on earth can equal genuine Vidalias, that kosher and sea salts are overrated, and that the biggest rip-offs in gastronomic history are overpriced extra-virgin olive oils and balsamic vinegars. Mother has always loathed catsup, and just in the past year, I've even noticed that I'm no longer squeezing it on my hamburgers. Don't ask me to explain.

While I've never subjected Mother intentionally to my emotional problems, she's quick to pick up on any mood changes, any hysterics, and any bouts with frustration and despair. Something so trivial as a glitch in our travel plans, a screwed-up restaurant reservation, or a punctuation change in a manuscript can so threaten my damnable perfectionism that I'm driven to distraction. And if I so much as casually allude to the problem, she still has that unique ability to grasp the issue immediately, empathize, and, if necessary, reprimand sternly.

> PARIS, MARCH 2001—
>
> *Mother and I here to celebrate her 85th birthday and returned to Lasserre for first time in almost 15 yrs. Terrine de foie gras (with glass of Suduiraut), huîtres gratinées, canard rôti aux mandarines, pommes soufflées, marquise au chocolat, and '90 Ch. Lascombes. I practically wept, not because the classic cuisine was as perfect and exquisite as ever, but because it simply no longer exists in ultratrendy New York.*

"As I used to tell your daddy," I've heard her bark more than once when she sensed that my complaint was exaggerated or foolish, "it's absurd to get so upset over something you can't do anything about. There're just too many other important things to worry about in this life to allow a bunch of nonsense to get you down. So shape up." Of course, it's shameful to realize that I'm still being addressed as a child, but curiously, after one of her facile but wise lectures, the distress does seem to disappear. As it should.

Where Mother and I do differ radically is in our individual lifestyles, a factor that creates some tension when we spend long periods of time together traveling or working on a cookbook. Alone in her apartment, she likes a noon lunch followed by her soaps, her thoughts begin dwelling on the Jack Daniel's bottle by late afternoon, and she prefers to dine no later than eight o'clock and retire early. I, by contrast, am accustomed at home to putting off lunch (especially when writing) till midafternoon, not starting cocktails till well after dark, eating around ten, and often not going to bed till two in the morning. Somehow we reach a compromise when she visits or we're traveling, but only after considerable haggling and her reminding me repeatedly how ridiculously eccentric and abnormal my way of life has become. Also, I must have an afternoon nap no matter where, which irritates her almost as much as her soaps drive me nuts. I've always suspected that this is what marriage must be like, and when I say so, she simply glares suspiciously, then rolls her eyes the way she does when I ask a dumb question about cooking.

Since we both religiously eat three well-balanced meals a day, much of our time together is spent either shopping for food and cooking or going to restaurants. Neither of us pays the least bit of attention to the possible dangers of excess weight, cholesterol, alcohol, and the like; and pity the poor soul who dares to bring up the subject of dieting around my mother.

"Listen," she once coldly informed a certain zealous health fanatic, "my mama lived into her nineties and ate bacon and cornbread every day of her life. I'm in my eighties and overweight, but I eat anything I want, I drink plenty of wine and hard liquor, I've never swallowed a single vitamin pill, and I'm still going strong. Jimmy never diets either, and if he'd just stop smoking those stinking cigarettes, he'd probably live as long as I have."

It's true that for her age, Mother is remarkably fit and independent, so much so that despite my worry and futile protests, she thinks nothing of loading the trunk of her big Buick with sacks of Southern flour, pickling ingredients, a country ham, fresh butter beans and tomatoes, an ice-cream churn, bottles of cut-rate Jack Daniel's, and Lord knows what else and driving seven hundred miles from Charlotte to East Hampton. Yet every time I notice the thinning silver hair and vaporous blue eyes, detect a momentary languor in her otherwise alert voice, or watch her bravely negotiate a set of stairs as the tyranny of time claims victory over her knees, I do wonder how many more berry-picking days are left.

When she complains occasionally about decrepitude, I simply tell her it's laziness or all in her head, and since this infuriates her, I go a step further and project that she'll outlive me—not an unlikely prospect given my reckless ways. The reality, of course, is that now I can't imagine a world without the mother who's always been there to teach, encourage, console, and accept what others can't tolerate. The author William Maxwell said it all when he spoke of the "shine" that disappeared from his life after his mother's death. That's no doubt a sobering insight, but at least for the time being, I know that as long as Big Mama is still around to roam farmers' markets, bake fruitcakes, put up pickles for friends, and remind me about chiggers, the universe remains a bright place where warm strawberry fields extend forever.

*In my element and
properly dressed:
aboard the QE2, 1999.*

*With maitre d' David Chambers and
muse Alex Birnbaum at my usual table
in the Queen's Grill aboard the QE2, 1999.*

*With Paula Wolfert
in Finland, 1988.*

AN OPTIMISTIC REBEL

F I WERE ASKED TODAY why I chose to devote most of my working life to food writing, my only honest answer would be first, that after abandoning the teaching profession, I was unwilling to make the enormous sacrifices necessary to test my worth as a novelist; and second, that I had the career virtually handed to me on the proverbial silver platter when, out of the blue and with minimum qualifications, I was made the food and wine editor of *Town & Country* in the early seventies. That I've never considered my craft to be anything but a respectable way to make a living (and certainly no "art") should be taken for granted, but it's equally true that once I embarked on the vocation, my capacity for hard work and curiosity, literary ambition, and determination to cut a different cloth had no bounds. Given the highly subjective and elusive nature of the subject, writing about the sensual experience of eating and drinking has never been an easy task. As I learned early on, when a writer takes it upon himself, as I did, to relate gustatory pleasures to various social, cultural, and philosophical aspects of our lives, he walks a tight wire that can snap at any moment. Over the years, I've worked for—and with—some of the most brilliant magazine and book editors in the business, most of whom have respected my refusal to provide what amounted to one hundred ways to prepare chicken cutlets and do a laundry list of the hippest sushi restaurants in America, and who actually encouraged me to establish a distinctive platform, explore charted and uncharted territories, and produce material—no matter how unorthodox or unfashionable—that I felt would appeal to everyday readers. Sometimes my ideas have backfired, and topic discussions with colleagues could become heated, but even when I was guilty of poor judgment or a distorted point of view, rarely was I asked to compromise my basic standards pertaining to food and restaurants just to placate testy advertisers and inflated egos.

After serving all those years as the freelance food and wine editor of *Town & Country*, it became painfully obvious by 1999 that my fourth and final editor in chief and I had radically different perceptions of what the magazine's food-and-drink coverage should be. Despite the gastronomic revolution raging in every corner of the world, gone were the venturesome articles on ethnic and regional culinary traditions, exciting new food discoveries, enticing recipes, and great wines. It didn't take a wizard to recognize that essentially all I was expected to do was produce one fluff restaurant review after the next, profile restaurant celebrities, and repeat the same tired, predictable advice to readers on dining strategy and conduct found in every homogenized travel magazine in America.

And the irony was that, all the while, I was virtually starving to death. Actually, I can almost pinpoint the moment when I suddenly came to the sober and somber realization that, contrary to all the ecstatic proclamations by the ever-gullible food press, the proliferation of trendy cookbooks, and the wildly buoyant Zagat restaurant surveys, gastronomy in America had evolved into nothing more than a sick joke. The doleful epiphany began one night a few years ago in New York while I was dining at Lespinasse with the intention of reviewing the luxurious, putatively French restaurant for *Town & Country*. With me was the renowned Chicago restaurateur Jovan Trboyevic, the man who introduced nouvelle cuisine to America and in whose legendary restaurant, Le Perroquet, I'd once worked as an undercover table captain, an outrageous experience related in *Esquire*. Nobody had or has a more adventurous appetite and refined palate than Jovan, but when the menu was presented, the tortured expression on his face was equaled only by the sharp and foreboding chill that shot down my spine.

"I thought this was supposed to be a serious French restaurant, not a kindergarten," he snarled, pointing out a seared red snapper in an herbed broth seasoned with Asian five-spice powder.

My heart sank even more as I continued to struggle through the items on the menu. "All I can tell you is that the Swiss chef was born in Singapore, worked under Fredy Girardet, and is New York's most talked about recent young Turk," I volunteered. "Maybe that should tell us something."

Utterly baffled by most of the dishes yet determined to do my job, I finally settled helplessly on a concoction of fresh tuna mixed with two caviars, which came surrounded by strange, dense, colorful dots on an enormous plate, followed by some form of lamb immersed in a cloying carrot emulsion with no less than nine other ingredients. Thinking that *bouillon aux champignons* sounded relatively safe, Jovan ended up with a weird spicy-sour shimeji mushroom broth reeking of lemongrass and . . . pineapple juice, but even that abomination couldn't hold a candle to a bleeding piece of salmon perched atop fried strips of artichoke in a muddy wine reduction flavored with ground chestnuts and an Indian fruit identified as *kokum*. The wine we ordered, a fine French burgundy, was silly with this sort of food, and by the time the waiter returned to suggest a banana-chocolate soufflé, nausea had already begun to rumble in the pit of my stomach. Jovan returned to his hotel and finished a pack of Rolaids; I returned to my apartment and promptly vomited. Two weeks later, the *New York Times* proclaimed Lespinasse an extraordinary French restaurant and awarded it the highest rating of four stars. I was baffled, but then, what did I know?

Not, mind you, that I hadn't spent the last decade observing and criticizing the gradual fallout wrought by *la cuisine santé, la nuova cucina,* Modern British Food, and New American Cuisine, believing naively that such asinine notions would eventually fade away and that sanity would return to the kitchens of the world. From the beginning of my career, I'd championed all forms of traditional cooking while acknowledging the need for any cuisine to evolve slowly and sensibly. I'd called for a more probing investigation of regional foods and wines, and I'd railed against flippant novelty that was passing as important innovation and that sought to destroy what had taken centuries to develop worldwide. At first I was totally receptive to the intelligent concepts and exciting changes effected by Paul Bocuse, the Troisgros brothers, and other serious French exponents of the inaugural nouvelle cuisine, but when it became apparent that their original ideas were leading to total abuse and distortion in the childish hands of inexperienced, arrogant French, American, British, German, and even Italian chefs out to reinvent the kettle overnight, I was ready to wage battle when and where it was merited.

In this country, I'm sure I was the only food writer repelled by all of Alice Waters's fatuous hype about organic foods and "environmental consciousness," having not only been raised in the South on farm-fresh chickens and homegrown produce (like thousands of others), but exposed repeatedly to leading professional chefs like Pierre Franey, André Soltner, Richard Olney, and Madeleine Kamman—not to mention my own mother—who were as fastidious about the provenance and quality of their ingredients as about their classic approaches to cooking. I considered Wolfgang Puck and his contrived creations a national disaster, and with the single exception of Jeremiah Tower, who gradually developed a highly original but sensible style of regional cooking based on classic principles, I found virtually every practitioner of wacky "California cuisine" an embarrassment to the proud traditions upheld by James Beard, Julia Child, and Craig Claiborne.

If all the frenzy had remained contained in the unholy state of California, perhaps my trepidation and revulsion would have eventually dissipated, but the virus began to spread all across the country. Hordes of pubescent, brash, superstar chefs jumped on the pretentious bandwagon of *mâche*, cuttlefish ink, organic blue potatoes, exotic chili peppers, goat-cheese ravioli, raw duck breasts, tabbouleh, and cutesy pizzas. The health gestapo initiated its campaign against a host of culprits threatening the very future of mankind. Top food critics and cookbook publishers embraced any new culinary idea, any unfamiliar ingredient, and any offbeat cooking technique. And meanwhile, American food was being transformed into muck—all in the reckless name of novelty, novelty, novelty. By the mid nineties, the era of gastropornography was in full swing, and by the time I barely survived that splenetic meal at Lespinasse, chocolate martinis, tuna roe, vegetable foams, and ovo-lacto dishes were rearing their ugly heads from Santa Fe to Atlanta. Entire cookbooks on low-cal spa cuisine, salsas, weird grains, Pacific Rim food, and Italian bruschetta masquerading as cardinal components of American cookery were sprouting, and "The Naked Chef," "Iron Chef," "Molto Mario," and the two "Hot Tamales" would soon be proclaimed the new culinary masters of the universe.

Still, even while most of my peers were endorsing cheap celebrity and delivering messianic reports on beet sorbet with thyme gêlée and candied pomelo, sardine sushi, yellowtail tuna with Banyuls-ponzu sauce, and ragout of braised farro, I continued to applaud the exciting, often brilliant interpretations of both classical and regional fare tendered by such keen-minded experts in this country as Paul Prudhomme, Jasper White, Lidia Bastianich, Daniel Boulud, Joyce Goldstein, and yes, Emeril Lagasse. I respected the adult, cogent writing of John Thorne, Jay Jacobs, Jean Anderson, Betty Fussell, Barbara Kafka, John Mariani, and Jane and Michael Stern, and I rallied when the Food Network had the courage to broadcast the amazing Two Fat Ladies. Ignoring the cutting-edge poppycock of the IACP and James Beard Awards, I published traditional books on French provincial cuisine, regional American country cooking, gutsy stews, and my mother's Southern kitchen, and even though I no longer had the outlet at *Town & Country* to explore the food topics that interested me and that I felt appealed to ordinary Americans, I stuck by my guns and never missed a chance to seek out different gumbos in Louisiana and barbecue houses in Kansas City, catch up on what the chefs at Savoy Grill and Shepherd's in London, the Hofbrauhaus in Munich, and Da Ivo in

Venice were up to, and revisit Taillevent, Paul Bocuse, and dozens of unstarred bistros while traveling in France.

Forever open-minded if acutely apprehensive about the new wave cooking that seemed to be overtaking the globe, I also forced myself to ingest the much-heralded (and absurdly overrated) raw fish concoctions at Le Bernardin in New York, pistachio-crusted tuna with smoked tomato coulis and *"crème"* at La Tourelle in Memphis, sweet pea soup with a lobster ice cube at TRU in Chicago, undercooked spiced monkfish with a gratin of vanilla-flavored potatoes at Au Petit Montmorency in Paris, and a ghastly ravioli of bloody duck and sweet potatoes at Coast in London. Like listening to twelve-tone music or gazing at a Julian Schnabel painting, it all disgusted me, and when subsequently the demented notion of global fusion cuisine ushered in every conceit from South American pirarucu fish with coconut red curry vinaigrette to Peking duck pizza to pineapple-lemongrass ice cream, I realized not only that my days as a constructive restaurant pundit were over, but that I'd literally succumb to anorexia unless I changed my dining habits and spent more time cooking civilized food at my home in East Hampton. I mean, all around me was a gullible public actually falling for the claptrap: self-styled gourmets, magazine editors, cookbook publishers, TV chefs, glitzy socialites, and indeed, thousands of other illiterate palates actually pretending to enjoy these laboratory dishes that could only be called "interesting" and were instantly forgettable. Was I missing something? Had I simply become a gustatory philistine? Or was it merely a question of waiting till the lunacy had run its course in favor of a return to what is still being meekly heralded as "real food"?

No matter, for today if I've become conditioned to nothing else in this age that worships technology, SUVs, rap music, bottled water, and salad, I've become conditioned to the undeniable fact that I'm just not a man of my time—gastronomically, socially, politically, and culturally. I don't own a computer, cell phone, microwave, or pair of sneakers. I drink as much hooch as vintage Talbot, have never seen the inside of a gym, refuse to vote in public elections when I deem the candidates to be utter buffoons, and, abhorring the Wright Brothers' folly, utilize *Queen Elizabeth 2* as a shuttle between New York and Europe (sixty-six voyages by the last count). Although I still travel primarily to eat, I have no immediate plans to follow the foodies to Spain's Costa Brava to genuflect at the high altar of some new culinary priest whose specialties include ducks' tongues with chopped oysters and ravioli of lichees, nor do I intend to rush to California any time soon to sample the latest organic heirloom watermelon radish.

Indifferent to fanatical growlings about health, I have eggs, bacon, buttermilk biscuits, and other such toothsome breakfast staples at least four times a week as Providence designed, and on the rare occasion when I lunch in public, I find a bourbon manhattan plus a half-bottle of wine to be a sensible ritual. Since I no longer have the beastly duty of testing every popular gastronomic flophouse that opens, I'm now free in the evenings to join other tosspots (including a few high-power chefs) at old-fashioned steak and fish houses, smoky bistros and taverns, and unfashionable neighborhood havens serving chicken pot pie, *boeuf bourguignon,* and *stinco,* the only major rules being that, unlike those blokes who insist on dining with the chickens and passing food around a table, I won't dine before eight o'clock or share my grub. Although manners are now a street accident and styles of dress couldn't be any more coarse and plebian, I still maintain a respectful attitude of formality when I venture out and wouldn't dream of not wearing a jacket in even the most casual burger joints. For dining companions, I avoid foodies like the plague, no longer able to tolerate palaver about the hottest new chefs, ingredients, and restaurant decors and insisting on engaging individuals who have considerably more interest in British farmhouse cheeses, North Carolina country cured hams, and Alsatian wines than in what Chicago's latest wonder boy is doing with free-range ostrich, micro-arugula, and ciabatta bread. My stance hasn't made me exactly popular in the arch food world, but I no longer care, and at least my gustatory passion is once again intact.

Since my retro purview of gastronomy is not in tune with the "relevance" that most magazines and cookbook publishers strive to project, my crusade for regional and home cooking is geared primarily to a silent but enormous and hungry readership that couldn't care less about fancy high-tech ovens, omega-3 eggs, hydroponic black mint, and white truffle oil. Thanks to two or three magazine editors still brave enough to entertain food subjects that can hardly be deemed cutting-edge, I've recently had published some rather bold articles glorifying Southern pig, iceberg lettuce, canned tuna fish, the unholy act of carrying a flask of real booze to phony "cocktail" parties, and the like. Pieces like these I enjoy writing immensely, the public seems to eat them up much to the consternation and bewilderment of the culinary prima donnas, and so the next major ink I plan to spill will be an in-depth, slightly rowdy, definitive book on . . . casseroles. I do remain stubbornly and optimistically convinced that cooking everywhere will return to its basic roots, that public enlightenment will evolve from reexposure to the timeless tastes and values codified by James Beard, Paul Bocuse, Elizabeth David, and Marcella Hazan, and that the day is not far away when a truly well-prepared coq au vin, spaghetti carbonara, Wiener schnitzel, or bread pudding with bourbon sauce will once again be the hallmark not only of a great restaurant, but of the serious home kitchen.

ACKNOWLEDGMENTS

Despite all the exalted names, places, and experiences scattered throughout these memoirs, my life has been basically a rather private one devoted mainly to my work, my dogs, and a relatively small cluster of loyal, treasured, unsung friends and colleagues who have provided the very backbone of my personal and professional stability. Each has indulged my moody disposition, tolerated my bad habits and testy prejudices, and unselfishly tendered more support, understanding, and love than any maverick like myself has the right to expect.

Patricia Brown, former editor in chief of *Bon Appétit* and *Cuisine* magazines and my editor at Harper & Row, has been a steadfast mentor, champion, and beloved pal for more than three decades, and neither she nor her husband, John Brady, has ever failed once to succor and comfort. No one over the years has done more to promote my work than my cherished friend Marion Gorman, the most elegant and efficient publicist in the business and a seasoned gastronome in her own right. And without the heated challenges, unremitting encouragement, and tender hand-holding of my veteran *QE2* companion, Alex Birnbaum, this book would have been a very different beast altogether.

No persons will ever command my respect and affection more than the unique team with whom I worked so closely at *Town & Country* under Frank Zachary's stewardship: Jean Barkhorn, Marilou Doyle, Melissa Tardiff,

Dick Kagan, Kim Waller, Slim Aarons, and the late Arnold Ehrlich. For over twenty years, they were my extended family, and, except for Arnold, they continue to play a prominent role in my unhinged life.

Dining out worldwide with a professional food writer and restaurant critic may sound exotic, but it also requires a certain digestive and chivalrous stamina that few of my cohorts could maintain on a regular basis. Some who have survived the sybaritic ordeal and continue to share my table are Mary Homi, Anita Cotter, Alice Marshall, Mary Gendron, Scott Stone, and, most solicitous and rakish of all, Warren Picower. I toast each of them with a Jack Daniel's manhattan—straight up.

My thanks also to Ruth Reichl, Elaine Richard, and Zanne Stewart at *Gourmet* magazine and Barbara Fairchild at *Bon Appétit* for being receptive to my more offbeat ideas, as well as to Pam Hoenig, the editor of five of my books whose faith in my abilities has been unwavering for many years.

Robin Straus has been my literary agent since the day I published my first food book, and not once has she ever lost her temper with me. Ditto Gus Davis, who has handled much of my business on the home front often without knowing whether I was again on the high seas or lost in the truffle fields of Périgord.

I can't adequately express my admiration for and gratitude to Susan Wyler at John Wiley & Sons for believing in a highly provocative literary endeavor that would assuredly have terrified most other food editors. From the very beginning, Susan has counseled, prodded, cajoled, provoked, exhorted, and tempered—and what's embarrassing, dammit, is that she's always been right. She's also respected implicitly this book's purpose and integrity; she's consoled and pampered; and her enthusiasm has never been anything less than extravagant. What more could any author ask?

Finally, no doubt polishing off double portions of fresh beluga and magnums of vintage Krug at some upscale dining saloon in the sky are Craig, Elaine, Graham, Daddy, Mary, Pierre, and Philip, and I just hope they're saving a place for me at the august table.

INDEX

Restaurants are identified by city.